COVENANT
AND
COMMUNITY

*The Life, Writings and Hermeneutics
of Pilgram Marpeck*

by

WILLIAM KLASSEN

WILLIAM B. EERDMANS PUBLISHING COMPANY
GRAND RAPIDS, MICHIGAN

PREFACE

Modern theology has keen interest in the hermeneutical question. It is *the* critical question for modern theology because it underlies all that theology does.

One facet of the hermeneutical problem which lies comparatively neglected is the relation of the Holy Spirit to interpretation. What role if any does the Holy Spirit play in the interpretative process? Are there ways in which this subject can be studied? When we confront the New Testament texts with this question they are comparatively silent. Nevertheless, periodically within the history of the church there have arisen groups of Christians whose study of the Bible was driven by the conviction that the same God who had brought the Bible into being was also ready through his Spirit to lead in its study.

One such group were the Anabaptists of the sixteenth century. Since they are related to the whole free church tradition (Baptists, Church of the Brethren, Mennonites, etc.) their approach to the Bible has had a profound impact on the history of the church since the Reformation, and therefore it deserves further study. In this book a modest beginning is made with one of the outstanding leaders of the Anabaptists, Pilgram Marpeck. Until now no book has ever been published on him in English. The recent discovery of much new material from his pen indicates that what he had to say on this subject in the sixteenth century is clearly pertinent to hermeneutical study in our times.

Encouragement for this study has come from my friend and teacher, Professor Otto Piper of Princeton Seminary. Funds to support me in the research were provided by the Calvary Mennonite Church, Washington, Illinois, on two separate occasions. A generous publishing subsidy was provided by the Mennonite Historical Society, Goshen, Indiana, through its president, J. C. Wenger. Financial assistance was also provided by Paul Klassen and Jacob Driedger.

It is a pleasure to dedicate this book to my father, David D. Klassen, who not only first introduced me to the subject of hermeneutics and Bible study but also has been a constant source of encouragement. Although he was denied the opportunity of higher education he has always been an uncompromising searcher after truth. It was his insistence and his sacrifice which compelled me to continue to search the Scriptures. His ability to understand the Biblical writers and to translate their teaching into life has been a beacon to many and continues to be my profound debt, which it is a pleasure to record and to endeavor to repay.

My colleague, Clarence Bauman, graciously assisted in the final proofs; a student, David Schmidt, also rendered valuable assistance. Professor Hans Hillerbrand, Duke Divinity School, shared his discovery of one of the Marpeck booklets of 1531 with me. Many others, through conversations and correspondence, became, in Marpeck's words, my "partners in the tribulation and joy which is in the covenant and community of Jesus Christ."

—W. K.

Pentecost, 1967

TABLE OF CONTENTS

ABBREVIATIONS

AMBS	Associated Mennonite Biblical Seminaries, Elkhart, Indiana
ARG	*Archiv für Reformationsgeschichte*
ARG, Roth	Roth, F., *Augsburg Reformationsgeschichte*
Bayern I	Schornbaum, K., ed., *Quellen zur Geschichte der Wiedertäufer: Markgraftum Brandenburg, Bayern I*, Leipzig, 1934
Bekentnisse	Rothmann's *Bekentnisse* of 1533
Bericht	*Bericht auss der heiligen schrifft . . .* by Bucer *et al.*, 1534
BW	Schmeller's *Bayerisches Wörterbuch*
ChHist	*Church History*
Conf.	Marpeck's *Confession* of 1532
CS	*Corpus Schwenckfeldianorum*
CV	*Clare verantwurtung*, 1531, by Marpeck
ET	*Expository Times*
GCL	Goshen College Library
Gedenkschrift	*Gedenkschrift zum 400 Jährigen Jubiläum der Mennoniten*, Ludwigshafen, 1925
Glaubenszeugnisse, I	*Glaubenszeugnisse oberdeutscher Taufgesinnter*, Lydia Müller, ed.
HTR	*Harvard Theological Review*
Humanity of Christ	Marpeck's tract cited from *MQR*, XXXII (pp. 192ff.)
Institutes	Calvin, J., *Institutes of the Christian Religion*
KB	*Das Kunstbuch*
Krebs-Rott	*Strasbourg Täuferakten*, Manfred Krebs and H. G. Rott, eds.

KU	*Ain klarer vast nützlicher unterricht,* Marpeck, 1531
LM	*Glaubenszeugnisse,* I, Lydia Müller, ed.
ME	*The Mennonite Encyclopedia*
Menn. Geschbl.	*Mennonitische Geschichtsblätter*
ML	*Mennonitisches Lexikon*
MQR	*The Mennonite Quarterly Review*
NT	New Testament
OT	Old Testament
QF	*Quellen und Forschungen,* Loserth, ed.
RGG	*Die Religion in Geschichte und Gegenwart* (always third edition unless otherwise indicated)
The Recovery	*The Recovery of the Anabaptist Vision,* Hershberger, ed.
Schiess	Schiess, Traugott, *Briefwechsel der Brüder . . . Blaurer*
SL	Schwenckfelder Library, Pennsburg, Penna.
SW	Röhrich, T. W., "Zur Geschichte der strasburgischen Wiedertäufer"
TB	*Taufbüchlein,* also called *Vermanung,* by Marpeck and Scharnschlager
TE	Marpeck's *Testamenterleutterung*
Thes. Baum.	Thesaurus Baumianus
ThLtzg	*Theologische Literaturzeitung*
TWNT	Kittel's *Theologisches Wörterbuch zum Neuen Testament*
V	Marpeck's *Verantwortung* of 1544-1548
WA	*Weimarer Ausgabe, Deutsche Bibel*
ZdVGMS	*Zeitschrift des Vereins für die Geschichte Mähren und Schlesien*
ZSW	*Zwinglis Sämmtliche Werke*
ZhTh	*Zeitschrift für die historische Theologie*

INTRODUCTION

It is a comparatively recent development to speak of the hermeneutic of an Anabaptist. A hundred years ago Anabaptists were still referred to as stepchildren of the Reformation while others less kind called them "deformers." Fifty years ago they began to be considered a part of the great Protestant stream.

In his *History of Dogma* Harnack did not deal with the Anabaptists because he felt that they agreed on all essential points with the Protestant Reformation.[1]

With a better understanding of the Anabaptists has come also the recognition that they take their own path even in theology more frequently than is often recognized. The custom of defining theology in classical terms has receded; and it is evident now that even Luther in some ways was not a theologian but a practical Christian pastor and a superb exegete, whose thought is intuitive and dialectic rather than logical or systematic. If one can speak of the theology of Paul, of the New Testament, or of Luther, then it is equally permissible to talk of an Anabaptist theology.

Can the same be said about the subject of hermeneutics?

---

[1] Except that they were essentially untheological (*Lehrbuch der Dogmengeschichte* [Tübingen, 1910], III, 771), they were different only in that they stressed more Christian individualism (*Selbständigkeit*, p. 772). Furthermore he could not conceal his admiration for some outstanding Christians among the Anabaptists who were in sharp contrast to the "heroic Luther and the iron Calvin" (p. 773). Earlier he said: "Die mennonitische Kirchenbildung gehört nicht in die Dogmengeschichte, weil sie in der Glaubenslehre—anders verhält es sich mit der Ethik—wesentlich zu den Bestimmungen der alten Kirchen zurückgekehrt ist oder doch nichts Selbständiges dauernd bei sich durchgesetzt hat" (p. 768, footnote 2).

The hermeneutics of Luther and many others has been described by scholars; and where these writers themselves have
specifically written on hermeneutics, this task is made much
easier and is more clearly justified. The majority of Anabaptists, however, did not know the original languages of the
Scriptures and seldom studied the Bible in any concerted
way. They read the Scriptures, taking them by and large at
face value, and allowed them to speak to their condition. If
by exegesis we mean a study of the Bible based on the
original languages then there is a minimum of it among the
Anabaptists. And if one can speak of hermeneutics only
where there is technical exegesis then it is equally clear that
there is no such thing as hermeneutics among the Anabaptists.

There is, however, no reason to restrict these terms in this
way. Everyone brings certain presuppositions with him as he
studies the Bible and these presuppositions determine what
he will or will not find in it. If he presupposes the Bible to be
a mysterious book filled with esoteric secrets, this will influence his understanding. Basically hermeneutics deals with the
process of understanding. It is both an art and a science, but
it was certainly an art before it was a science and its domain
is much more broadly conceived in this work than merely the
specific study of Scripture.[2]

In varying degrees it has been recognized that the Anabaptists have a place in the history of hermeneutics. Wilhelm
Dilthey saw the place of the Anabaptists in hermeneutics as
being one of the stimuli that provoked Matthias Flacius to
develop his famous *Clavis* (1567). According to Dilthey, Flacius fought against the assertion of the Anabaptists that the
Scriptures are a dark book.[3] Dilthey was apparently not
aware that Flacius engaged in extended literary debates with
Caspar Schwenckfeld about the same time that Marpeck was
parting ways with Schwenckfeld. On the question of the
clarity of Scripture Marpeck and Flacius both opposed
Schwenckfeld! There is no support for the assertion that the
Anabaptists held the Bible to be a dark book; they only

[2] Justification for such a broad conception of hermeneutic is provided
in *The New Hermeneutic*, ed. by J. M. Robinson and John B. Cobb
(New York: Harper and Row, 1964).
[3] Wilhelm Dilthey, "Die Entstehung der Hermeneutik," in *Philosoph-
ische Abhandlungen, Christoph Sigwart zum siebzigsten Geburtstag
gewidmet* (Tübingen, 1900), p. 195.

asserted what the church has always asserted, that without the work of the Holy Spirit in its interpretation, it is a book like any other book. One recent author has noted that the Anabaptists should have a place in the history of Bible study, and has picked perhaps the least representative Anabaptists, Hans Denck and Balthasar Hübmaier.[4]

Recognition that Anabaptists have a distinct hermeneutical approach has been growing remarkably in the past decade. Doctoral dissertations at Oxford and at Harvard Divinity School have given major attention to the Anabaptist hermeneutic.[5] In his monumental work, *The Radical Reformation*, George Huntston Williams gave some attention to their hermeneutic, concentrating however, as has been traditionally done, on "their hermeneutical principles."[6] Our study leads us to conclude that we are justified in speaking of an Anabaptist hermeneutic and that such a hermeneutic is worthy of consideration in contemporary theology.

The method most commonly used in Anabaptist writings is itself an illustration that they believed in the basic clarity of the Word, for their proof-text method loses all validity once it is asserted that words have a hidden meaning or that a key is necessary in order to understand the message. Beyond this it will be seen that Marpeck does grapple seriously with the meaning of certain concepts in Scripture and their usage, and the basic hermeneutical principle of contextual consideration figures largely in his approach to the Scriptures.

The purpose of the present work is to describe the hermeneutic of Pilgram Marpeck with special reference to his use of the Old Testament. This should be borne in mind especially in Chapter IV, which is basically descriptive. It does not assume that analogy necessarily indicates genealogy.

---

[4] James D. Wood, *The Interpretation of the Bible* (London, 1958), pp. 99-101. They receive no treatment in the article "Hermeneutik," *RGG*, III, cols. 261ff.

[5] Walter Klaassen, "Word, Spirit and Scripture in Early Anabaptist Thought" (Oxford, 1960), and Alvin J. Beachy, "The Concept of Grace in the Radical Reformation" (Cambridge, Mass., 1961).

[6] (Philadelphia: Westminster Press, 1962), pp. 828-831.

I

THE LIFE AND WRITINGS OF PILGRAM MARPECK

A. THE PLACE OF PILGRAM MARPECK IN ANABAPTIST RESEARCH

The place that has been allotted to Pilgram Marpeck in the current upsurge of Anabaptist studies has been quite modest. Considering that the literary production of this South German representative of the Anabaptist wing of the Reformation surpasses that of Menno Simons, it is somewhat puzzling that he has been thus neglected. Certain possible reasons for this neglect can be adduced, the first of which is that Marpeck did not acquire a prominent place in the historiography of the Reformation period itself. His experience with the Hutter-ites[7] and also the lack of any reference to him in the Ana-baptist hymns may be partly responsible for this. Apart from a few studies, Marpeck's position has never been assimilated either by the Mennonites or by students for whom Anabap-

---

[7] As recorded by *Die älteste Chronik der Hutterischen Brüder* (Ithaca, N.Y., 1943), ed. by A. J. F. Zieglschmid, pp. 223f. The exact description of the incident is as follows: "In [1541] a man named Cornelius [Veh] came to Schäckowitz. Similarly, soon after that a man came in all haste and with much fuss whose name was Pilgram. This one claimed that he had come into the land in order to unite all people who were divided by reason of articles of faith. But immediately he evidenced the opposite, for his presence gave the appearance as though he wished to foster unrest and confusion, as his calumniations and slanders showed. When the congregation was gathered at the same place in order to strengthen itself with the Word of God, and had kneeled in one spirit to pray, this man also wished to bring prayer before God with them. This the congregation did not allow, and described as a great folly, since he had first despised the congregation with reviling and slanders, but now desired to pray with them. He tried to say much, but the congregation did not hear him, but instead prayed for him. Thus he became embittered at the congregation and said openly that he would rather join himself to the Turks and the Pope than to this congregation and withdrew with great impetuosity."

tism is a subject of purely historical interest. An example or
two may illustrate this.

In the larger historical studies that have included (or attempted to include) the total Anabaptist movement, the paucity of references to Marpeck is striking. In the book *The
Anabaptist View of the Church*, generally regarded as the
standard treatment of the Anabaptist view of the church,
Marpeck receives only slightly more than a passing reference;[8] i.e., he is given credit for his contribution in joining the
issues and helping to achieve the final unification of the
Anabaptist tendencies, but his writings are not once drawn
upon to assist in arriving at a balanced and representative
"Anabaptist view." Indeed it seems unfair to speak of an
"Anabaptist view" when the references are so weighted in
favor of Swiss, Dutch, and Hutterian sources, as is the case in
Littell's treatment. The absence of Marpeck is equally conspicuous in Fritz Heyer's work on the Anabaptist doctrine
of the church.[9] One of the most important publications
of Anabaptist source material in recent time, *Spiritual and
Anabaptist Writers*, [10] bypasses the writings of Marpeck
and his brotherhood altogether, an omission that indicates
that the editor relied too heavily on secondary Anabaptist
research. Anyone studying Anabaptism *de novo* could not
overlook South German Anabaptism so completely, even if he
did decide to omit Marpeck.

The same neglect of Marpeck characterizes the studies that
have been carried on from an antagonistic point of view. An
outstanding illustration is Ulrich Bergfried's book on responsibility as a theological problem among the Anabaptists.[11]
Bergfried has deliberately chosen other sources than Mar-

[8] Franklin H. Littell, *The Anabaptist View of the Church* (American
Society of Church History, 1952), p. 37. This is not corrected in the
second edition (Boston: Beacon Press, 1958).

[9] *Der Kirchenbegriff der Schwärmer* (Leipzig, 1939).

[10] Vol. XXV of *Library of Christian Classics*, ed. by George H.
Williams and Angel Mergal (Philadelphia, 1957). Apart from wrongly
attributing a writing of Hübmaier's to Marpeck (p. 288) the editor
shows no awareness of Marpeck's significance, although in a more recent
work, *The Radical Reformation* (Philadelphia: Westminster Press,
1962), much attention is given to him (pp. 273-76, 454f. 466-76). W.
R. Estep (*The Anabaptist Story* [Nashville, Tenn., 1963], pp. 79-82)
sees something of Marpeck's role.

[11] *Verantwortung als theologisches Problem im Täufertum des 16.
Jahrhunderts* (Wuppertal-Elberfeld, 1938).

peck, on the ground that in spite of Marpeck's greater importance for the South German Anabaptists he is not referred to
as much as Stoffel Eleutherobios (n) because: (1) Marpeck's
Vermanung was written fifteen years later; (2) Marpeck
quite clearly based his writing on the former work; (3) Eleu-
therobion's work is inaccessible today and hence not used as
often; (4) his writing is considerably shorter, more precise in
its formulation, and, above all, more popular than Marpeck's,
having the form of a catechism rather than a theological
treatise; it therefore, relative to its total content, has exerted a
greater influence.[12] These somewhat strange reasons for ac-
cepting certain sources and rejecting others allowed Bergfried
to confirm his previous negative view of this movement.

B. A HISTORY OF MARPECK RESEARCH

The credit for the discovery of Pilgram Marpeck in modern
times belongs to John Loserth, who did extensive work in
Tirolese Reformation history. Camill Gerbert, in his history of
the sectarians in Strasbourg, included a brief section on Marpeck;[13] and T. W. Röhrich printed some important sources
pertaining to Marpeck in his treatment of the sectarians in
Strasbourg,[14] but no one devoted so much attention to his life
as Loserth. The earliest evidence of this interest is an article
written in 1895 that gives a brief sketch of Marpeck's life
noting among other things his interest in gynecology.[15] In
much greater detail Loserth painstakingly described the major events of Marpeck's life in the *Mennonitisches Lexikon*,[16]
a description that appears without any significant changes in
the *Mennonite Encyclopedia*.[17] The importance of Loserth
for Marpeck research is seen most clearly in his exact publication of the text of the *magnum opus* of the Marpeck group

[12] Bergfried, *op. cit.*, p. 224, footnote 48.
[13] *Geschichte der Strassburger Sectenbewegung* . . . (Strassburg,
1889), pp. 97-106.
[14] "Zur Geschichte der strassburgischen Wiedertäufer . . . ," *Zeitschrift
für historische Theologie*, 1860, pp. 3-121.
[15] "Zwei biographische Skizzen . . . ," *Zeitschrift des Fernandeums
für Tirol* . . . , XI (1895), 277-288.
[16] *ML*, III, 28f.
[17] *ME*, III, 491-502.

namely, the *Verantwortung*.[18] The publication of this volume
made it possible for scholars to evaluate the theology of this
South German group, and it remains the best single source for
the study of their theology. Loserth's work is characterized by
exacting scholarship and by restraint in evaluating or criticiz-
ing. As an objective historian he left to the theologian the task
of interpreting.

The work of John C. Wenger is different in this respect.
Wenger begins with a painstaking account of Marpeck's life,
sparing no effort in tracing down all the relevant sources
available to him.[19] Then he attempts to describe Marpeck's
theology, using as a basis the classic categories of theology.[20]
Finally in the publication of the text of Marpeck's *Confession*
of 1532,[21] and in the translation of Reublin's Letter to Marpeck of 1531, Wenger has given the historian invaluable assistance toward an understanding of Marpeck by making primary source material available.[22] Unfortunately, Wenger was
able to conceal neither his sympathy toward Marpeck nor his
desire to vindicate Marpeck as an orthodox theologian, and
his transcription of the *Confession* at several crucial junctures
is inaccurate; but in spite of these limitations Wenger has
greatly furthered our knowledge of Marpeck. Wenger's con-
cluding plea that "historians must now turn to these writings
[Marpeck's] if they wish to paint a true picture of Anabaptism"[23] was ignored for two decades.

A major advance in Marpeck research was made by the
Dutch historian Jan J. Kiwiet, who devoted his doctoral dis-
sertation to the study of Pilgram Marpeck.[24] In giving Mar-
peck his proper place in the larger Anabaptist movement,
Kiwiet rejects the thesis of John Horsch, Harold S. Bender, and
Wenger that Marpeck was a member of the group of Anabap-

[18] *Quellen und Forschungen zur Geschichte der oberdeutschen
Taufgesinnten im 16. Jahrhundert, Pilgram Marpecks Antwort auf
Caspar Schwenckfelds Beurteilung des Buches der Bundesbezeugung
von 1542* (Vienna and Leipzig, 1929), pp. 60-578.

[19] *MQR*, XII (1938), 137-166. See also *ChHist*, IX (1940),
24-36.

[20] *Ibid.*, pp. 205-256.

[21] *Ibid.*, pp. 168-202.

[22] *MQR*, XXIII (1949), 67-75.

[23] *ChHist*, *loc. cit.*, p. 36. It is surprising that Wenger did not as
much as mention Marpeck in his attempt to write a theology (*An Introduction to Theology* [Scottdale, Penna., 1954]).

[24] *Pilgram Marbeck* (Kassel, Oncken Verlag, 1957).

tists called Swiss Brethren. Instead, Kiwiet argues for a South German Anabaptist group which owes its origin to Hans Denck, independent of the Grebel, Manz, and Sattler group in Switzerland.[25] Kiwiet is the first to note the significance of Marpeck's residence in Strasbourg, both for Marpeck's own development and for the Anabaptist movement as a whole. Furthermore his development of the section of his thesis that deals with an analysis of Marpeck's theology is greatly enhanced by the principle of organization he has followed.[26] Rather than employ the classical categories as Wenger does, he allows the materials to suggest the organizing categories inductively. As a result he organizes his materials around the idea of "order," and states that the covenant is the concretization of the abstract concept of order among the South German Anabaptists. Kiwiet's weakness is that he builds too elaborate a structure upon mere hypotheses. His work also suffers from being based too much on the studies of others (notably Hulshof).

Two important recent discoveries have furthered Marpeck research immeasurably. The first was Wray's discovery that the *Vermanung*, which had hitherto been attributed to Marpeck, is actually a translation of Bernhard Rothmann's *Bekentnisse van beyden Sacramenten* of 1533. He showed that the major revisions were additions to the Rothmann text and indicated in what respects the changes reflected the individual theology of the South Germans. The knowledge that this is a translated revision helps the historian to see what views were peculiar and important to the Marpeck group, and for the most part it must be assumed that they agreed with those passages which they took over unaltered into the *Vermanung*.[27]

More important for an understanding of Marpeck and his theology is the discovery of the *Kunstbuch*, which Heinold Fast has brilliantly described in the *Archiv für Reformationsgeschichte*.[28] This valuable codex of the sixteenth century

[25] *Op. cit.*, pp. 43f.

[26] *Op. cit.*, pp. 84-148.

[27] "The 'Vermanung' of 1542 and Rothmann's 'Bekentnisse,'" *ARG*, 47 (1956), 233-251.

[28] "Pilgram Marbeck und das oberdeutsche Täufertum," 47 (1956), 212-242.

contains sixteen letters written by Marpeck himself, and all of the material in it somehow relates to the Marpeck group. The way in which this discovery relates to an understanding of Marpeck, his indebtedness to others, and his sphere of influence are carefully described by Fast. In spite of the fact that both Kiwiet and Torsten Bergsten used parts of the *Kunstbuch*, the present study is the first to use all of the source material available in ascertaining Marpeck's position.

A good contribution to Marpeck research is the study of the controversy between Pilgram Marpeck and Caspar Schwenckfeld made by Torsten Bergsten. [29] This is a model of scholarly exactness and originality. Bergsten describes the lines of controversy between Marpeck and Schwenckfeld and treats both with utmost fairness (even though he admits that at times the issues they bandied about are somewhat trivial). As over against Kiwiet, Bergsten would place Marpeck closer to the missionary type of Anabaptists (Hans Hut) than to the spiritualistic type (Denck). Bergsten contributes to the discussion of these issues not only through his exacting work in the dating of the writings and his careful description of the salient points of the controversy, but also in the way in which he defines spiritualistic tendencies. His work ranks among the most reliable of all the research on Marpeck's theology.[30]

Through the encouragement of Bergsten, Olof Källstigen wrote his licentiate dissertation on the theology of Marpeck. He appropriately called it "Der Mensch Christus als Eckstein," and in it analyzed both the Christology and concept of the church represented by Marpeck. Written in Swedish, the dissertation uses all the major works of Marpeck, although only slightly the books of 1531. The title is drawn from a sentence in one of Marpeck's works and accurately portrays a significant element in Marpeck's theology.[31]

The last major piece of Anabaptist research undertaken by

[29] "Pilgram Marbeck und seine Auseinandersetzung mit Caspar Schwenckfeld," *Kyrhohistorisk Årsskrift*, 1957 and 1958 (Uppsala, 1958), pp. 39-135 (offprint).

[30] The review article, "Pilgram Marpeck in Recent Research," *MQR*, XXXII (1958), 211-229, goes into greater detail in evaluating the work of Wray, Fast, Kiwiet, and Bergsten.

[31] Olof Källstigen, "Der Mensch Christus als Eckstein, En analys av kristologi och församlingssyn i Marbeckskrifterna" (Stockholm, 1964).

the late Harold Bender was devoted to a study of Pilgram Marpeck. Although Bender did not consult Marpeck's own writings to any extent his article is a competent drawing together of various research items. He is especially concerned that the division between Marpeck and the Swiss Brethren not be pressed beyond the evidence. He availed himself of an earlier form of the present work in the writing of his article.[32]

The Reformation and the Bible

During the period of the Reformation there was an urgent and genuine attempt to arrive at an adequate understanding of the authority and the significance of the Old Testament. When Adolf Harnack implies that the Old Testament should have been rejected at the time of the Reformation he attributes its retention in the church's canon to an unavoidable "fate."[33] While any official action by a church council was, of course, out of the question, a rediscovery of the Bible and, above all, putting it in the vernacular into the hands of the man on the street, could only lead to a violent encounter with the problem of the relationship of the Old Testament to the New.

It should therefore not be too surprising that the Anabaptists crucially confronted the problem of the Old Testament. On the one hand, since the birth of the Anabaptist movement a reaction had set in against Zwingli's virtual identification of the Old and the New Testaments,[34] a position that was most fully stated by Zwingli's successor in Zürich, Heinrich Bullinger.[35] Calvin, perhaps the greatest exegete of the Reformation period, shared the position of Bucer and Zwingli and

[32] Harold S. Bender, "Pilgram Marpeck, Anabaptist Theologian and Civil Engineer," *MQR*, 38 (1964), 231-265.

[33] *Marcion* (Leipzig, 1921), p. 248. The text runs: "*The thesis, which I shall attempt to prove in what follows is: to reject the OT in the second century was a mistake which the Catholic Church rightly avoided; to retain it in the sixteenth century was a fate which the Reformation could not avoid, but to conserve it as a canonical source in Protestantism since the nineteenth century is the result of a religious and ecclesiastical malady*" (his italics).

[34] Most clearly stated in his *Von der touff* . . . ZSW, IV, 188-337, especially the section "Vom kindertouff," pp. 292ff.

[35] *De testamentarum unitate seu uno testamento* (1534).

asserted that the two covenants were *"idem in substantia."*[36]

It has long been known that in some way the Anabaptists were related to the rise of "covenant theology" in the period of the Reformation. Where it originated and who gave it the greatest impetus has never been determined.[37]

The present work is meant to contribute to the increased interest in Reformation hermeneutics and to the increased interest in the problem of the relationship between the Old and New Testaments.[38] To determine Pilgram Marpeck's possible contribution to this discussion in his day would require a treatise that would test his solution with the Biblical data. The purpose of the present work is rather to describe the development and the outlines of his hermeneutic, with special attention to his use of the Old Testament.

[36] Bucer uses these words in Krebs-Rott, p. 419. On Calvin, see Olavi Castrén, *Die Bibeldeutung Calvins* (Helsinki, 1946) and the thorough study made of one facet of his hermeneutics by H. H. Wolf, *Die Einheit des Bundes. Das Verhältnis von Altem und Neuem Testament bei Calvin* (Neukirchen, Kreis Moers, 1958). Heinrich Bornkamm has studied Luther's use of the Old Testament in his monograph, *Luther und das Alte Testament* (Tübingen, 1948).

[37] Compare the indecisive conclusions of Champlin Burrage in *The Church Covenant Idea, Its Origin and Development* (Philadelphia, 1904), pp. 13-25. Gottlob Schrenk (*Gottesreich und Bund im älteren Protestantismus, vornehmlich bei Johannes Coccejus* [Gütersloh, 1923], p. 36) attributes the entrance of the idea into Reformed theology to Zwingli's encounter with the Swiss Anabaptists. L. J. Trinterud ("The Origins of Puritanism," *ChHist*, XX [1950], 27-37) asserts that the covenant principle "came quickly to be the organizing principle of the entire Rhineland Reformation movement. . ." (p. 41), and that the Anabaptists took it from Capito (p. 56, footnote 28). This theory of the origin of the covenant idea in Anabaptism remains to be documented. W. Hollweg accepts Schrenk's view of its origin and offers extensive evidence of its importance in North Germany in "Bernhard Buwo, ein ostfriesischer Theologe . . . ," *Jahrbuch der Gesellschaft für bildende Kunst und vaterländische Altertümer zu Emden*, 33 (1953), 71-90.

[38] For evidence of current interest in this relationship see J. Coppens, *Vom christlichen Verständnis des Alten Testaments* (Louvain, 1952), in particular the extensive bibliography. H. Richard Niebuhr remarks, "The relationship of the Old Testament to the New is a central issue in Biblical studies, and in the interpretation of the nature of Christianity" (*The Advancement of Theological Education* [New York, 1957], p. 70). See also Bernhard Anderson, ed., *The Old Testament and Christian Faith* (New York: Harper and Row, 1963).

C. THE LIFE OF PILGRAM MARPECK[39]

1. TYROL: THE FREE CHURCH, ca. 1500-1528

Of all the South German Anabaptist leaders, none is so remarkable in so many aspects as Pilgram Marpeck.[40] Pilgram was born of a noble family in the city of Rattenberg on the Inn River in the Tyrol. The date of his birth can be assumed to be about 1495. The Marpecks were a prominent family in Rattenberg. Henry Marpeck was a member of the City Council and was listed as mayor in 1511; in 1514 he was still a member of the Council. Pilgram, along with his wife, enrolled in the Brotherhood of Mining Workers (*Bergwerkbruderschaft*) of Rattenberg on February 26, 1520. He was active in the civic affairs of the city, first as member of the Lower Council after February 24, 1523, then as member of the Upper Council after June 11, 1525.

His position of responsibility may account for his being sent to Cardinal Matthew Lang as a representative of the city to intercede for Stephen Agricola, who was imprisoned at Mühldorf (Upper Bavaria). This trip took place on March 1, 1523, and on April 18 he was sent again, this time to visit Agricola himself.[41] It may be that this visit with Agricola was the beginning of Marpeck's break with the Roman Church. In any case he became a Lutheran first, but the libertinism that he found there caused him to reject the Lutheran way and join the Anabaptist movement. When he made this change is not known;[42] but on April 20, 1525, he was still a

[39] All European scholars except Widmoser write "Marbeck," while J. C. Wenger, on the basis of Marpeck's autograph supplied by the archivist at the Landesarchiv of Tyrol at Innsbruck, adopted Loserth's earliest usage, "Marpeck" (in *Zeitschrift für Fernandeum*). All the signed letters in the *Kunstbuch* support Wenger's usage.

[40] *ME*, III, 491-502; John C. Wenger, *op. cit.*, pp. 137-166; Jan J. Kiwiet, *op. cit.*, pp. 19-30; Eduard Widmoser, "Das Täufertum im Tiroler Unterland" (Innsbruck: L. Franzens Universität Diss., 1948), pp. 41-49; and his article, "Das Tiroler Täufertum," I *Tiroler Heimat*, XV (1951), 45-89; II, *ibid.*, XVI (1952), 103-128. Marpeck is discussed on pp. 107-08.

[41] Widmoser, Diss., p. 42. This Agricola is confused by Neff (*ME*, I, 23) with John Agricola of Eisleben, who only briefly visited at Augsburg (see Roth, *ARG*, I, 127f., 332f., *et passim*).

[42] It is known that Anabaptists were active in the Tyrol quite early. According to the testimony of Hans Hut given on September 16, 1527, Anabaptists were active in the Inn valley prior to May 20, 1526 (cf. Christian Meyer, "Die Anfänge des Wiedertäuferthums in

Catholic, for on that date he was hired (service beginning June 7) as a director of mines with an annual wage of sixty-five pounds. He must have attained some wealth, for in 1524 he was assessed for two houses; by 1530 this assessment was missing.

The issue that led to his removal from the office of mining director was apparently his refusal to use his office in assisting the government to determine who were Anabaptists,[43] asserting that this was not included in his duties.

The position of director of mines was a responsible one since he was responsible for the ore, for the payment of the miners, for the general productivity of the mines, and the general welfare of the miners. The director represented the king directly. The office of director of mines itself goes back to the thirteenth century. About 1477 there were five different mining directors in the Inn valley. If this was still the case in 1520 Marpeck had one of the most responsible positions available in government.[44] Stolz describes the work of the mining director in the following words:

> The mining director, in the Austrian areas as well as in other lands, is the official who is commissioned within certain limits to administer the mining laws of the local regent. Accordingly he has to lease new mining pits or strips, to settle legal controversies relating to mining and those relating to the personal affairs of the people working in the mining and smelting locations, with the exception of criminal law which the local regent alone can settle. Further he must supervise the adherence to the mining code and collect the revenues

---

Augsburg," *Zeitschrift des Historischen Vereins für Schwaben und Neuburg*, I [1874], 224). Since Hut asserts that his baptism took place on May 20, 1526, after having become persuaded by Caspar Färber who had told him of Anabaptists active in the Inn valley, we must assume that some Anabaptists were active there prior to May, 1526. Heinold Fast (*ARG*, 47 [1956], 220, note 30) rejects this as evidence, but without sufficient grounds. No doubt those who were baptized constituted a small group until later.

[43] Johann Loserth, "Der Anabaptismus in Tirol," in *Archiv für österreichische Geschichte*, 78 (1892), 457; Widmoser, Diss., pp. 42f.

[44] See the informative essay by Otto Stolz, "Zur Geschichte des Bergbaues im Elsass im 15. und 16. Jahrhundert," *Elsass-Lothringisches Jahrbuch*, XVIII (1939), 116-171, especially p. 122.

pertaining to the mining royalty for the royal treasury and keep a record of that as well as of the loans and judgments, as well as of the royalties, keeping an exact record of all through the services of an accountant. A beadle of his own assists him in this.[45]

For Maximilian I (1459-1519) the miners were considered of great military significance. For this reason he did much to make the mining directors a more prominent force.[46]

In January, 1528, Marpeck had to relinquish his post as mining director, and he left Rattenberg with his wife to find a living elsewhere.[47] He left his daughter and three adopted children behind, and it was not until 1530 that the disposition of his Rattenberg property was settled. No doubt his daughter received at least a part of it.[48]

2. STRASBOURG: PURIFICATION OF ANABAPTISM, 1528-1532

An Anabaptist writer of the early seventeenth century states that Marpeck went to Augsburg after his dismissal from his home town. [49] In view of the fact that the records indicate that Marpeck was a citizen of Strasbourg in September, 1528, it is plausible to assume that Walch confused Marpeck's Augsburg and Strasbourg residences and inverted their correct order. Certainly it was impossible for Marpeck to accomplish at Augsburg between February 1 and September 15 the

[45] Stolz, op. cit., pp. 125-26.

[46] See Eberhard Gothein, "Beiträge zur Geschichte des Bergbaus im Schwarzwald," Zeitschrift für die Geschichte des Oberrheins, N. F. II (1887), 436.

[47] It is supposed by Widmoser (Tiroler Heimat, p. 108), Loserth (Gedenkschrift, p. 138; QF, p. 2), Christian Hege ("Pilgram Marpeck," p. 250), and Gerhard Goeters (Ludwig Hätzer, 1957, p. 112) that Marpeck attended the "Martyrs' Synod" at Augsburg in the summer of 1527. It is probable that Ludwig Keller is responsible for this assumption, for which no evidence has yet been adduced (Die Reformation [Leipzig, 1885], p. 427).

[48] Widmoser, Diss., pp. 45f.

[49] Johannes Walch, Decas fabularum, humani generis sortem, mores, . . . (Strasbourg, 1609): "Pilgramus Marpeck, Tirolensis, vir pius ac praestans, reipublicae studiosus, ingenio ac plurimis artibus excellens, cum patria ac bonis ob religionis causam pulsus esset, Vindelicorum Augustam primum instruxit; . . ." (cited by Krebs-Rott, p. 186).

work that Walch credits to him.[50] By September 19 he had his Strasbourg citizenship.[51]

Strasbourg was the home of many dissenters, and here Marpeck met men like Caspar Schwenckfeld, Sebastian Franck, and Johannes Bünderlin of Linz, who at one time was a leader of the Anabaptists of Linz. Marpeck attended the Anabaptist meetings and likely took a prominent place in organizing an Anabaptist congregation. He worked for a salary in the city forest. It is known that Anabaptist meetings were held in his home.[52]

Undoubtedly Marpeck put his talents to work in the area of Strasbourg. The mining director in the Tyrol as well as in Alsace had supervision over the use of the forests; in fact, he had been given more authority over the forests through the reforms of Maximilian earlier in the sixteenth century. The regulations on cutting, transporting, and selling the wood were complex and it was the mining superintendent's responsibility to see that they were observed.[53] The fact that Alsace followed Tyrol in these regulations may have made it much easier for Marpeck to find employment here; for that matter he may even have been instrumental in bringing some of the tried methods from Tyrol and instituting them in the valleys of Alsace.[54]

[50] The value that Walch ascribes to Pilgram's work is likely also exaggerated. Compare the negative judgment of his work in Paul Stetten, *Lebensbeschreibungen zur Erweckung und Unterhaltung bürgerlicher Tugend* (Augsburg, 1782), p. 451. While Walch aims to describe the unusual, Stetten appears to be somewhat too negative. That the Council continued to use Marpeck's method of getting wood down from the mountains indicates that they were not as disappointed in the results as Stetten indicates (see Stetten, *op. cit.*, p. 422, where a report for the year 1557 indicates that Marpeck's method was still used).

[51] According to the lists of citizens, Marpeck bought his citizenship on September 19, 1528. See C. Wittmer and J. Charles Meyer, *Le livre de bourgeoisie de la ville de Strasbourg 1440-1530, Texte II* (Strasbourg, 1954), p. 788. It is not clear why Kiwiet says that Marpeck moved to Strasbourg in 1530 (*op. cit.*, p. 27).

[52] Krebs-Rott, *op. cit.*, p. 185.

[53] See Eberhard Gothein, "Entstehung und Entwicklung der Murgschifferschaft," *Zeitschrift für die Geschichte des Oberrheins*, N. F. IV (1889), 401-455.

[54] The close connections between Tyrol and Alsace are demonstrated by Otto Stolz who says: "Die Bergwerke im Elsass haben von den etwas früher und stärker entwickelten Bergbauen Tirols die Grundzüge eines einheitlichen Bergrechtes und ebenso auch der Betriebsweise übernommen" (*op. cit.*, p. 171).

In the city he became an honored member of the religious society so important in the Reformation times. Men like Wolfgang Capito and Martin Bucer spoke highly of him, and Bucer said the Anabaptists honored him like a God(*numinis instar*).[55] He built a water system for the city and wood-floating flumes in the surrounding valleys, whereby Strasbourg, which lacked wood, attained access to the wealth of the Black Forest.[56] The opinion of the religious leaders was not determined by his secular achievements. While Bucer admitted on August 17, 1531, that Pilgram was of unblamable conduct, he nevertheless insisted that Marpeck was intent on his own pleasure and his own supposed knowledge. On the ground of his obstinate opposition to infant baptism, which he called a sacrifice to Moloch, and his prominence in the city, Bucer charged him with misleading the citizens, and Marpeck was imprisoned. Capito's intercession, and perhaps Marpeck's record as a public servant, restored him his freedom without the regular oaths to renounce Anabaptist company and doctrine.

At the beginning of December, 1531, the events in Marpeck's life took on a faster tempo. He requested the Council's permission for a public debate with the clergy. This was refused. Instead, on December 9, 1531, Marpeck was granted a colloquium before the Council and the "committee of twenty-one." In twenty-eight articles Marpeck presented his doctrine; the main point that Marpeck defended was adult baptism. Bucer was his leading opponent. Marpeck accused the clergy of not preaching freely under the cross of Christ but under the protection of princes and cities; hence one should not be surprised that there was still no Christian order in Strasbourg and the Word of God was bearing no fruit.

The Council decided in favor of Bucer and ruled that if Pilgram persisted in his opinion and was planning to overthrow infant baptism and set up a separate church, he must leave the city and region, not to return unless he forsook his

[55] Traugott Schiess, *Briefwechsel der Brüder Ambrosius und Thomas Blaurer* (1908), I, 316. The letter by Bucer is dated January 19, 1532.

[56] The reference to the "Black Forest" goes back to an erroneous reading of the Akten entry by Röhrich. It is corrected by the careful research of Krebs-Rott, p. 185, footnote 8. It accounts also for the confusion about his place of residence (cf. Williams, *Radical Reformation*, p. 253, following *ME*, III, 493).

error. These proceedings took place on December 18, 1531. Two days later Marpeck notified the Council that he would leave the region; but he could not guarantee that he would not return, since he would follow wherever God would lead him. Also he asked for a short period of grace, three or four weeks to sell his little household; and he requested the payment of the wages that still were his due. This was granted, along with a statement of the Council's displeasure at his insistence that infant baptism could not be proved by Divine Scripture.

On December 18, 1531, the Council informed Countess Elizabeth of Fürstenberg that Pilgram had been dismissed.[57] Actually they did not ask him to leave until December 19, when he stated that he would not desist from teaching the correctness of adult baptism.[58] On December 20 he appeared before the Council again and thanked them cordially for their fatherly way of dealing with him, assuring them that he never had any intention of changing the political order in Strasbourg, but only desired to have freedom in the spiritual realm.

On December 29 Marpeck met Bucer and asked him for a written statement of his reasons for infant baptism. Bucer complied.[59] Marpeck then asked whether he might reply to it, and Bucer asked him to do so. On January 10 Marpeck appeared and said he had responses to his articles which he would like to discuss with them, in hope that thus the truth might come to light more fully. Bucer presented a request for this discussion to the Council since they did not wish a surreptitious discussion. He asked for Pilgram's presence at the discussion, for Pilgram was complaining that his time in Strasbourg was running short.[60]

A disputation was then held on January 12, 1532, at the close of which Marpeck handed a copy of his *Confession* to Bucer and the Councillors present, with the rebuttal of Bucer's booklet appended.[61] Bucer did not allow Marpeck the last

[57] Manfred Krebs, *Quellen zur Geschichte der Täufer*, Vol. IV, *Baden und Pfalz* (Gütersloh, 1951), p. 365.

[58] Krebs-Rott, pp. 361f.

[59] *Ibid.*, pp. 395-411.

[60] *Ibid.*, p. 531 of January 12, 1532.

[61] This is the verbose epistle of which Bucer speaks in a letter to Blaurer on January 19, 1532 (Schiess, I, 316), and also the whole book of which Blaurer writes in a letter to his brother on February 2 (*ibid.*, p. 321).

word, even if he was about to be banished from town, so he refuted the *Confession* phrase by phrase.[62] When Marpeck's four weeks expired, he undoubtedly left Strasbourg, soon after January 12, 1532. Before doing so he wrote a moving letter to the City Council, which has also been preserved.[63] Where he went from Strasbourg is not clear. Widmoser assumed that he returned to Rattenberg to see his daughter, but this remains conjecture.[64]

When Pilgram Marpeck arrived in Strasbourg in 1528, he found the Anabaptist movement badly in need of leadership and direction. The spiritualism of Clemens Ziegler had had its effect, and the leadership of Wilhelm Reublin was only partially effective in steering the little brotherhood through some perilous days. The fact that Strasbourg was such a haven for the discontented and the poor complicated matters. Soon there arrived in the city men like Hans Bünderlin, Sebastian Franck, and Caspar Schwenckfeld, none of whom did much to strengthen the Anabaptist brotherhood.

On Marpeck's arrival the leadership was still largely in the hands of Wilhelm Reublin. Not much is known about Reublin's views at this time, but that his relationship to Pilgram Marpeck was most cordial is evident from a letter he wrote to Marpeck in January, 1531.[65]

It is evident that a major parting of the ways of various Anabaptist groups with their leaders took place in Strasbourg during the years 1528-1532. Involved in this parting of the ways was Clemens Ziegler, a strange person, who appears to have been a "fringe" Anabaptist. He must be considered a speculative Anabaptist, for he joined himself to men like Hans

[62] When Bucer says, "Peregrinum nondum absolvi," on February 2, 1532 (in a letter to Ambrosius Blaurer, Schiess, I, 322), he is no doubt referring to this rebuttal. The *Confession* was broken down into 284 "Articles" by Bucer, not by Marpeck as Röhrich thought (*Geschichte der Reformation*, III, 73). Fortunately this rebuttal has been preserved and is contained in Krebs-Rott.

[63] Published first by Röhrich in *ZhTh* (1860), pp. 57ff., then by Ludwig Keller in *Monatsheft der Comenius-Gesellschaft*, V (1896), 311-13. It appears also in Krebs-Rott.

[64] Diss., p. 46.

[65] Printed in C. A. Cornelius, *Geschichte des Münsterischen Aufruhrs*, II (Leipzig, 1860), 253-59 (trans. by John C. Wenger in *MQR*, XXIII [1949], 67-75).

Denck, Jacob Kautz, and Hans Bünderlin.[66] No doubt it was his work and that of Jacob Kautz, rather than Denck's explicit statements, that gave the Anabaptists the reputation of believing in universal salvation. Ziegler seems to have propagated the belief that the body is evil and the spirit alone is good, a view that was repeatedly rejected by Pilgram Marpeck.[67]

Closely related to Ziegler was Jacob Kautz, a fiery preacher who had come to Strasbourg from Worms. In his statement of faith there are a number of articles that were later rejected by Marpeck. It is, no doubt, a valid assumption that already in the Strasbourg period Marpeck did not share Kautz's division between the inner and the outer word, and in particular the division between the inner desire and the external act of eating the fruit of Adam.[68]

However, a real break was not forced upon the Anabaptists in Strasbourg until the coming of two more persons to that city, namely, Melchior Hofmann and Hans Bünderlin. Hofmann forced the Strasbourg Anabaptists to decide two important issues: apocalyptic eschatology and Christology. These issues involved Marpeck directly at this period, and also his friend and co-worker, Leupold Scharnschlager. In the Christological discussions Scharnschlager sided against Hofmann's Valentinian Christology, a fact about which Hofmann complained to the Strasbourg Council.[69]

More important for Marpeck directly was the parting of the ways with Hans Bünderlin. The fact that none of the sources indicates a direct contact between these two men does not mean that there was no such contact. In fact, exceedingly few details about the inner workings of the Anabaptist congregations are known to us. But there is evidence of a clash in various indirect sources. For one thing it is known that the

---

[66] Röhrich, op. cit., p. 21.

[67] Ibid., pp. 64f. For a complete study of Ziegler, see Rodolphe Peter, "Le maraîcher Clément Ziegler, l'homme et son oeuvre," Revue d' histoire et de philosophie religieuses, 34, 1954 (pp. 255-282).

[68] The seven articles of Kautz are found in Manfred Krebs, op. cit., pp. 113f., and in Krebs-Rott, pp. 91-115. The date of these articles is June 13, 1527, and they were sent to the Strasbourg Council by the Worms Council on November 3, 1528.

[69] Röhrich, op. cit., p. 71.

Anabaptist congregation meeting in Fridolin Meiger's house read a Bünderlin book in their assembly.[70]

Bünderlin's stay in Strasbourg was very brief; he no doubt left in 1530 to return only intermittently, if at all. Nevertheless his type of thinking lived on in Strasbourg, in a milder form in Schwenckfeld, and in its more extreme form in Clemens Ziegler. Bünderlin's last book, dealing with the sacraments and the external church, was published in 1530, perhaps not at Strasbourg, but near enough that the Anabaptists there felt its impact. His highest praise came from Sebastian Franck, who was also at Strasbourg during these years.[71]

Bünderlin came to Strasbourg and called together the brotherhood, perhaps with the desire to unify the movement and rally it around himself as one of the apostles.[72] Even in his later books Pilgram Marpeck speaks of the "bünderlinischen," which may indicate that they were an independent group in Strasbourg.[73] About this time Schwenckfeld wrote that the Anabaptists called Bünderlin a squabbler.[74]

Finally, it is clear that Marpeck viewed the Strasbourg period of his life as a time when a major parting of the ways took place. Writing in 1542 in the Preface to the major confessional volume of the Marpeck brotherhood, the *Vermanung*, the writers refer to the manifold splits and sects which are a terrible error and which have been accomplished through the guile of the serpent, "now into the twelfth year."[75] This is doubtless a reference to the Strasbourg period; and the context makes it clear that the sects are being caused by false

[70] The Council report is dated March 16, 1529. But already in September, 1528, it is reported that Meiger and Marpeck allowed themselves to be found in the Anabaptist meetings, and met with the Anabaptists in a house in the city of Strasbourg, "und daselbst eine ordnung machen wollen, wie ihre brüder und secten zu underhalten" (Krebs-Rott, *op. cit.*, pp. 185f.). For the report of the reading of the Bünderlin book, see Röhrich, *op. cit.*, p. 48, No. 13; Cornelius, *op. cit.*, II, 272; Nicoladoni, *Johannes Bünderlin* (Berlin, 1893), pp. 105, 132ff.

[71] See Franck's letter to Campanus (printed in *Spiritual and Anabaptist Writers*, ed. by G. H. Williams and Angel Mergal [Philadelphia: Westminster Press, 1957], pp. 145-160) of Strasbourg, 1531, and also the discussion of his position in Sebastian Franck's *Chronica* (1531), fol. 451b.

[72] Röhrich, *op. cit.*, p. 48.

[73] V, 149:37.

[74] *CS*, IV, 254.

[75] *TB*, 187:3.

apostles of Satan *within* the true members of the covenant, that is, among the Anabaptists themselves.[76]

3. SWITZERLAND AND MORAVIA: THE UNITED CHURCH, 1532-1544

John C. Wenger has aptly termed these years of Pilgram Marpeck's life "the obscure years,"[77] for little indeed is known of this period. No trace of his movements from Strasbourg has been left, although he continued his connections with the Strasbourg brotherhood as a leader and a co-worker of Leupold Scharnschlager.[78] Scharnschlager was unable to fulfill a request for baptism because of the temporary suspension of baptism ordered by the churches of Moravia. The cause for this is discussed above, but his subsequent correspondence shows that Marpeck did not break his relationship with the Strasbourg brotherhood.[79]

Although it is not known where Marpeck lived in these years, there are some traces of his activity. It is unlikely that he returned to his homeland, Tyrol,[80] except perhaps for a short visit. It is possible that he was serving as an apostle sent

[76] The tensions of the Strasbourg Anabaptists in 1530f. resulted in a temporary cessation of baptism, according to the testimony of Michel Leubel on January 8, 1533. The reason he gives is that some of the Anabaptists "den geseurten taig under das ungehefelt gemischt," and that this suspension of baptism was to last "bis got weiter gnad und zeit gebe" (Krebs, *op. cit.*, 424:11f.). In all likelihood this refers not to severe persecution, but to "das Einschleichen unlauterer Elemente" (Gerhard Hein, "Täufer in Speyer," *Beiträge zur Geschichte der Mennoniten*, I [1938], 54). On a similar suspension, but for different reasons, see Friedrich Otto zur Linden, *Melchior Hofmann* (Haarlem, 1885), p. 263. The case of Hans Bot, a Moravian Anabaptist, bears only a superficial resemblance (Rudolf Wolkan, *Geschicht-Buch der Hutterischen Brüder* [Vienna, 1923], pp. 101f.). Evidence for the heterogeneous character of Strasbourg in these years comes also from the request of the ministers to the Council for legislative support in dealing with divergent religious deviants. Incidentally, this document also sheds considerable light on the relation between church and city government (Krebs-Rott, pp. 357f., dated soon after December 16, 1531).

[77] *Op. cit.*, p. 155.

[78] Krebs, *op. cit.*, p. 422.

[79] See above, footnote 76.

[80] As suggested by Kiwiet (*op. cit.*, p. 35) on the basis of a letter written July, 1533, by Ludwig Fest. The "Marpeckin" referred to both by Fest and Jacob Huter is in all likelihood not Pilgram's wife, but Gilg Marpeck's wife (see Widmoser, Diss., p. 46).

by the Moravian church. But he did not neglect his natural talents; he built a fulling mill at St. Gall, and was probably responsible for conducting water around the mountains for the rapidly expanding weaver's craft in that city. One of Marpeck's closest associates in Augsburg in the later years, Jörg Propst Rothenfelder (also called Maler), for fourteen years a weaver in St. Gall and Appenzell, became acquainted with Marpeck there through his genius at construction.[81] No doubt Marpeck nurtured this friendship with Maler, for he wrote a letter in 1543 in an attempt to iron out the difficulties between Maler and the Swiss.[82] Other letters written from Switzerland include one written December 21, 1540, from the Grisons (to Strasbourg) and one to the brethren in Württemberg on August 15, 1544, from Chur.[83] If a home base must be assumed, it would seem most logical to suppose that Marpeck spent most of his time from 1532 to 1544 somewhere in Switzerland, where contacts with Scharnschlager made it possible for the two to undertake the revised translation of the Bekentnisse. According to the Hutterian Chronicle he undertook a trip to Moravia in 1541 in an attempt to unite the Anabaptists there with the South German and Swiss groups.[84] Schwenckfeld's inability to send him a letter because he did not know where to find him[85] also indicates that Marpeck's dwelling place in these years was not fixed.[86]

[81] For the weaving situation in St. Gall, as well as the water shortage and its remedy, see Johannes Kessler, *Sabbata* (modern edition by Emil Egli and Rudolf Schoch, St. Gallen, 1902), p. 434. While Marpeck's name is not mentioned, Kessler indicates that the water flumes were constructed in 1535 or after. Maler left Augsburg on April 15, 1535, and went to St. Gall. His point of contact was that he had been attracted to Marpeck through his fame "als der Schöpfer des dortigen Walkwerkes (fulling-mill) . . ." (Roth, *ARG*, IV, 616). On Maler see *ME*, IV, 365-67.

[82] No. 8, *Kunstbuch*.

[83] Nos. 5 and 33 respectively in the *Kunstbuch*.

[84] See above, footnote 7. Strangely, for the year 1551 Kiwiet (*op. cit.*, p. 66) accepts Wenger's (*op. cit.*, p. 157) reading "Pilgram" instead of "Pilger" corrected by Zieglschmid (*op. cit.*, pp. 53, 328, 968). See also Fast, *op. cit.*, p. 230, footnote 77. "Pilger" is correct; see J. Andreas Schmeller, *Bayerisches Wörterbuch* (Leipzig, 1939), I, 385.

[85] *CS*, VIII, 618 (May 37, 1543).

[86] Will-Erich Peuckert assumes that Schwenckfeld, Franck, and Marpeck were at Ulm in 1533 (*Sebastian Franck* [München, 1943], p. 203), but gives no evidence.

In view of Marpeck's leadership in the Anabaptist movement, there can be little doubt that Marpeck worked hard to
unify the movement in these years. His concern about the
schisms among the Anabaptists is understandable when it is
remembered that one of the reasons he gave for his break
with Lutheranism was the difference that existed between
Luther and Zwingli.[87] It would hardly do to have a part in a
movement that was even more badly splintered than the
Reformed movement, if one of his basic objections to the
Reformed party had always been that of disunity.

The concern for the united church strongly based upon a
united confession resulted in the publication of the *Vermanung*. The true members of the covenant were called to
rally around the banner of the spiritual general, Jesus Christ,
and to take strength from his leadership. By their own admission, the editors used other confessions, but purified, corrected, and cleansed them of all error, for in their estimation
nothing was as deadly as truth mixed with error.[88]

4. AUGSBURG: THE WITNESSING CHURCH, 1544-1556

Marpeck settled in Augsburg at a most convenient time. The
city records reveal that Augsburg had always been plagued
by a wood shortage, and hence they could well use his services.[89] The water flumes of the city were also in need of
repair, so he was hired, first on a temporary basis, then later
on a full-time basis.

One reason why Marpeck could live in Augsburg in relative
peace was that he was recognized as an asset. His coming at a
time when the city was concerned about the possibility of an
attack by the Turks, and his dwelling there during the Smal-
kald War and the period of the Interim, all worked to his
advantage. The Council minutes indicate that the major concern during most of these years was not Anabaptism, but the
Schwenckfelders. And yet even his contemporaries were surprised that he was allowed so many years of fruitful work in

[87] Röhrich, *op. cit.*, p. 53.
[88] *TB*, pp. 187-190.
[89] Paul von Stetten, *Geschichte des Heiligen Römischen Reichs
Freyen Stadt Augsburg*...(Franckfurt und Leipzig, 1743), pp. 310,
370, 384.

Augsburg.[90] Schwenckfeld is certainly correct in assuming that the Council was looking after the advantage of the city in retaining him as an employee.

Another reason why he could remain at Augsburg was that he was more cautious about creating offense to the authorities than he had been in Strasbourg, especially in administering his duties to the congregation.[91] He appears also to have been gone from Augsburg some of the time, and may have used the press and the pen as his means of strengthening the body of Christ.

It is, however, misleading to speak of the Anabaptist brotherhood at Augsburg as a "quiet type of conventicle-Christianity" or to say that Marpeck "died in the quiet and seclusion of his residence in Augsburg, no longer disturbed by any of the authorities in his last years."[92] As early as 1545 his religious activities were under suspicion, and the Council sent him a number of warnings. These are dated July 16, 1545; May 6, 1550; September 26, 1553; and September 25, 1554.[93] The first was an order that the mayor was to relay to him, that he was to allow his sect to be idle.[94] The second time they wished to check on the veracity of Seifried's statement relative to the publication of the *Testamenterleutterung;* but this book bore no indication of its author, and appeared to be a relatively harmless concordance; and perhaps it was not written by Marpeck, but rather by Scharnschlager. The third entry ordered an investigation to see if he was holding meetings; if so that he be punished.

[90] As seen by the remarks of Schwenckfeld in a letter to Sibilla Eisler after September, 1551: "Lenhart (Hieber) schreibt, pilgram hab sein Buch (editorial footnote says *Vermanung!*) mussen vor Ratth einlegen. Ich hab nicht gedacht das Er da mehr sey. Also ist ein ding umb den eigen Nutz, Ein Ratth wurd ihn sunst langsam beherbergen; Aber es soll ie jrrthumb in dieser Wellt platz haben, die Gerechtigkeit aber, und warheit Nicht in dieser wellt sonder in der Newen" (*CS*, VII, 657). Hans Uhrmacher was also allowed to remain in the village of Znaim because of outstanding service to the city (see "Uhrmacher" in *ME*, IV, 1131).

[91] He was aware that some people had done harm to the Anabaptist cause by their rashness. Compare his thoroughly objective statements about the role of government in No. 15 of the *Kunstbuch* (*MQR*, XXXII [1958], 203).

[92] So Robert Friedmann, *Mennonite Piety Through the Centuries* (Goshen, Indiana, 1949), pp. 10, 22.

[93] Roth, *ARG*, II, 279.

[94] *Ibid.*, "Missig" meaning "müssig."

The entry under September, 1554, reads: "When (If) it is ascertained that Pilgram is spreading his error, he shall be told to go and spend his penny elsewhere."[95]

Two years later he died, apparently a natural death. The exact date of his death is not known, but it is probable that it occurred sometime during the last three months of 1556. He received his salary for the first three quarters of that year, but under the payment of December 16, 1556, are written the words: "Is dead."[96]

D. THE WRITINGS OF PILGRAM MARPECK

1. THE TWO BOOKLETS OF 1531

The Strasbourg censors, Christian Herlin and Jacob Bedrotus, in their report of 1531 listed *"Duo etiam libelli germanica lingua scripti* (Pilgerinum autorem ferunt) *anabaptistarum dogmata continent, nempe quod credentibus tantum baptismus sit conferendus. Addit idem libelli autor se ideo baptismum recepisse, quia ita scriptum etc."*[97] The censors do not recommend these books to be sold to the public.

It is generally supposed that neither of these booklets is extant.[98] Through a marginal reference in the Thesaurus Baumianus it has come to be assumed that a book by Marpeck perished in the Strasbourg fire of 1870, but Baum preserved at least the title for posterity. The Dutch historian Hulshof is responsible for the conjecture that the book referred

[95] *Ibid.* "Do man auch in erfarung käme, das der Pilgram seinen irtumb ausbraitet, soll ime gesagt werden, seinen pfennig anderstwo zu zeren." Wenger (*op. cit.,* p. 165) translates "Do" as "since" and is baffled that Marpeck remained in the city employ until his death. If "Do" is given a contingent meaning, as the use with the subjunctive mood would suggest, and as it is used in the line preceding it (and on pp. 277 and 283 of the same volume), then it is easier to explain. The Council could not prove its charges against Marpeck to its own satisfaction, and hence he remained.

[96] Wenger, *op. cit.,* p. 165.

[97] Krebs-Rott, p. 335. Röhrich (SW, p. 52) also prints it with only one variant, i.e., "quod ita scriptum."

[98] The comprehensive treatment of Pilgram Marpeck's life, writings, and theology by Kiwiet (*op. cit.,* p. 50) simply repeats the assertions of former scholars.

to by Baum may be one of the Marpeck booklets of 1531,[99] a conjecture based on a statement Baum attributes to Schwenckfeld. Nicoladoni, apparently the only other historian besides Baum who knew of the book, ascribed it to an Anabaptist "biblischer Richtung" on the basis of the title.[100]

After a futile attempt to locate a copy of this book in continental European libraries, the director of the University Library at the Freie Universität, Berlin, Professor Dr. Wieland Schmidt indicated that there was a copy in the British Museum. This is presumably the only extant copy of this booklet. The exact title is: *Ain klarer/ vast nützlicher vnterricht/ wider ettliche Trück / vnd schleichendt Geyster / so jetz in verborgener weisz auszgeen/ dadurch viel frommer hertzen verirrt vnd verfürt werden / kürtzlich / getrewer warnungweisz herfür gebracht.*

On the title page there appears also a table of contents:

i Betreffendt das Apostelampt.

ii Das Bischoff ampt.

iii Die Ceremonien Christi.

iv Vnderschiedt der gotheyt vn menscheyt Christi.

v Die sendung vnd wart [*sic!*] eines newen Propheten.

vi Gebet vnd gut werck Corneli.

Beneath the table of contents appears Proverbs 21:15, the statement, *"Nit was/sonder das,"* and the date MDXXXj.

There are a number of indications that this is one of the booklets condemned by the censors in 1531.[101] The first of

---

[99] Abraham Hulshof, *Geschiedenis van de Doopsgezinden te Straatsburg van 1525 tot 1557* (Amsterdam, 1905), p. 99.

[100] Alexander Nicoladoni, *op. cit.*, p. 128.

[101] Kiwiet (*op. cit.*, p. 80), following Hulshof (*op. cit.*, p. 100), reasons that the description of the contents given by the censors makes it unlikely that it is to be identified with the *Klarer Unterricht*. Now, of course, we can judge the book according to its contents. More work needs to be done, however, on the whole area of censorship of Anabaptist books. Is Hege's assumption correct that after a book was censored it did not circulate at all ("Pilgram Marpeck. . . ," *ARG*, 37 [1940], 250)? This hardly seems likely in the tolerant city of Strasbourg. Karl Schottenloher says that there were three attitudes toward censorship in Strasbourg. One party said that the books should not be printed before they were approved by the Council, another said that no books were to be allowed in the city without the author's name, and a third party felt that leniency should be the course to follow. The matter was increasingly referred to the ministers of Strasbourg, who became more conservative, especially after Hofmann's arrival in Strasbourg and

these is the presence of the motto *"Nit was/sonder das"* just
above the date on the title page. Possibly it represents an
abbreviated translation of the words of Seneca, *"Non quis, sed
quid dicatur, attende"* and occurs on at least one other title
page of the sixteenth century.[102] It is worthy to note that the
same slogan occurs in the *Kunstbuch*, inserted there apparently by the sixteenth-century editor, Jörg Propst Rothenfelder.
This may indicate that some relationship exists between the
booklet of 1531, *Klarer Unterricht,* and the *Kunstbuch.*[103]
The fourth item in the table of contents deals with the difference between the humanity and deity of Christ, and the writers of the *Verantwortung,* Leupold Scharnschlager and Pilgram Marpeck, assert that in order to maintain the true
almighty God in Christ in (or with) his two united natures,
"we contended for several years against certain spirits which
denied that some time ago."[104] The reference could be to
Scharnschlager's opposition to Melchior Hofmann's Christology

---

his publications of 1530, and also because of Sebastian Franck. With
respect to the five books censored in 1531 Schottenloher reports that
they were found in "einem Buchgewölbe des Buchhändlers Wendelin
Richel, das sich in den unteren Geschossen des Strassburger Rathauses
befand" ("Beschlagnahmte Druckschriften aus der Frühzeit der Reformation," *Zeitschrift der Bücherfreunde,* N. F. 8 [1916/17], 316f.).
F. Husner("Zwei unbekannte Wiedertäuferdrucke?" *Stultifera Navis,
Mitteilungsblatt der Schweizerischen Bibliophilen-Gesellschaft,* III
[1946], 84-88) adds nothing to our knowledge of these two books. F.
Ritter ("La police de l'imprimerie et de la librairie a Strasbourg. . . ,"
Revue des Bibliotheques, 32 [1922]) deals only cursorily with our
period (161-65), without shedding any new light on the problem of
censorship of Anabaptist publications.

[102] See CS, XVI, 283, and XIX, 349f. The Latin form appears on
the title page of a book published in 1558. The general idea is
contained also in some modern writers, as e.g., Gerhard von Rad,
Theologie des Alten Testaments, I, 340: "Des weiteren, unterscheidet
sich unser Werk von dem älteren durch sein gesteigertes Interesse an
dem instrumentalem Wie der göttlichen Geschichtslenkung, denn der
älteren war es vielmehr um das Dass gegangen."

[103] On the *Kunstbuch,* its discovery and significance, see Heinold
Fast, *op. cit.* It occurs in this codex on fol. 12b in the introduction
written by Rothenfelder. On Rothenfelder and his relation to Marpeck
see *ME,* IV, 365.

[104] Cf. J. C. Wenger, *MQR,* XII (1938), 269f. The *Verantwortung*
is published in *Quellen und Forschungen. . . ,* ed. by Johann Loserth
(Vienna and Leipzig, 1929). This statement appears on p. 507:41f.
and, if written by Marpeck, was written sometime between 1544 and
1556.

in 1532,[105] but could also refer to the book under discussion.

The last piece of external evidence comes again from the Thesaurus Baumianus where Baum has written after the transcription of the title the following:

Ad haec ultima verba "Nit was s. das" manu coaeva quadam, Schwenckfeldii ut opinor, adscripta reperio quae sequuntur: "Ich sag, das soll u. müss man glouben, will man selig werden." Also pflegen alle Secten Bapst, Luther, Teuffer zureden, hat jede etwas usserlichs daruf sye jr seeligkeit sezt, u. welcher eben dasselbig usserlich nit annimt und glaubt nach jren furgeben, der muss [des] Teuffels seyn, ob er schon sonst so gottesforchtig u. fromm waere als er immer seyn moecht. Also thut auch der dichter dieses buechlins. Ich acht das es der Pilgram sey. Es lat sich kein Sect benugen an der forcht Gottes oder am glauben daran sich doch gott benugen lath. Sye henken all etwas usserlichs dran, ein jeder nach seim verstandt, wider den anderen verwirfft u. verdammt jn einer dem anderen sein verstandt, haben alle geschrifft für sich.[106]

In line with this is the internal evidence of the book, *Klarer Unterricht*, which refers often to "Stillstand"; its appeal as well as its danger.[107] The tone of the above quotation, which Baum took from the Strasbourg copy of the *Klarer Unterricht*, seems to agree with the supposition that Schwenckfeld wrote this. Positive proof is, of course, lacking. Nevertheless it would seem that one is justified in assuming that this book is the one that Schwenckfeld referred to when he said that the Anabaptists had published a book against him.[108]

In determining whether there is any internal evidence of Marpeck's authorship it is risky to compare this book with his writings of 1542ff., partly because the eleven intervening years would probably have caused a change in his style and

[105] T. W. Röhrich, *op. cit.*, p. 71.
[106] Thes. Baum. (ms. 662, fol. 388 verso in Bibliotheque Nationale et Universitaire, Strasbourg; cf. Hulshof, *op. cit.*, p. 99, note 3.) Dr. Rott kindly supplied the writer with a photocopy of this page. It is now reproduced in Krebs-Rott, p. 298.
[107] A iib, *bis;* A viii; C a; C b; C iiib; D iiii.
[108] September 24, 1531, in a letter to John Bader, CS, IV, 259:25f.

his thought, and partly because he had always had a collaborator. Materials known to have been written by Marpeck
without a collaborator are his letters in the *Kunstbuch,* all but
one of which are dated after 1540. The same is true of his
Confession submitted to the Strasbourg Council in the early
days of 1532, which, though drawn up in haste, is no doubt
most reliable for literary comparison.

One question that needs to be dealt with is whether the
content of the *Klarer Unterricht* agrees with the description
by the censors. For instance, the censors reported that Marpeck had asserted that baptism should be administered only
to believers, and that he himself had been thus baptized. In
the *Klarer Unterricht* the author makes the corresponding
statement: "*Ja eben darumb das es geschrieben stet/ hach* [!]
ich mich tauffen lassen / ."[109] In this instance external and
internal evidence agree remarkably.

Another booklet that might be of help both in the solution
of the problem of the authorship of these two books, and also
in locating the two books written by Marpeck in 1531, is the
Clare verantwurtung, which has hitherto been attributed to
Hans Bünderlin. The complete title is: *Clare verantwurtung
ettlicher Artickel/ so jetz durch jrrige geyster schrifftlich vnnd
mündtlich ausschweben / von wegen der ceremonien dess
Newen Testaments / als Predigen / Tauffen / Abendtmal /
Schrifft, etc. zu trost vnd sterck warhaffter Christen/ newlich
aussgangen. Auch betreffent Christi befelch/ sein jüngern
gethan. Vnnd die aussgiessung des heyligen Geysts. Gegründt
in heyliger schrifft.* The date at the end of the book is
MDXXXI, but the place of publication is not given.

Camill Gerbert was the first to ascribe this booklet to Hans
Bünderlin but he did so without indicating in any way that he
was acquainted with the book.[110] Nicoladoni joined Gerbert

---

[109] *KU,* C v. Kiwiet (*op. cit.,* p. 80) is therefore mistaken when he
says that the censor's description does not fit the *Klarer Unterricht.*
Compare especially the sentence: "Addit idem *libelli* (note the singular)
autor, se ideo baptismum recepisse, quod (or quia) ita scriptum etc."
(*vide supra,* p. 36).

[110] *Op. cit.,* p. 96. He states that the *Klarer Unterricht* is a
"Gegenschrift" to Bünderlin's *Erklärung durch vergleichung* (1530), a
suggestion he likely took from the Thesaurus Baumianus, III, 388 *recto,*
but in doing so confused the *Clare verantwurtung* with *Klarer Unterricht,* for Baum states that the former was a reply to *Erklärung durch
vergleichung* (Thes. Baum., fol. 388r.).

in ascribing it to Bünderlin without basing his assumption on Gerbert, but also without showing any knowledge of the contents of the book.[111] This lack of description of content is surprising, since Nicoladoni gives a synopsis of all of Bünderlin's other writings. What led these two men to assume Bünderlin's authorship of this booklet is a mystery, since a careful comparison of its contents with any of three works that bear Bünderlin's name shows clearly that he could not have been the author of the *Clare verantwurtung* because it expresses a position diametrically opposed to his. His writings call for the cessation of all the ceremonies of the church, on the ground that they were instituted only as concessions to the Jews.[112]

A comparison of content and of print shows that both the *Clare verantwurtung* and the *Klarer Unterricht* were printed by the same printer who, however, apparently did not print any of Bünderlin's known works.[113] Furthermore, the tone and style of these two writings, while not identical, is sufficiently similar to suggest a common author. Neither book is consistently organized, although they are written in a less rambling style than any of the other books generally attributed to Pilgram Marpeck. As to their contents, it would appear from the sharper tone and harsher condemnation of the "false spirits" in the *Clare verantwurtung*, from its rejection of the

[111] *Op. cit.*, p. 126. G. H. Williams also ascribes the *Clare verantwurtung* to Bünderlin (*Spiritual and Anabaptist Writers*, p. 156), while Ernst Crous (*RGG*, I, 1496) describes it as his last writing against which Marpeck replied in the *Klarer Unterricht*!

[112] The books that bear his name are: *Aus was ursach...*(Strassburg, 1529); *Eine gemeine berechnung* . . . (Strassburg, 1529); *Erklärung durch vergleichung* (s. 1., 1530). The fourth writing, *Eine gemeine Einleitung* . . . (s. 1., revised ed., 1529), is so similar to Bünderlin's other works that there is little doubt concerning his authorship. The head librarian of the Dresden Royal Library kindly supplied microfilm copies of these works. The work which most clearly states his position with regard to sacraments, etc. is *Erklärung durch vergleichung* (1530), although the desire to be done with all ceremonies is present in all of his works. See C. R. Foster, "Hans Denck and J. Bünderlin," *MQR*, XXXIX (1965), 115-24.

[113] Such a comparison can now be made since Dr. Hans Hillerbrand discovered the only known copy of *Clare verantwurtung* in the Stuttgart Library. See "An Early Anabaptist Treatise on the Christian and the State," *MQR*, XXXII (1958), 29, footnote 5. A comparison of typography shows that Beck, who printed some of Hofmann's writings and also Franck's *Chronica* in 1531, did not print the *Klarer Unterricht*.

argument that length of time weakens the strength of the sacraments, and especially from its use of some of Bünderlin's favorite phrases, that it was directed against Bünderlin, who had just left Strasbourg after causing considerable stir. It was, of course, inevitable that the spiritualism that he represented, bordering on pantheism, and his rejection of Antiochan methods of exegesis, would clash with the sober hermeneutics of the Anabaptists represented by Marpeck. When Marpeck arrived in Strasbourg, the works of Bünderlin were being read in some of the Anabaptist meetings and a showdown between these two types was inevitable. The *Clare verantwurtung* is the statement of the Anabaptist brotherhood, who opposed Bünderlin with vigorous arguments.[114]

On the basis of the content of these booklets the present writer has been led to conclude that they were written either by Marpeck himself or in collaboration with Scharnschlager.[115] Several striking similarities found in Marpeck's later writings appear here.

(1) The stress on the humanity of Christ.

(2) The serviceable nature of the sacraments and ceremonies, including the life of Christ and the Scriptures.

(3) The insistence that the coming of the Holy Spirit and Pentecost are related and that prior to Pentecost no one received the Holy Spirit.

(4) The definition of baptism not as metaphysical but as experiential. The significant thing about baptism is not that it is a symbol (*Zeichen*) but that it is a witness (*Zeugnis*). It is the witnessing response of the believer to God's gracious act in Christ.

(5) Marpeck was one of the few Anabaptists who stressed the practice of feetwashing, and in the

---

[114] For description of the contents of these two booklets and some evidence for Marpeck authorship, see *MQR*, XXXIII (1959), 18-30.

[115] Scharnschlager undoubtedly lived in Strasbourg by this time, although there is no indication that Felicitas Schernschlegerin, who purchased her citizenship on October 16, 1527, is related to Leupold (Ch. Wittmer and J. C. Meyer, *op. cit.*, 2 [1954], 770, No. 8458). On Leupold, see *ME*, IV, 443-46 and literature there cited. According to Reublin's letter to Marpeck of Jan. 26, 1531 (Cornelius, *op. cit.*, II, 253f.), he was in Strasbourg then.

Klarer Unterricht it is repeatedly mentioned, as well as in his later writings.[116]

In the opinion of the present writer all the evidence points to Marpeck's authorship of both of these booklets. The situation addressed in them fits the religious picture in Strasbourg in 1531, and the literary style shows similarity to that of Marpeck. Either Marpeck read these two booklets and was deeply influenced by them in 1531, or else he wrote them, the latter being the more plausible. There is every reason to use them as important sources for Marpeck's theology.

The discovery of these two booklets by Marpeck not only gives us a fuller view of his theology in these important years, but makes it necessary to rethink our whole perspective on the differences between spiritualism and Anabaptism. While it is granted that Sebastian Franck and Bünderlin parted ways with Anabaptism in about 1530, scholars have been more reluctant to draw the lines of distinction between Schwenckfeld and the Anabaptists. On the basis of this newly discovered material, however, it is necessary to make the distinction between spiritualism and Anabaptism earlier and sharper. It is certainly inaccurate to say that Marpeck "did not at this time (1531) engage in controversy with either Schwenckfeld or Hofmann."[117]

[116] Taken by themselves these similarities may not be convincing, but the evidence is cumulative. In addition to the few stylistic similarities given in the *MQR* article cited above one could add the following: the use of the argument that since Christ did not shun the use of mud in healing the blind man, the church ought not to despise external means (*KU*, C viiib; *V*, pp. 76f., 80:30; 184); that Christian judgment must not be premature, but wait for the fruit (*KU*, A vi; *KB*, No. 7); that the spiritualists, like the Jews, wait for some glorious manifestation of Jesus, and miss him because he comes as a carpenter's son (*KU*, A ivb; *QF*, 55:28). That the *Clare verantwurtung* was written against Bünderlin would appear to be supported also by the presence of the term "Ubersprung." Bünderlin's goal was "einen vbersprung auff/ das geistlich thun" (*Ein gemayne Einleittung*, 1529, p. 84) while the *CV* argues that when the true King comes at the second coming "wirt erst der recht vbersprung sein/ da die Ceremonien/ eusserlich leer schrifft vnd alles stückwerck vnd tunckel wort/i. Cor. xiii auffhörn vnd nicht mer von nöten sein werden" (fol. a iii). A little later: "Aber diese geister/ wolten das reich Christi hie in dieser zeit gar zu geistlich machen/ und eynen zu weiten vbersprung thun/ wie es der Antichrist im gegentail gar zu fleischlich hat gemacht" (fol. a viib).

[117] Williams, *Radical Reformation*, p. 274. Although referring to my article on these two books (*MQR*, XXXII, 1959) he apparently never

2. THE CONFESSION OF 1532[118]

As a result of his continual discussions with the religious leaders of Strasbourg Marpeck crystallized his thinking and took issue with Bucer's position in particular. The two booklets of 1531 had defined his position over against Bünderlin and Schwenckfeld. Now, as the Council made it increasingly clear that unless he gave up his Anabaptist views he was *persona non grata* in Strasbourg, he wrote a confession of his faith.[119] He wrote the bulk of the *Confession* either in December, 1531, perhaps during the last three weeks, or during the first two weeks in January of 1532; the appendix, which deals with Bucer's views on infant baptism, could not have been written before December 31. It was presented to the Council on January 18, 1532.

This *Confession* is introduced by a series of propositions and is, to a large extent, a defense of these propositions. It makes abundant use of Scripture and names no other writer,[120] except for one passing reference to Luther in which Marpeck seeks to claim Luther's authority for his position.[121] It reiterates two themes again and again. One of these is the radical separation between the Old and New Covenants, evoked by Bucer's position on this question. The second theme deals with the nature of baptism; Marpeck repeatedly makes the point that baptism is not to be considered a sign (*Zeichen*) but rather a witness (*Zeugnis*).[122]

The value of the *Confession* as a source lies not in its evidence of reflective thinking, but in its indication of the direction of Marpeck's thinking at that time in his life. The rebuttal by Bucer is valuable for its insight into Bucer's methods of countering the arguments of this Anabaptist leader.

---

read it, otherwise he could not say that I "discovered and edited" the two books, nor that both are directed against Bünderlin (*ibid.*).

118 Wenger, *op. cit.*, pp. 154f. Kiwiet, *op. cit.*, pp. 71f.

119 He called it a "Rechenschaft." It was first published by Wenger (*op. cit.*, pp. 167-202), more recently by Krebs-Rott (pp. 416-527).

120 This is hardly sufficient grounds for saying that it was written in prison as does Kiwiet (*op. cit.*, p. 71).

121 Page 196. Kiwiet's statement (*ibid.*) that Marpeck does not mention a single theologian thus needs correction.

122 Kiwiet errs in attributing this view to Denck (*op. cit.*, p. 134, followed by Bergsten, *op. cit.*, p. 105). Denck uses the term "bezeugnis" to be sure, but in an entirely different way.

Although it is unfortunately not very perspicuous, as a source for the study of the theology of the early Marpeck the *Confession* is invaluable.

3. THE TAUFBÜCHLEIN OF 1542[123]

In an attempt to unite the splintered Anabaptist movement and to encourage those who were tempted to become weary, the Anabaptist brotherhood in South Germany revised and translated the *Bekentnisse van beyden Sacramenten*, published by the Wassenberg preachers of Münster in 1533 under the leadership of Bernhard Rothmann. The *Bekentnisse* presented a concise and clear defense of the position against infant baptism.[124] Rothmann and the other preachers at Münster had sought discussion of this point for some time, and finally a major disputation was held at Münster on August 7 and 8, 1533.[125] Although neither Rothmann nor any of his associates at this time were Anabaptists, they spoke out openly against the practice of infant baptism. As a result of the disputation and the publication of the *Bekentnisse* a book was written by the Strasbourg clergy in 1534, entitled: *Bericht auss der heyligen geschrift von der recht gottseligen anstellung und hausshaltung Christlicher gemeyn, eynsatzung der diener des worts, haltung und brauch der heyligen Sacramenten. Vom heyligen tauff. . . . Von dem h. sacrament des leybs unnd bluts unsers herren Jesu. . . .* [126] This book extends to over one hundred pages, and appears first to have been written as a letter to the preachers at Münster, then published at the Augsburg Council's request.

Since the *Vermanung* is a revised translation of the Münster *Bekentnisse* one is tempted to see it as a contribution to this discussion. However, the editors nowhere refer to the *Bericht auss der heyligen geschrift*, nor indeed to the *Bekentnisse*

[123] Wenger, *op. cit.*, pp. 158f. Kiwiet, *op. cit.*, pp. 72f. Bergsten, *op. cit.*, p. 47. See also *ME*, IV, 816.

[124] An excellent introduction to this writing and a modern edition have been supplied by Heinrich Detmer and Robert Krumbholtz in *Zwei Schriften des Münsterschen Wiedertäufers Bernhard Rothmann* (Dortmund, 1904). The *Bekentnisse* appears on pp. 1-85.

[125] H. Detmer reports on this disputation in: "Das Religionsgespräch zu Münster am 7. und 8. August 1533," in *Monatshefte der Comenius-Gesellschaft*, IX (1900), 273-300.

[126] Copy in the Krauth Library, Lutheran Theological Seminary, Philadelphia, Pennsylvania.

from which they took two thirds of their material![127] Another
alternative is to view it as a polemic against Caspar Schwenckfeld, and to assume that the latter's propaganda instigated
its publication of the *Vermanung*.[128] Its main purpose was
to build up and unite the brotherhood, and since the book
was of a confessional nature it was published anonymously
from an unknown place with another confession as a basis.[129]
At a number of points the *Bekentnisse* suffered drastic
revision; these points are precisely the ones that show the
Gemeindetheologie of the Marpeck brotherhood at work.
Since it is confessional, the individual authorship must not be
too greatly stressed. In actual fact, it is next to impossible to
distinguish between Scharnschlager and Marpeck as authors.
Unless otherwise noted, all references to the *Vermanung* in
the present study do not appear in the *Bekentnisse*.

The outline of the *Vermanung* is simple. It deals first of all
with the term "sacrament" and whether or not it is a legiti-
mate one. Then follows a lengthy discussion on baptism, and
a summary treatment (about twenty pages) of the Lord's
Supper.

The importance of the book lies in the fact that it is an
attempt to unite the Anabaptists on a platform other than the
Hutterite one and that it is an explicit rejection of the Münsterites and their program of force (even though no compunction
was felt about using Rothmann's *Bekentnisse* as a basis).
Since the *Bekentnisse* was written prior to Rothmann's commitment to believer's baptism (a commitment that incidentally
never led to his acceptance of the suffering church), the logic

---

127 Frank J. Wray, *op. cit.*

128 Bergsten (*op. cit.*, p. 47) attributes this view to Loserth without
documentation, and, arguing from internal evidence, rejects it. On the
whole Bergsten tends to stress the friendliness between Marpeck and
Schwenckfeld before the publication of the *Vermanung*. That Schwenckfeld felt it was directed against him is clear from a remark he makes
in a letter to Helene von Freyberg (May 27, 1543) about "das
buechlin von Pilgram, welchs er wider uns geschriben..." (*CS*, VIII,
618). The editors of the *Corpus* mistakenly identify it as the *Verantwortung* (*CS*, VIII, 617).

129 Kiwiet's statement that the editors of the *Corpus* indicate Froschauer in Zürich as publisher "ohne weitere Begründung" (*op. cit.*, pp.
72f.) needs correction. According to *CS*, VIII, 162, the editors rely on
Arnold Kuczynski, *Thesaurus Libellorum Historiam Reformationis Illustrantium Verzeichniss einer Sammlung von nahezu 3000 Flugschriften
Luthers und seiner Zeitgenossen* (Leipzig, 1870), p. 272; admittedly
an unreliable source.

of believer's baptism is not at all inherent in the *Bekentnisse*. Its value for Marpeck was its systematic rebuttal of the arguments for infant baptism, which he used to establish his case for believer's baptism.

All that is known regarding the circumstances of the writing[130] of this book comes through Schwenckfeld's comments. Two copies are extant, one in the British Museum, discovered there by John Horsch and photocopied for the Goshen College Library, and one in the Württemberg Landesbibliothek, from which a modern edition has been prepared.[131] A manuscript copy was discovered by Robert Friedmann among Hutterite codices in Austria. It is not clear how widespread its influence was in the sixteenth century, but Marpeck mentioned in a letter of 1553 that he was sending twenty *"Bundszeugnisse"* to Moravia.[132] Since the *Vermanung* was also called *"das buch der bundesbezeugung,"* it is quite likely that it is here meant.

4. THE VERANTWORTUNG[133]

The *Verantwortung* is the finest single source of the theology of the South German Anabaptists, having been composed from the years 1542 till 1556. Some parts may be even older, but it was surely finished by 1561. Since it came out in two installments (it was not published until modern times), the first installment being completed hastily by 1544, it is customary to designate the two parts as V I and V II.

a. Verantwortung I

The publication of the *Vermanung* brought the tension between the Schwenckfeld circle of friends and the Marpeck brotherhood into the open and resulted in a vigorous literary

[130] Christian August Salig (*Vollständige Historie der Augsburgischen Confession und derselben zugethanen Kirchen,* III [Halle, 1735], 1113f.) also knows of it only through the references to it in Schwenckfeld.

[131] By Christian Hege in *Gedenkschrift zum 400 Jährigen Jubiläum der Mennoniten* (Ludwigshafen, 1925), pp. 178-282. A photostatic reproduction of the British Museum copy was used to check Hege's remarkably reliable edition.

[132] *KB,* fol. 167.

[133] Wenger, *op. cit.,* p. 160; Kiwiet, *op. cit.,* pp. 74f.; Bergsten, *op. cit.,* pp. 56f.; *ME,* IV, 807f.

battle, which continued for nearly two decades.[134] The first reply to the *Vermanung* was Schwenckfeld's *Judicium*, which was meant to circulate only among the Anabaptists, and was ostensibly written at the request of some in Schwenckfeld's group. It was meant as a quiet correction of Anabaptists.[135]

The contents of the *Verantwortung I* consist of a rebuttal of the *Judicium* written by Schwenckfeld. It makes no reference to other books, but gives extensive citation from Scripture. Large sections of the *Judicium* are printed in full, then vigorously refuted.

The publication of the correspondence between Schwenckfeld and Marpeck shows that there was a variety of factors in the parting of the ways between the spiritualists and the Anabaptists.[136] Nevertheless the *Verantwortung* would probably not have been written, were it not for the *Judicium's* biting criticism of the poor uninstructed Brethren who wrote the *Vermanung*. The *Judicium* was completed by August 21, 1542;[137] and upon receiving it the Anabaptists immediately began to refute it.

There is considerable difference of opinion as to when the first part of the *Verantwortung* was completed and sent to Schwenckfeld.[138] The fact that at the conclusion of the first part of the *Verantwortung* mention is made of the haste with which that part was completed and sent out suggests that it must have been completed in a relatively short time after the receipt of the *Judicium*.[139] Marpeck dated the letter written to accompany *Verantwortung I*, "*Newenjahrsabent anno 1544.*"[140] It seems plausible to assume that the date meant is December 31, 1544.[141] But this would mean that over two years elapsed between the receipt of the *Judicium* (1542)

[134] It is still reflected in the correspondence between Schwenckfeld and Daniel Graff (see *CS*, XVI, Doc. No. MCXXIX).

[135] It was not published until 1927 (*CS*, VIII, 161-214) and exists also in the edition of the *Verantwortung* by Johann Loserth in *Quellen und Forschungen* (see Bibliography).

[136] As shown by Bergsten (*op. cit.*, pp. 5-8).

[137] *CS*, VIII, 222.

[138] The date of its completion must be the same as that of the letter to Schwenckfeld (*QF*, pp. 55-59). The dates of January 31, 1544, found in *ME* (III, 494) for the letter and January 1, 1544 (III, 496), for the completion of *V*, I, are corrected in *ME*, IV, 1146.

[139] *V*, I, 174.

[140] *QF*, p. 59.

[141] So Loserth, *QF*, pp. 20, 54.

and the Anabaptist reply. This hardly seems possible in view of the reference to haste at the end of *Verantwortung I*. Consequently, the phrase has been interpreted to mean the evening of New Year's Day.[142] The question is further complicated by the change of the beginning of the New Year; one authority even suggests that from 1544 South Germany changed New Year's Day to January 1.[143] The exact date of the beginning of the New Year is not of great consequence, since there would only be about a week's difference. Customary usage would indicate that *Newenjahrsabent* refers to the date following, namely, the night before the festive day.[144]

It is therefore most probable that *Verantwortung I* was written during 1543 and completed at the end of that year, though the exact date and month cannot be determined.[145]

[142] John Wenger was the first to suggest this, conjecturing that Marpeck might have written Silvestri if he meant New Year's Eve (*op. cit.*, pp. 160, 164). The other alternative he suggests is December 31, 1543. Kiwiet makes the date "um Weihnachten 1544" (*op. cit.*, p. 62) or "An Weihnachten" (p. 74), citing the authority of Fritz Blanke that it refers to the evening preceding New Year, supposedly December 24, 1544. Kiwiet's statement that Marpeck wrote V, I "in a little more than a year" (p. 62) therefore is questionable. Bergsten accepts the judgment of Blanke with reference to the meaning of "Newenjahrsabent" but attempts to make a clear case for the date 1543 by using a reference in a letter that Schwenckfeld wrote February, 1544, in which he speaks of books by Marpeck (*CS*, VIII, 866). Unfortunately he relates the date of V, I, to the *Dialogus* (*op. cit.*, pp. 54, 58). It is clear (*CS*, VIII, 862) that the *Dialogus* is not another book written by Schwenckfeld against Marpeck, but rather a summary of a dialogue that Schwenckfeld and Pilgram had about the *Vermanung*. At the complaint of Pilgram that Schwenckfeld never did justice to his comments (and Pilgram appears to have been somewhat verbose—while Schwenckfeld was plagued with deafness) the latter wrote up this *Dialogus* (see also CS, XVI, Doc. MCXXIX and CS, XVIII, 47).

[143] *The Catholic Encyclopedia* (New York, 1913), III, 739.

[144] According to H. Grotefend (*Taschenbuch der Zeitrechnung des Deutschen Mittelalters und der Neuzeit*[4] [Hannover und Leipzig, 1915], p. 18) the term "abend" always relates to the day following. Hence "Neujahrsabend" must be the *same* as Silvestri, and cannot refer to the evening of the first day of the New Year (p. 83).

[145] According to Schmeller (*BW*, I, 1209), it was the custom to use the year number of the following year ("Das New-Jar, oder vielmehr blos die Zahl des nächstfolgenden Jahres, wurde bis ins 14te und 15te Jahrh. oft schon vom Weihnachtstage des laufenden Jahres angefangen"). See also the illustration he gives on col. 1206 where "1318 an St. Johans tage ze Weihennacht" actually means 1317.

b. *Verantwortung II*

The best available source for a study of South German Anabaptist theology is the second part of the *Verantwortung*. The date of its completion has also been the subject of debate, J. J. Kiwiet having advanced the theory that the second half of the *Verantwortung* was written after 1550, since it makes abundant reference to the *Testamenterleutterung*, which was not finished until 1550.[146] One of the problems related to this theory is that there is no sure evidence of the date of the completion of the *Testamenterleutterung*. By 1550 it was already known and no doubt published,[147] but it may have been ready earlier. The statement of the author of the *Testamenterleutterung* that he did not work alone leads to the assumption that it was published earlier than is generally thought. Schwenckfeld said on May 1, 1547, that he had seen a large book made by the Anabaptists, which dealt with the faith of the patriarchs.[148] Since the first part of the *Verantwortung* does not use the *Testamenterleutterung* and the second part does, it is logical to conclude that while *Verantwortung I* was being written the *Testamenterleutterung* was not yet published. In view of the nature of the *Testamenterleutterung* it is not impossible, however, for both *Verantwortung I* and the *Testamenterleutterung* to have been written by May 1, 1547. If this is the case, Schwenckfeld's reference to a "big book" may refer to the *Testamenterleutterung*, a book which is indeed large and which deals almost exclusively with the faith of the patriarchs.[149] Since *Verantwortung I* hardly touches upon the faith of the patriarchs at all, the reference must be either to *Verantwortung II* or to the *Testamenterleutterung*, the latter being the more likely. Hence the date for *Verantwortung II* comes after May, 1547, and the date of its completion is uncertain. It was certainly completed by 1561, possibly even by the time of Marpeck's death in 1556. If there is a difference in style in the second part, this may indicate that Scharnschlager had a larger hand in its

[146] *Op. cit.*, p. 76.

[147] According to Seifrid's testimony recorded in Roth, *ARG*, IV, 640.

[148] *CS*, XI, 21. Bergsten (*op. cit.*, p. 61) was the first to suggest that this refers to the *TE*, although the present writer had arrived at this conclusion prior to reading Bergsten.

[149] *Vide infra*, pp. 51f.

preparation than in the first part. Only a careful stylistic study could shed light on this problem, and this falls beyond the scope of the present work.

In the second part there is an extensive array of contradictions between the early and the later Schwenckfeld, which could only have been written by someone well acquainted with some of Schwenckfeld's works. The references to the *Theologia Deutsch*, to Franck's *Paradoxa*, and the *Testaments of the Twelve Patriarchs* point toward Scharnschlager's authorship, since his writings in the *Kunstbuch* as well as his confession before the Strasbourg Council indicate wide reading and an inclination to point up contradictions in authors.

The manuscripts of the *Verantwortung* were completed by Scharnschlager after they had been approved by the leaders of the brotherhood, but the work as a whole was not published until modern times.

5. TESTAMENTERLEUTTERUNG[150]

The work that followed the *Verantwortung I* chronologically is the concordance called *Testamenterleuttterung*, which was written between the two parts of the *Verantwortung*. This book exists only in two extant copies, one at the Zürich Library[151] and one formerly at the Prussian State Library, Berlin. This also appeared anonymously, partly because of popular over-concern with the names of authors. Such information might hinder the readers in getting an understanding of the Bible.[152] The date also is missing, but on the basis of court testimony given by the Anabaptist George Seifrid and some remarks made by Schwenckfeld it is possible to determine an approximate date. Seifrid testified on May 6, 1550, that he attempted to get a book from Pilgram that the brotherhood had made on its printing press, which they called "*Das Buch von gestern und heute.*"[153] It is, of course, possible that it was not yet finished; but this is not likely. Bergsten is apparently correct in dating this book earlier than is generally

[150] Wenger, *op. cit.*, pp. 161f.; Kiwiet, *op. cit.*, pp. 77f.; Bergsten, *op. cit.*, pp. 59f.; W. Wiswedel, "Die Testamentserlaüterung," *Blätter für Württembergische Kirchengeschichte*, 41 (1937), 64-76; *ME*, IV, 699f.

[151] The Zürich copy on microfilm was used for this study.

[152] See the Preface, published in *QF*, pp. 579-584.

[153] Roth, *ARG*, IV, 460.

done; a safe assumption is that it was written before May, 1547.

More important than its date are the nature and structure of the book. It is in the nature of a topical concordance which seeks to relate the Old and New Testaments. A series of 118 topics are selected and then Scripture passages quoted fully to shed light on them. The basic distinction is between "yesterday" (Old Covenant) and "today" (New Covenant). At times a third category is introduced with the heading "longed for yesterday." At the end of each section there appear *"Beireden,"* which vary considerably in length and which the reader is asked to ignore if they do not agree with his views.

The reasons for compiling the book are given in the Preface. They are as follows: (1) It was a commonly held opinion that Christ's suffering worked retroactively into the Old Testament period; to hold such a position is to deny the sentence in the universally held Apostles' Creed that Christ descended into hell, for there would have been no need for Christ to proclaim redemption to the patriarchs if they had already received all the gifts of salvation. (2) The suffering and resurrection of Christ are slandered if their benefits are projected into the Old Testament. (3) Since the New Testament is clear on the point that redemption came only through Christ, to be vague on the distinction between the Old and New Covenants means to lessen the authority of Scripture and to imply that it contradicts itself. (4) Through a confusion of the relation of the two covenants earthly power is perverted from its rightful use and is used against God's divine purpose.

The abundant use of the *Testamenterleutterung* in the second part of the *Verantwortung* and the fact that its viewpoint is never called into question, as well as the evidence given by Seifrid, point in the direction of its emanation from the Marpeck brotherhood. Gerhard Hein attributes it to Leupold Scharnschlager on the basis of a reference in a letter to a book by Scharnschlager on *"Underschaid."*[154] While the word *"Underschaid"* does occur in the title of the *Testamenterleutterung*, this alone would hardly prove Scharnschlager's au-

[154] "Leupold Scharnschlager," *Menn. Geschbl.*, 4 (1939), 6-12. Also *ME, sub voce.*

thorship; but perhaps all the evidence taken together points in his direction.

The influence of the book in the sixteenth century is hard to estimate. Its influence seems apparent in the discussion on the Old and New Testaments held at Franckenthal in 1571,[155] for even though the *Testamenterleutterung* is never referred to in those discussions, the position defended there is substantially that found in the *Testamenterleutterung*. The presence of one of Marpeck's close co-workers at this colloquium supports this surmise.[156]

Its influence is also suggested in the warning by Jacob Andrea, a Lutheran minister, against the Anabaptist book "Today and Yesterday" in his sermons at Esslingen, Württemberg.[157] Beyond that there is no evidence that the book has had any influence or circulation.

6. THE LETTERS OF MARPECK

In addition to the books and Marpeck's *Confession*, nineteen letters are extant, which are also useful as a source for the theology and hermeneutics of Marpeck. The farewell letter that Marpeck drew up for the City Council at Strasbourg[158] has already been discussed.

The next letter, on the theme of the unity of the church,[159] dated December 21, 1540, was written to the believers around Strasbourg. The same theme prompted a letter to the Swiss Brethren, who were threatening the unity of the church by their proclivity toward quick judgments. This is one of the longest letters in the *Kunstbuch*; it should probably be dated about 1541.[160] Shortly after this, in the spring of 1542, the

---

[155] *Protocoll: Das ist/ alle handlung des gesprechs zu Franckenthal* (Heidelberg, 1571), pp. 19, 44, 45, 87-90, 272f., 601f. It is the first point for discussion (see *ME*, II, 374).

[156] Hans Büchel (see *ME, sub voce,* and Fast, *op. cit.,* p. 226).

[157] *Drey und dreissig Predigen Von dem furnembsten Spaltungen in der Christlichen Religion. . .* (Tübingen, 1568), Part 4, Sermon 5, pp. 101f. According to Kiwiet (*op. cit.,* p. 80) a reference to it occurs also in Andreas Ambergius, *Disputatio contra Anabaptistarum errores* (Wittenberg, 1598), p. A 2.

[158] *Vide supra*, p. 29.

[159] *KB*, No. 5.

[160] No. 7, fol. 27a-62b. The date on the letter is 1531, but Fast has rightly called it into question and suggested instead the date 1542 (*op. cit.,* p. 227). The error is more easily explained if it is assumed

Vermanung was published, which also had as a major concern the unification of the Anabaptists. The reluctance of the Swiss Brethren to accept Marpeck's proffers of union and their disagreements with the close associates of Marpeck, Rothenfelder and Uli Scherer, prompted the second epistle to the Swiss Brethren, which is much briefer than the first; its last pages are missing. [161] He deals with the same problem from a different angle in his writing to the Anabaptists in the Grisons, Appenzell, St. Gall, and Alsace, dated February 1, 1547, when he discusses the humility of Christ.[162] Another epistle dealing with this same theme is directed to the Brethren in the Grisons and Appenzell and is dated August 9, 1551.[163] Since Rothenfelder was directly involved in these tensions, there is evidence that he slanted the headings for the letters somewhat; but nevertheless their content makes clear that Marpeck was much concerned with the over-zealousness of the Swiss Brethren.

Related to this is the concern that the reaction against legalism should not degenerate into libertinism, a danger that appears to have plagued the Strasbourg Anabaptist churches. To counteract this Marpeck sent an epistle to the churches in Moravia and in Strasbourg on the theme of Christian freedom.[164] Two other epistles were written to the Moravian churches, both dealing with the church, one with the inner church[165] and one with the service and servants of the church.[166] An epistle to the Brethren in Württemberg dated August 15, 1544, at Augsburg deals with the same theme, namely, the difference between the Christian church and the Hagaric church.[167]

In this group there are three more or less personal letters. Two of these were written to Magdalena von Pappenheim,

---

that Maler simply changed the "4" to a "3." It is quite impossible to imagine this letter having been written in 1531 in view of the available sources, so 1541 seems most likely.

[161] No. 8, dated 1545. Fast, on the basis of the style, attributes it to Marpeck even though the signature is missing (*op. cit.*, p. 228).

[162] *KB*, No. 35.

[163] *KB*, No. 34.

[164] *KB*, No. 3, dated Augsburg, 1544.

[165] *KB*, No. 37, to Austerlitz and elsewhere, 1553? (*MQR*, XXXII [1958], 201-05).

[166] *KB*, No. 16, dated Augsburg, 1553

[167] *KB*, No. 33.

one, dated at Augsburg, 1545,[168] concerning those who are dead in their sins, and the other, dated December 9, 1547, dealing with the kinds of people who find themselves in judgment, and with the nobility.[169] The third more or less personal letter is addressed to Leupold Scharnschlager and is the only extant bit of correspondence between these two men. It is apparent from this letter that they had a close working relationship.[170]

Furthermore there are four epistles without indication of recipient, three of which are preserved without indication of date. One of these deals with the subject of love,[171] one with the love of God as shown in Christ Jesus,[172] and another with the five kinds of fruits of true repentance.[173] Finally there is a theological treatise on the humanity of Christ, a subject that was dear to Marpeck and on which he often made extensive statements.[174] The discovery of the *Kunstbuch* thus has made available sixteen hitherto unknown letters and treatises by Marpeck, which throw invaluable light on this church leader. He is now seen not merely as a controversialist against his opponent Schwenckfeld, but also as a leader dealing with deviants within his own group and as a pastor trying to strengthen his flock.[175]

Two more known letters are not included in the *Kunstbuch*. One of these is the letter to Schwenckfeld that accompanied the first part of the *Verantwortung* at the beginning of 1544.[176] The second was written to Helena Streicher defending his position over against Schwenckfeld's.[177]

---

[168] *KB*, No. 2.

[169] *KB*, No. 38.

[170] *KB*, No. 29, dated 1545, and dealing with the inheritance of sin (not "original sin," *MQR*, XXXIII [1959], 214). This relationship dates from about 1530 (see *Bündnerisches Monatsblatt*, 1916, p. 80, and Krebs, *op. cit.*, p. 424).

[171] *KB*, No. 4.

[172] *KB*, No. 13.

[173] *KB*, No. 18, published by H. Fast in *Der linke Flügel der Reformation* (Bremen, 1962), pp. 105-117.

[174] *KB*, No. 15, dated Augsburg, January 22, 1555, possibly the last extant writing of Marpeck. *MQR*, XXXII (1958), 205-210.

[175] For a fuller description of these new sources, see Heinold Fast, *op. cit.*

[176] Published by Johann Loserth in *Quellen und Forschungen* (Vienna and Berlin, 1929), pp. 55-59.

[177] Also published by Loserth in *Quellen und Forschungen*, pp. 170-188. Both of these sources are cited as *QF* and page references.

Even before the discovery of the *Kunstbuch* and the *Klarer Unterricht* and the identification of the *Clare verantwurtung*, Kiwiet ascertained that there is available four times as much source material for Marpeck as for Menno Simons. Even allowing for difference in page sizes and for the fact that the *Testamenterleutterung* is not a very valuable source, it is nevertheless true that the extent of source material available for the study of Marpeck is richer than for any other Anabaptist leader.

The value of these sources is heightened by two factors. In the first place, they span nearly thirty years of the Anabaptist movement, 1530-1560, and open to our view the developing thought of a man who was an Anabaptist almost from the beginning. Secondly, they reveal a very wide range of reflection. Not only are the positions of the major Reformers, such as Luther, Zwingli, Calvin, Bullinger, and Bucer, here evaluated, but the various Anabaptist emphases are considered and discussed. Hutterite communism, the Münsterite rebellion, Swiss concern for external details, the spiritualism of Hans Denck and of Caspar Schwenckfeld—all are here evaluated and discarded. Marpeck, though indebted to many predecessors, emerges with an amazingly independent position singularly his own. One of the objectives of this study is to determine the factors in the development of this position in the area of hermeneutics.

A final word should be said about the use of the sources. No attempt will be made to differentiate in detail between Marpeck and his co-workers in the composite books. Besides the great difficulty involved, it is quite obvious that Marpeck felt it most important that individualism be tempered by the interaction of the Christian brotherhood. Hence, no attempt will be made to unravel the various strands that comprise this *Gemeindetheologie*. Nevertheless Marpeck's leadership within the group was dominant enough to qualify him as the subject of this study.

II

REGULATING PRINCIPLES IN MARPECK'S HERMENEUTICS

A. THE FORMAL PRINCIPLE: *SOLA SCRIPTURA*

Since Marpeck's writings are not meant to be systematic, and since he rarely discusses his view of the Scriptures,[1] we must arrive at his attitude toward them on the basis of his use of them.

It is already clear in his *Confession* that the Scriptures are to be his only authority. This made Bucer cautious in his use of the evidence of tradition and resulted in his confining himself to the Bible in his arguments for infant baptism.[2] A cursory glance over the *Confession* shows what a battery of Scripture texts and allusions it contains, not all of which are listed on the margin. The *Vermanung*, insofar as it is reworked by Marpeck and his associates, shows, however, a recession from the amassing of Scriptural citations.

Though the *Verantwortung I* appears to use Scripture references less frequently than does *Verantwortung II*, both parts abound in Scriptural references. The same is true of the letters in the *Kunstbuch*. In the *Testamenterleutterung* the

---

[1] V, pp. 108f., 294-316, 517-530; *KB*, fol. 59b-61b.

[2] Krebs-Rott, pp. 398:14f., 402:27, 510:17. In his reply to the Schwabach articles of Luther, Bucer also assumed that understanding in doctrine can best be accomplished simply when the "artikel alle mit bublischen worten und ufs clerest und curtzest gefasst wurden" (*Quellen und Forschungen zur Geschichte des Augsburgischen Glaubensbekenntnisses*, I:2, ed. by Wilhelm Gussmann [Leipzig and Berlin, 1911], p. 289). When the diversity of interpretation became more apparent he began to attach more significance to the exegesis of the Church Fathers. In addition to Scripture there must then be the "solidus consensus cum ecclesia Christi" (compare the introduction to the third edition of the Gospel Commentary and F. R. Lammert, "Martin Bucer's Activity for a United Protestantism," University of Chicago Diss., 1941, pp. 139-140). On Bucer's Biblicism see also J. Müller, *Martin Bucers Hermeneutik* (Gütersloh, 1965), pp. 150-162.

reader is advised, if he so desires, to ignore the editorial comments, and pay heed only to the Biblical evidence.

His apparently mechanical array of texts does not, however, indicate a blind devotion to Holy Scripture, but rather a conviction that the very nature of Holy Scripture is such that it does not call for complex arguments of rhetoric and sophistry (*schriftgelerten kunst*). As in Holy Scripture, so also in the words of the apostles and the Lord himself, one can discern that they were not spoken according to rhetoric and "*schriftgelerter kunst, weisheit und spitzigen reden*" (V, II, 510:24ff.).

Marpeck countered Schwenckfeld's argument distinguishing between a physical and spiritual Abraham by saying: "Therefore we do not go beyond the evidence of Holy Scripture, and since it calls him simply Abraham, and distinguishes between physical and spiritual promises to him, so do we" (V, II, 373f., cf. 528). The readers of the *Vermanung* are urged to "judge it according to the chalk line of Holy Scripture" (*TB*, 252 from Rothmann, but omitted from *Bekentnisse*, 2). To Schwenckfeld's criticism that the Anabaptists do not have a catechism, the writers of the *Verantwortung* reply: "we freely admit that we . . . have no such catechism but we do have Peter (as an example?) Acts 2, 3, 4, 5, 10 and the Holy Scriptures of the whole Old and New Testaments . . ." (*V*, 74).

Marpeck's appeal to the basic simplicity and clarity of the Bible comes to energetic expression in his letter to Schwenckfeld upon finishing the first part of the *Verantwortung* (*QF*, 56-57). No doubt referring to Schwenckfeld's seeming pride in his learning, Marpeck states that one had better learn the simple language of the common man before one begins to exercise "*kunst*" with the Scriptures; and he disparages the learning of the classical languages if one does not allow the "*kunst*" and wisdom of God to be revealed through his Holy Spirit. He says that it is the true nature of the serpent to distort the simple text of God's Word to such an extent that the simple are confused, but this manner of dealing will be put to shame under the feet of Christ.[3] It is the nature of Holy

_____
[3] *QF*, p. 57. Marpeck taught that human reason is prone to disguise itself as an angel of light, "sonderlich die schriftgelehrte Art" (Humanity of Christ, p. 207). The opposite extreme "grobe fleischliche Einfalt," which usually assumed a self-chosen spirituality and which results in sects, is repudiated by Marpeck as waterless clouds (*ibid.*, cf. *QF*, 56:23, but especially *V*, p. 469). Ever since Hübmaier, Anabaptists

Scripture to be clear (*Hayter*), and faith must bow in its presence and accept its direction. "*Die geschrift richt sich aber nit nach eins yeden glauben*" (*V*, II, 510:24f.). If Scripture could be broken or were false, Paul's faith would have been wrong, for he says he believes all that is written in the Law and the Prophets (*V*, II, 504).

The nature of God's Word is such that it challenges tradition and calls for renewal. To Schwenckfeld's complaint that the efforts of the Marpeck brotherhood to reform the church had not been confirmed by miracles, Marpeck retorts that they are still living in the New Testament age, and that the preaching, teaching, word, and gospel of Jesus Christ have been abundantly confirmed through miracles, so that whoever reads or hears the gospel of Jesus Christ read, can as easily come to faith through it as if he heard Christ, Paul, or Peter orally; for such empowering, evangelical, apostolic writings, as well as all other Biblical, prophetic writings have been written for us that they may serve for our instruction until Christ's return (*V*, II, 436-447). Since God does not desire anyone to perish, Marpeck's argument continues, the will of God is given for our attention and understanding in the Old and New Testaments, before and after the "*vermenschung*" of Christ (*V*, II, 437:42ff.).

What is it that gives the Holy Scripture this authority? Marpeck refuses to distinguish between the oral and the written Word of Christ because the Holy Spirit has written the Gospels and apostolic writings through the hands of the evangelists and apostles. But it is not for Marpeck the ink and paper, or the perishable, creaturely parts of books, or human speech that is God's Word; rather the "meaning, written or spoken, that it contains." It is faith that makes the written Word become spirit and life in the heart of the recipient.[4]

---

refused to be enslaved by the new popery of the linguists who wished to be the authorities to settle doctrinal questions. One Moravian Anabaptist observed that "those who crucified our Lord knew Latin, Greek and Hebrew" (John Horsch, "The Faith of the Swiss Brethren," *MQR*, V [1931], 20, footnote).

[4] *V*, II, 518ff.; 521ff.; 529ff. Torsten Bergsten is correct when he says: "Marpeck vertritt . . . nicht einen orthodoxen Verbalinspirationsglauben, man könnte stattdessen seine Auffassung als eine Kombination der Real- und Personal- inspirationstheorie, charakterisieren" (*op. cit.*, p. 35). This is true of the Anabaptists as a whole(compare Paul Peachey's statement: ". . .Anabaptist Biblicism in modern times has become widely identified with the Fundamentalist view of Scripture. It is the view of

Again it is in the Scriptures themselves that Marpeck finds support for his view. Marpeck sees Scripture as having been used in three different ways by Christ, Moses, the prophets, and the apostles. The first is didactic, i.e., for the purpose of imparting *information*, and is related primarily to those who know nothing of God's witness and his Word. The second function is *admonition* and serves to help those on their way who have already learned but need assistance so that they can truly bear fruit. Marpeck singles out the book of Deuteronomy as being especially valuable in this area, as well as the parenetic sections of the Epistles written by the apostles.[5] Thirdly, there is the function of *threat* (*Gebot und Verbot*); where these threats are not heeded the punishment and wrath of God are sure to follow. This threatening aspect of Scripture often results in hope and repentance for the believer and in that way the Scripture realizes its true purpose. In case the reader does not heed the Scripture or denies his faith and becomes apostate he must be handed over to Satan. Pilgram concludes that "whoever does not use the Scriptures with these three distinctions cannot deal in Holy Scriptures with certitude, and especially where the true teacher, the Holy Spirit does not precede in all knowledge of Christ, there all of (Scripture) is misused when one desires to admonish where there has been no instruction, or punish where there is no knowledge of sin, or make sin where there is no commandment."[6]

It was the intent of Pilgram Marpeck both to avoid the Charybdis of spiritualism in which the authority of the Word is lost, and also to avoid the Scylla of arid Biblicism, which makes the New Testament an enslaving letter.[7] Some principles that guided him in his hermeneutics will now engage our attention.

---

the present writer that few outside influences have so adversely affected modern Mennonites as this confusion" [*The Recovery of the Anabaptist Vision*, p. 333]).

[5] Marpeck calls Deuteronomy "Wiedereroeffnung," which was its Swiss-German title according to Schmeller, *sub voce*.

[6] *KB*, fol. 60b f.

[7] Compare his statement: "Gott wolle die so jetzt zu unserer Zeit durch die Gnad Christi abgesondert sein von neuen Menschensatzungen bewahren und verhueten das sie nicht ein neuer Raub widerfahr. Collo 2" (*KB*, 48b). On the margin stand the words:"ungenannte evangelische vnd täufferisch."

B. THE MATERIAL PRINCIPLE: THE HUMANITY OF JESUS[8]

Marpeck's Christology is definitely a logos-Christology with the major emphasis falling upon the humanity of Christ. For both Luther and Calvin the central criterion for the use of a given book of the Bible is whether or not it promotes Christ, and the purpose of much of their Old Testament exegesis becomes the promotion of Christ. Marpeck refuses to find the human Christ in the Old Testament and minimizes the presence of the divine Christ. Instead, he finds in the historical books evidence of God's dealing, in the Law the negative preparation for Christ, and in the Prophets the positive preparation for his coming. In the poetical literature he finds some themes which appeal to him and which he applies (often in an allegorical or highly imagistic way) to the church today.

One reason why Marpeck uses the Old Testament this way is the importance that he attaches to the principle, strange at first sight, that the external key to the Scriptures is the humanity (*Menschheit*) of Christ (*KU*, A vib). He makes many references to the humanity of Christ, stressing that even the devils believe in the deity of Christ and tremble, and that only faith in the humanity of Christ brings salvation.

The development of this principle must be seen also as a conscious substitution for the keys to Scripture suggested by his opponents. He refused, for example, to admit that human preparation and gifts suffice to understand God's Word. On the other hand, he recognized these human gifts or training as gifts of God; languages and other natural talents are not to be depreciated but rather to be used in the true humility of Christ. Further they are to be used in such a way that the educated will become too proud to sit at the feet of the better in the divine wisdom. The constant danger that the educated will become too proud to sit at the feet of the twelve-year-old boy Jesus (*QF*, 57) can be averted by letting the simplicity of Jesus always be the instructor even of the learned. In spite of this warning to Schwenckfeld that learn-

---

[8] Källstigen (*op. cit.*, pp. 60f.) offers valid criticisms of Kiwiet's attempt to make the concept of order central in Marpeck's position. Apart from the 1531 booklets he has convincingly shown that the cornerstone for Marpeck is Christ the Man.

ing alone cannot assure one of the truth of God's Word, Marpeck is obviously aware that his own lack of training is a disadvantage in his conversations with the spiritualists (*KU*, A iib); nevertheless he is comforted by Christ in the simplicity of faith, and "this faith is a master of all artistry (*kunst*), reason (*vernunft*), wisdom and teaching" (*ibid.*). He willingly calls his opponents masters in the Scriptures, adding: "But the believers shall remain pupils and disciples of Christ, in which may the Lord preserve us through his grace" (*ibid.*).

It is the physical voice of Christ that still is heard by the true believers. Marpeck rejects the position of the false spirits that God could have revealed himself without the revelation and knowledge of Christ (*KU*, A vib). The physical voice of Christ is heard today through men and through the Scriptures (*KU*, A biv f.). The Scriptures have been preserved for us and witness to Christ (*ibid.*).

One reason for Marpeck's stress on the humanity of Christ was that in 1531 three positions appeared to be prevalent, none of which he could accept. The first spoke glorious things about the godhead of Christ and his glorious majesty and made others feel guilty who talked about his lowliness, such as the beginning of his teaching, baptism, the Lord's Supper, laying on of hands, ban, rebuke, and the service of Christ.[9] The second position rejected the incarnation of Christ (*Menschwerdung Christi*) and proclaimed salvation outside of it. The third position made use of the external ceremonies in a mechanical way without the spirit, such as the papists and others (*KU*, B iib). What strikes one is the fact that the final one should come into the category of Christology; it indicates that for Marpeck Christology issues directly in one's attitude toward the rites of the church. Stress on the deity and glory of Christ tends to depreciate the ceremonies of the church; if the incarnation is rejected there is no need for the ceremonies at all. In Luther, Schwenckfeld, and Marpeck, Christology is intimately related to their understanding of the Lord's Supper. The pivotal point of the controversy between Schwenckfeld and Marpeck was Christology, their differences on

---

[9] Then Marpeck makes the strange assertion: "darauss folgt das die menschhait Christi höher weder sein gottheyt geacht, erhebt, vnd also dz obrist zeundrist, vn das nidrist zu höchst gekert wirt" when exactly the opposite would seem to follow (*KU*, B iib).

other matters being merely adumbrations of their basic disagreement on Christ.[10]

Marpeck agrees that the scandal in the Christian church is
the same as that found in Christ—a carpenter's son forgiving
the sins of people, and a church of imperfect beings, lowly,
foolish people given the authority to forgive sins (*KU*, B iib).
The carnally minded who pride themselves in their knowledge object to having their sins forgiven by such despised
persons, whom Marpeck identifies with Christ himself when
he adds, "that is, the physical Christ, or the humanity of Christ
(to speak according to the members which are his body)"
(*KU*, B iii; C v). Just as the Jews were angered at Jesus when
he forgave sins, so these wise people resent the humility of
Christ's physical body.

Marpeck insists that the mysteries of God lie concealed in
the humanity of Christ (*KU*, iii), which comes to expression
in his external speeches, words, deeds, and ceremonies.
Whoever would search out the secrets of God apart from them
rejects (as did the Jews) the means given to us by God,
namely, the humanity of Christ (*KU*, B iiib). It is the humanity of Christ, not his divinity, that is a mediator between God
and man (I Tim. 2; *KU, loc. cit.*). The life of the physical
Christ is not meant as an example for the Christian, but rather
to serve us.[11] All the ceremonies also serve us; we do not serve
them.[12] This service of Christ will last as long as the world
lasts and is made manifest to men through the body of Christ,
the church (*KU*, B v). The false spirits miss it because they
do not know the physical Christ (*ibid.*). Christ became man

---

[10] Bergsten (*op. cit.*, p. 116 [offprint]) has noted this point, and on
Luther see Prenter, *op. cit.*, pp. 266f. Paul L. Maier has most recently
dealt with Schwenckfeld's view in *Caspar Schwenckfeld on the Person
and the Work of Christ* (Assen, 1959).

[11] "dann das gantz leiblich leben Christi, ist der warglaubigen
diener, sein geist ir herrscher" (*KU*, B ivb).

[12] This remarkable statement of the place of the ceremonies is rare
in Anabaptism, where the emphasis generally falls upon obedience to
Christ's commands. In *KU* the ceremonies are considered as gifts from
God that serve us (A iiib; B iib; B ivb). The same position is clearly
stated in *CV*, B vib and also in *V*, pp. 141f., where even the
commandments of Christ, "the greatest and the least, each in its order is
necessary and serves (*dienstlich*) for our salvation" (*V*, 142:24f.).
Schwenckfeld takes much the same position (*CS*, XII, 49; XIII, 194),
and it may be that both are dependent upon the Bohemian Brethren
(see Erhard Peschke, *Die Theologie der Böhmischen Brüder* [Stuttgart,
1940], I, 199ff., 227ff., 250ff.; II, 143ff., 152ff.).

for the sake of humanity, not for the spirit or angelic world (*KU*, B vib), and therefore became a natural man using the external means at his disposal to help people penetrate to spiritual realities (*ibid.*). Only when the end has come and man moves out of history can he forego the use of external means, for then Christ the slain Lamb has conquered all. The "*dienstbarkeit*" of the humanity of Christ does not terminate until that time.

But Marpeck does not overlook the spiritual Christ. "Now the whole world is full of Petrine and Iscariotic Christians who promise to defend the physical Christ with the sword" (*KU*, C iib). "They confess only the mortal and physical Christ, but very few believe and confess the risen Christ with their lives" (*KU, ibid.*). These Christians constitute a grave threat to the faithful, in whom "the spiritual Christ lives and reigns through faith and witness of the resurrection" (*KU*, C iii).[13] Just as John the Baptist prepared the way for Christ, so the physical Christ prepares the way for the spiritual Christ through his physical teaching, life, word, and ceremony. Through his physical coming all respect of person, nationality, or place of worship is done away with (*KU*, C vib).

Marpeck admonishes his readers to allow Christ to cover their eyes with clay as did the blind man, so that (*KU*, C viiib; cf. V, 76f.; 80:39; 184) through these lowly means of the physical, human Christ all their pride and reason will be subjected to Christ and they will not repeat the error of Peter, who thought that Christ should never wash his feet. "The man Jesus whom God has sent has begun a work of clay now in our time, has touched my eyes and the eyes of many others, sent us to the pool of Siloam to wash in pure faith in Christ and now we see" (*KU*, D). To learn the humanity of Christ is the milk of the Christian life and elemental knowledge that the erring spirits have not yet learned. Marpeck's conclusion of his booklet of 1531, which deals with this theme, repeats his stress on the humanity of Christ thus:

> (The erring prophets) despise the elemental rudiments (Hebrews 6) also the milk (I Cor. 3), choking themselves with their food, do not wish to go and learn

[13] The resurrection of Christ is called "the most important article of our faith" in this connection (*KU*, C iiib). It is not clear whether this is Marpeck's evaluation or that of the erring spirits, but it appears as though it is Marpeck's.

from the humanity of Christ, as children at the bench (Matt. 11) do not humble themselves under the bench, but seat themselves on top of it and exalt themselves but will be humbled (Luke 18). They are not sick, therefore they despise the physician, the humanity of Christ (Luke 5), through which God himself is despised (Luke 10), without which humanity it is impossible for them to come to God (John 14, 15) neither can they recognize the divinity (Matt. 11, John 14, II Cor. 4, I John 5). Further, without this door they cannot enter into the sheep barn (John 10). It is through this corner-stone that they either stand or fall (Luke 2, 20). So they accuse us that we want to preach Christ according to the flesh, when after all Paul says (II Cor. 5) "We no longer know Christ after the flesh." Answer: As they are minded, so also they understand Paul, they themselves understand Christ only after the flesh as the unbelieving Jews recognized him who considered his humanity, deeds, and words only in a physical manner, nor did they use it for any improvement, but despised and rejected it. The believers know, consider, and use the humanity of Christ, his words, works, deeds and ceremonies no longer according to the standard of carnal but of spiritual understanding (D ii) for edification. Not that we recognize him as in the world in the way that he was before the resurrection but until his return we recognize him according to the spirit and the new creation of his spiritual body planted through faith, since the old carnal nature has passed away and the (Christian) man is spiritually minded according to the humanity of Christ (*KU, ibid.*).[14]

Eleven years later, in a striking addition to the Rothmann *Bekentnisse*, Marpeck's view of the humanity of Christ is explicitly related to his view of the Trinity and to the external

[14] Marpeck's view of the *imitatio Christi* is stated negatively in spite of his mystic influences because for Bünderlin the whole purpose of the incarnation was that Christ would serve as an example for us. By imitating this example man becomes regenerate (*Aus was ursach*, p. 13). Marpeck rejects this type of discipleship as only a cloak for works-righteousness.

ceremonies of the church. Struggling with the problem of sign
and essence, he argues that where the truth is in the heart
there the sign disappears and becomes fused with the essence
(*TB*, 207:20f.). He supports this with the statement:

> For what the Father does, that the son of man
> does at the same time, the Father as Spirit internally,
> the son, as man externally. Therefore the external bap-
> tism and Lord's Supper is no sign in Christ but the
> external work and essence of the Son. For what the
> Son sees the Father doing he immediately does also. . . .
> Thus also the children of the birth of the Spirit and
> essence in Christ, what the Father does through the
> Spirit in them in the inner man, they also do (as mem-
> bers of the Body of Christ) in the outer man, in every-
> thing, baptism and Lord's Supper. . . . what the Father
> works inwardly as Spirit, that the Son of man also works
> externally. Accordingly in Christ there is no sign any
> longer, only essence, one baptism, one faith, one God,
> Father of us all. Therefore baptism is in the name of the
> Father, the Son (208), and of the Holy Spirit, for the
> Son of Man is not without the Father and Spirit, nor
> Spirit and Father without the Son of Man. For that
> reason the external essence of the Son is one essence and
> action in Father and Spirit (*Ein wesen und werck im
> Vater und Geist*), Consequently if a spirit comes which
> does not bring the external teaching, baptism, and
> Lord's Supper of Christ the man (*abentmal Christi des
> Menschens*) he denies the Son of Man and is not the
> Spirit of the Father. Again whatever man steals external
> teaching, deeds, baptism, and Lord's Supper as a thief
> merely out of the Scriptures and practices these things
> without true faith on hearsay alone (faith being the
> correct, true cowitness of the Father and the Holy Spirit)
> truth does not dwell in him (*TB*, 207:30-208:14).

This quotation clearly states the reason for Marpeck's insistence on external ceremonies as based on his view of the
Trinity, though it incidentally also indicates that he feels
caught between Zwinglian symbolism and Lutheran
sacramental realism. As is shown throughout the *Vermanung*,
he did not resolve the tension between these two approaches,

but probably accepted it as a part of the givenness of life that can never be completely resolved.[15]

C. THE INTERPRETER AND THE HOLY SPIRIT

Article V of the *Confessio Augustana* of 1530 condemns the Anabaptists "and others, who imagine that the Holy Spirit is given to men without the outward word, through their own preparation and works."[16] At this time Marpeck had not yet begun to write; but in spite of some evident spiritualistic tendencies among the early Anabaptists, this charge seems preposterous. The charge indicates a confusion in the minds of Luther and Melanchthon between spiritualists and Anabaptists rather than the Anabaptist attitude toward the outer Word.

The Anabaptists profusely annotated their writings with references to the Scriptures.[17] Confronted with this evidence of Anabaptist devotion to the written Word Lydia Müller assumes that the Anabaptist use of Scripture is a methodological adaptation to the Reformation controversies and that the Scriptural support of their assertions does not mean that all the assertions grew out of their Bible study. "Not the Scriptures are *regula fidei*, but the Spirit which speaks in the elect's Seelenabgrund."[18] She says that in a situation like this

---

[15] Bergsten (*op. cit.*, p. 108) notes this and discusses the categories "Inner and Outer Man" in Marpeck (pp. 92-95). Hans Urner (*op. cit.*, col. 341) stresses a different aspect of the importance of the incarnation for the sacraments: "Von daher (the incarnation) nehmen wir die Gewissheit, dass Er Seiner Gemeinde in irdischen Zeichen Seine göttliche Hilfe darreicht." Marpeck might question the use of the preposition "in" although his position is not very far from this statement.

[16] *ME*, I, 186.

[17] In-group scholars speak with a measure of pride of Ánabaptist "Biblicism," a term that is about as elusive as the term "Anabaptist" itself. E. Schott questions whether the term ought to be used at all, while G. Gloege concludes: "The expression biblicism is not serviceable . . . except as designation of an error" (*RGG*, I, 1263). One wonders whether Anabaptist-Mennonite scholars should use such a negatively charged term. See John C. Wenger ("The Biblicism of the Anabaptists," *The Recovery of the Anabaptist Vision* [Scottdale, 1957], pp. 167-179) who used the term apparently to designate simply *usage* of the Bible.

[18] *Der Kommunismus . . .* , p. 27.

authoritarianism is apt to grow, finding its support either in a gift of the Spirit or in the natural gift of leadership.

Over against this judgment of Dr. Müller's that the Anabaptists only paid lip-service to the Scriptures but in actual fact were led by the subjectivity of their own spirits, John Howard Yoder states that the Anabaptists first shared the formal principle with Zwingli, but that Zwingli soon denied the authority of the Scripture over the outward things, like the mass, tithing, and usury. The ultimate authority in these matters was the magistracy. Yoder concludes that the other Reformers were "less able than Zwingli to take for granted such an Hellenistic view of the relationship of 'inward' and 'outward,' but it remained generally characteristic that whoever undertook to refute the Anabaptists began by limiting the authority of Scripture."[19]

For Marpeck the Holy Spirit is integral to the Christian life and is second in emphasis only to the human Christ.[20] He refused to discredit God's revelation in the Bible either by bringing in the category of "inward" and "outward" or by allowing the Spirit to speak a message that was in no way

---

[19] "The Prophetic Dissent of the Anabaptists," *The Recovery*, pp. 95f. Hans J. Hillerbrand has rightly criticized this statement as not going beyond the surface differences and failing to penetrate to the differing hermeneutical presuppositions that lie at the basis of the disagreement ("Die gegenwärtige Täuferforschung, Fortschritt oder Dilemma?" in *Lebendiger Geist, Festschrift für Schoeps, Beihefte der Zeitschrift für Religion und Geistesgeschichte*, IV [Leiden-Köln, 1959], 48-65. On Anabaptist Biblicism, see especially pp. 57f.). While the early Bucer thought strongly in terms of "inward" and "outward" the later Bucer and certainly Calvin differed with the Anabaptists mainly on the degree of authority ascribed to the OT. Gordon Rupp has observed that in the early years of the Reformation even the radicals did not have much to say about the Holy Spirit (*op. cit.*, p. 13). Just when the "early years" end is not stated, and in any case it would be difficult to prove that Anabaptism ignored the doctrine of the Holy Spirit. Evidence for their occupation with this theme is much more bountiful than would appear from *ME*, II, 795f.

[20] When the Strasbourg Council demanded a promise never to return to that city he replied that he had always been obedient to the Council and would continue to obey "wo er aber durch den geist gottes jn khunfftigm getriben vnnd hieher gefüert würde do wolt er nichts zugesagt oder begeben haben vnnd alsdann was jme gotte der herr deshalb zuschigkt gedulden" (Krebs-Rott, p. 361, December 19, 1531). Marpeck could not promise not to return lest the Spirit drive him back, but if the Spirit did bring him back he was willing to pay the price.

related to the Scriptures. The same Spirit who leads in the study of God's Word also inspired it at the time of its writing.

With a strong logos-Christology and a trinitarian Christology it is to be expected that Christ, Spirit, and Word converge in Marpeck's thought.

> The transfigured Lord, the man Jesus Christ, is, according to both united natures, true God in, through, and with the word, but otherwise there is a difference between the attributes of the two natures. This transfigured (*verklert*) Lord, as Man Jesus Christ dwelling as one God in heaven speaks the word through his Holy Spirit from heaven into the inner ears of the hearts of believing men as a living word of God, which word and spirit God and Christ himself are (John 1:8; II Cor. 3; Rev. 19) through which word all things were made (John 1)" (*V*, 516:22f.).

He says further that God's Spirit was active also in creation (Ps. 33; Job 13).

This quotation shows that Marpeck does not view the Spirit as a part of the human anatomy (identifying it with man's reason or intuition), but as a part of the godhead and as part of God's act in Christ; in no way identified with any gift, virtue, or quality inherent in human nature. Only through him can Christ be present in his church (*V*, 508). Since the Spirit is in some way bound to the incarnation Marpeck asserts in the strongest terms that the Holy Spirit was not given to the believers of the Old Testament (*V*, 245, 381; *KU*, D iib), but admits that the Spirit did work in the Old Covenant (*V*, 305). Sometimes he identifies this Spirit with the Spirit of the New Testament, but using a different manner of dealing with people (*V*, 318); [21] at other times he asserts that the Spirit possessed by the ancients was not the Spirit of Promise found in the New Testament (*V*, 377; *TE*, Chapters 70, 74, 81). What they had was a foretaste (*Vorgeschmack*) (*TB*, 235; 15f.); even the disciples did not have the Holy Spirit until Pentecost except as a foretaste (*V*, 314:40; 245:46; 381:20;

---

[21] "Gleichwie gestern und heut ein heiliger geist was und ist, wie nur ein gott, aber in der wirkung . . . weit underschidlich, also was (war) und ist auch gottes wort gestern und heut weit von einander zu underschaiden in der wirkung" (*V*, p. 296).

KU, D ivb); not in the same measure as after the glorification of Christ (*CV,* c ib; *Conf.,* 176, 186; *V,* 160:24f.; *TB,* 227:40f.). The disciples could not endure the words of Christ before the coming of the Holy Spirit (*V,* 301f.), nor did the mere words of Christ suffice without the Holy Spirit in understanding the Old Testament (*V,* 367). The physical words of Christ prepared the way for the coming of the Holy Spirit (*V,* 298). The actual power of Christianity consists in the Holy Spirit (*V,* 314:44).

The Holy Spirit is sent to lead Christians into all truth (*V,* 366).[22] He is not some pantheistic spirit that floats around the universe, or an inner light, but is specifically given to us and related to us (*V,* 486, 508, 509, 519). Thus the work of the Spirit is not some ecstatic phenomenon unpredictably and unrelatedly laying hold of the individual in a spectacular way, but related to the Scriptures. The Spirit is given us in history through external means and for this reason oral preaching must be accompanied by the Scriptures (*V,* 522).

What Marpeck said about the danger of learning obstructing a true understanding of the Scriptures in connection with the humanity of Christ he says also with reference to the Holy Spirit (*QF,* 56). The learned come with all their preparation and their artistry and present themselves as having been taught by the Holy Spirit, as though he would teach through no one but them. Their wisdom and artistry (*vernunft und kunst*), however, interfere with the working of the Holy Spirit; and this type of wisdom will never be favored with an unveiling of the wisdom of Christ and the rule of his Spirit until they lay themselves at the feet of Christ (*QF,* 57).[23] The Holy Spirit does not look upon rhetoric or hairsplitting distinctions (*V,* 468), and the scholastic distinctions of theology have resulted in nothing but persecutions and murders in the name of Christ (*V,* 468).

Without the Holy Spirit the Scriptures cannot be explained or interpreted:

> Through faith one receives in sequence both kinds of bread for eternal life, the bread which is from heaven, from God the Father, which is Jesus Christ according

[22] Wenger (*op. cit.,* p. 214) is correct in seeing this as Marpeck's favorite designation for the Holy Spirit (*V,* pp. 363, 366 *et passim*). The term "inner light" never occurs in Marpeck's writings.

[23] The other extreme, crass ignorance, is no better (*V,* p. 469).

to his divine nature; thereafter the bread which the Lord, the man Jesus himself, gave us, his flesh which he gave on behalf of the world. These two kinds of bread received through faith serve together to one purpose; the first (as the Holy Spirit) interpreting the second and witnessing to it in the heart as a comforter along with apostolic teaching or witness, John 15. For without such Holy Spirit (as reminder and guide into all truth) it could not interpret itself or explain itself in the heart (V, 486).

Even at the time of the Lord's Supper Christ spoke parabolically; his appearance to the Emmaus disciples after the resurrection was still not enough (V, 367), but now after his ascension "the Lord speaks out freely through reminding and instruction of his Holy Spirit (as the spirit of truth) in our hearts, that we may understand the sense of his words whether it be in the institution of the Lord's Supper or elsewhere" (V, 458). The Holy Spirit is the inner teacher and comforter (KB, 292b).

In 1547 in his Christological writing Marpeck emphatically expresses the same point of view:

We want to note well our calling as well as the one who called us, for we did not choose Him but He chose us from the terrible darkness of this world and opened to us the will of our heavenly Father having taught and instructed us with full understanding. He also sent us the inner teacher and comforter, to comfort and instruct us with the words which He had spoken before. (The Spirit) strengthens, leads and instructs us, anointing us with the oil of gladness, . . . so that it is not we who live, but Christ Jesus lives within us. We have learned Christ not only through a human voice and the letter about the physical teaching of Christ and the apostolic preaching of the gospel, but rather instructed by God, the Holy Spirit (as Divine and not human) who took it from Father and Son as if from their treasures and poured love into our hearts, as the true and only understanding and meaning of Christ. Only that which Christ spoke before and taught, and no other word does the Spirit recall or instruct by way of wisdom to His own. Those who add to or reject the Word or Teaching are false spirits, regardless of how saintly they may appear (*KB*, 293f.).

Where the Holy Spirit does not precede as true teacher in all knowledge of Christ there (all Scripture) is badly misused (*KB*, 60b f. to the Swiss Brethren).

Is this working of the Spirit automatically guaranteed whenever Scripture is read or preached? By no means!

Those are not taught of God who merely hear the word from the mouth of Christ, the apostles, or other saintly men, or who read their writings merely in a literal sense (*nach blossem Buchstaben*) without the instruction and reminder of the Holy Spirit. Instead they are thieves and robbers coming before and after Christ, that is, they run ahead of the Holy Spirit, by their own ingenuity (*kunst*) and imaginations from the Scriptures, before they are driven by the Holy Spirit (*KB*, 293f.). . . . These are clouds without water driven about by the whirlwind, and not driven by the Holy Spirit or instructed by Him (*KB*, 293b; cf. also V, 297, 525; Humanity of Christ, 207).

A lack of this inner call is likened by Marpeck to drawing water from foul cisterns. Such men are as decisively rejected as those who refuse to have anything to do with the lowly means used by the Spirit to prepare the way for his perfect work (*KB*, 293b f.; V, 525).

Marpeck relates the external ceremonies not only to the humanity of Christ, but also to the work of the Spirit. On this point he returns with full force to a critique of the spiritualists. Within the context of history the Holy Spirit is restricted to the use of external means, which are the antecedents of the real work of the Spirit just as the physical words of Christ served to prepare the way for the coming of the Spirit (V, 298; *KB*, 294f.). More often Marpeck asserts that inner and outer are identical. "God's Word and Spirit are and work with and alongside each other" (V, 516).

Because God promised to send the Holy Spirit and did so after the resurrection Marpeck asserts:

Therefore all external service of Christ and those who belong to him is in this time of mortality (*Sterblichkeit*) an assistance and preparation (*Behilfung und Wegberaiter*) to the Holy Spirit. (He lists external proclamation, instruction, miracles, baptism, footwashing, the Lord's Supper, discipline, rebuke, admonition, ban as part of true fellowship in separation from the world and exclusion from the body of Christ, which is remembered in the Lord's Supper, i.e., the true love of Christ shown in the act of love when he laid down his life, the basis for all genuine fellowship for true believers.) Where this service of Christ is not allowed to precede and man allows himself to be served by Christ in this manner and thus prepare for the Holy Spirit; there the Spirit has no place to move. Nor will he move there where people take Peter's attitude and think that they cannot allow Christ to wash their feet. To all such Christ says even today that they have no part in his kingdom. Because the Holy Spirit neither can nor will find a place to move without the preparatory instruction (*Lehr*) and all those things wherewith man is prepared according to the admonitions of Christ and through opening of his understanding, that is the key of David. Knowledge (*Erkenntnis*) can open the earthly man's understanding.[24]

Even when a man scrupulously obeys the admonitions of Christ, Marpeck maintains, the Spirit is not thereby brought or moved to action, for the Spirit is sovereign and moves where he wills. Even when man has done all, "yet the Spirit

---

[24] *KB*, p. 295. The position here expressed would seem very similar to Luther's in all important aspects, assuming that Regin Prenter has accurately portrayed it in *Spiritus Creator* (Philadelphia, 1953), pp. 254f. The statement: "Aber das alles, der massen und der ordenung, das die eusserlichen stücke sollen und mussen vorgehen. Und die ynnerlichen hernach und durch die eusserlichen kommen" (*op. cit.*, p. 291), which Prenter quotes from Luther, would agree for the most part with Marpeck's position, although Marpeck struggles to unite the external and the internal both temporally and experientially. Thus on the issue of faith and works of faith, which Marpeck related to the problem of inner and outer man, he asserts: "that they are one and the same thing and one essence not according to the elements but according to their effect" ("der wirkung und nit den elementen nach" [V, p. 166]). Luther insists on the necessity of faith in partaking of the Lord's Supper and initially in baptism; but the pressure was too great at this point and he yielded, not without some major inconsistencies (as shown by Karl Brinkel, *Die Lehre Luthers von der fides infantium bei der Kindertaufe* [Berlin, 1958]).

moves in glorious freedom given him by God the Father and
the Son, just as he gives the growth, increase and prosperity
to whom He wills" (*KB*, 295; cf. also fol. 277).

Not only is Marpeck convinced that the interpreter cannot
force the Spirit but must acknowledge his sovereignty; he is
also aware that one of the most subtle temptations besetting
man is to ascribe to the Holy Spirit what is actually one's own
human opinion or desire to instruct the Holy Spirit (*V*,
578).[25] Thus he remarks in one of his epistles:

> (The believers) know also through the Holy Spirit
> that all their commissions and omissions are governed
> and led by Christ, so that they do not live . . . but Christ
> lives in them and accomplishes the good pleasure of the
> Father. Hence St. Paul says that he dares speak nothing
> but what Christ works in him. . . . Our words also shall
> be so, that we do not speak, read, write, run, gather or
> assemble unless the Lord himself do it. Without that
> truly all is in vain and has not the good pleasure of God
> the Father. . . . We must simply in all our committing
> and omitting stand idle ourselves, as dead in ourselves,
> if Christ is to live in us. . . . For human wisdom can
> disguise itself as an angel of light, especially of the
> scribal (*schriftgelerter*) kind, indeed also it is often
> coarse carnal simplicity that it deems its simplicity to be
> a self-chosen spirituality out of which it runs. . . . These
> the apostle calls clouds without water (understand the
> waters of the graces of Christ, His Holy Spirit) driven
> about by the whirlwind. Ah, my brethren, how diligent-
> ly and carefully we have to take heed that we do not
> consider our own impulse the impulse of the Holy Spirit,
> our own course (*Lauf*) the course and walk of Christ.[26]

After he has given several criteria by which one can judge
the leading of the Holy Spirit he adds:

[25] The writers of the *Verantwortung* describe Schwenckfeld "als der
den h. geist, ja den herrn Jesum Christum, darumb das er nit überall
gleich nach der schnuer oder nach seinem synn hat geredt, straten und
geen schuel will fieren" (*V*, p. 300; cf. pp. 306, 468).

[26] "Concerning the Humanity of Christ," *MQR*, XXXII (1958),
197f.

> Therefore it behooves us to give diligent heed
> that we distinguish sharply, diligently and well, our own
> drives from the drives of the Holy Spirit.[27]

The criteria that Marpeck says will assure the certainty of
the leading of the Holy Spirit seem to concern the practical
ethical life of the Christian rather than his approach to the
Scriptures. But Marpeck does not separate these two domains;
for him life was a unit and the Scriptures were to be studied
only for the purpose of applying them.

In introducing these criteria Marpeck stresses the importance of differentiating between the natural goodness that
man has as a result of divine creation and that which the
Holy Spirit imparts to him. Through reading the Scriptures
and in his own experience he has noted that the natural man
often hates the evil and desires the good, but this is not to be
interpreted as the working of the Holy Spirit (Humanity of
Christ, 207). Paul's persecuting the church and Peter's chop-
ping off the ear of Malchus are examples of this natural piety;
Marpeck feels that many illustrations of this can be found in
his own day. In the early church there were those who were
zealous to keep the laws of the Sabbath and circumcision;
while their zeal was commendable and they were convinced
that they were driven by the Holy Spirit, this was not the
case. In part their actions were of God, but not under the
office of the Spirit of Christ (*ibid.*, 208); rather, God uses such
servants even today to prepare the way (*forlouff und
wegberaiter*) for those who are truly driven by the Holy Spirit
of Christ. These servants, he said, contributed to the splitting
up of Christ's church in his day in order that those driven by
the Holy Spirit might be more clearly revealed.

Examples of men who were truly Spirit-led, cited by Marpeck, are Peter at Pentecost, Paul going to Rome to preach the
gospel to the Gentiles, Philip going to the eunuch, and Peter
to Cornelius; they and their followers are led by the Spirit
according to the measure of their faith. They know what their
Father and Lord plans to do (John 15:15), and they also
know thoroughly the reason of their drive through the Holy
Spirit.

The assurance of this motivation is most important and can
be distinguished in four ways:

[27] *Loc. cit.*, p. 199.

(1) Love for God and for one's fellow men
(2) The depreciation of life and the willingness to suffer for Christ and the gospel's sake
(3) The recognition of God's open doors and refraining from entering where God has not opened the door— for the office of the Holy Spirit must remain free and absolute (*frei und alein*)
(4) Purity and freedom in teaching and judgment (that is, the Christian dare not lose the freedom of the Holy Spirit's direction by serving the state or other interests).[28] In his dealings with the Swiss Marpeck described the leading of the Spirit as it relates to the ethical sphere.

The practical slant of all of these criteria is surprising. In the first he agrees with the early Luther, and his insistence that the basic love commandment is central to the understanding of the Holy Spirit's work among the believers.[29] In the second he criticizes the attitude of Schwenckfeld and the more radical spiritualists who were spared much suffering by withdrawal into a conventicle type of Christianity (cf. V, 568f. and Schwenckfeld's advice that the Anabaptists could have spared themselves much suffering by being more quietistic).[30] In the third he describes a missionary principle basic to his approach; namely, that Christians should not cast their pearls before swine. In the fourth, he undoubtedly has in mind Bucer's policy of church and state union, and possibly also Luther.

These four criteria helped Marpeck distinguish those who were really under the office of the Holy Spirit from those who were not yielded to that office. The criteria can be restated in the questions: (1) Does he love? (2) Is he willing to suffer? (3) Does he recognize the sovereignty of the Spirit? (4) Is he pure and free in his teaching?

At the point where Marpeck notes disagreement between

[28] Humanity of Christ, pp. 208f.
[29] Prenter, *op. cit.*, pp. 3f.
[30] One sees the spiritualist evaluation of Anabaptist martyrdom in *KU*, A iff. where we are told that the spiritualists used the suffering of the Anabaptists as evidence that the latter were not under the command of Christ. The cross they bore is not that of Christ "sonder ain stroff von Gott" (*KU*, A iib).

himself and his fellow Christians he proceeds very cautiously
and slowly, even though he feels a strong urge of the Spirit.

> Not that I seek to resist the urging of the Spirit, far be
> that from me, but this is my reason, to put the urge to a
> thorough test, not for the sake of the Holy Spirit, but for
> my sake. Human weakness, human inability, human fool-
> ishness, human indecision and lack of stability make
> this necessary (*KB*, fol. 273).

Human weakness must be strengthened by divine power and
human wisdom displaced by divine wisdom; only then does
he take upon himself the urge of the Spirit, and even then only
with fear, concern, and trembling; for only after a thorough
self-examination can he proceed with certainty (*KB*, fol.
273b).

Marpeck did not arrive at these criteria or this certainty
alone, nor did he apply or test them alone, for he recognized
that the subjective element as seen in the individualism of the
spiritualists was contrary to the work of the Holy Spirit. The
most important single factor that helps the interpreter remove
the subjective element from his interpretation is the community that the Holy Spirit has called into being, and he who is
not willing to submit to the discipline of that community has
not yet learned to know Christ.[31]

D. THE INTERPRETER AND THE CHURCH

Marpeck's conviction that individualism finds its correction
in the Christian community comes to concrete expression in
that most books attributed to him were written in collaboration with someone else. The only works of which he was the
sole author are his *Confession* (1532, which was not meant to
be published or circulated beyond the City Council of Strasbourg) and, presumably, the two booklets of 1531. The letters
and epistles in the *Kunstbuch* were meant to circulate among
the churches and provoke discussion so as to reach some
measure of agreement.

---

[31] Spirits, of whom Schwenckfeld is one, who do not submit to the
discipline of the true mother, the bride of Christ, are called bastards
(*V*, p. 297). For Marpeck the Spirit brings both liberty and chastise-
ment.

Marpeck's leadership among the South German Anabaptists is obvious. Schwenckfeld recognized it in singling him out again and again, for he knew that Marpeck spoke for the brotherhood and not merely for himself.

Already in Strasbourg, Marpeck assumed that since the gospel had been preached there for some time, his position, having been derived from the Bible, needed only to be stated to be convincing and acceptable. For this reason he pressed for an open hearing to be conducted outside the halls of the City Council. This was not granted. But the insistence with which Marpeck pleaded for a public hearing indicates his reluctance to submit his faith to the jurisdiction of the City Council. The church, not the state, was to judge the validity of his position.[32] Marpeck's separatism was forced upon him when the Council decreed that he either obey them or give up his faith.[33] Bucer's basic charge against Marpeck was not doctrinal heresy, but rather disruption of the unity of the community, which for him meant the union of state and church.

Marpeck believed that the Scripture becomes more clearly understood as it is compared and studied,[34] and that such study can only be conducted by the regenerate within the

[32] On December 9, 1531, when he was before the Council, Marpeck said he had requested an open discussion often (*dickermal*, Krebs-Rott, p. 352). Since this had been refused and he was called to meet with the Council he made it clear that "this matter is not subject to any human court and that he is not speaking alone with Bucer and the preachers but with all Christians" (Krebs-Rott, p. 351). Bucer states that he too desired a discussion (Krebs-Rott, p. 353), and there is evidence that the ministers pressed for an open disputation but the Council refused to grant it (*op. cit.*, pp. 356f.; 359f.; 530). In his farewell letter to the Council, Marpeck addresses the Councillors "not as lords (*oberherrn*) but as listeners of the disagreement concerning the word of God between me and the ministers" (Krebs-Rott, p. 528). Apparently Anton Engelbrecht, the learned pastor at St. Stephan's church, shared Marpeck's position. He was released in 1534 because he denied the city government the right to interfere in religious matters (Krebs-Rott, p. 51, and § 373).

[33] Krebs-Rott, p. 531. John Howard Yoder has abundantly illustrated this same desire to converse among the earliest Swiss Anabaptists, in Switzerland, in his dissertation (*op. cit.*). Note also the tone of the farewell letter Marpeck wrote to Strasbourg when he was forced to leave in January, 1532 (*vide supra*, pp. 29f.). The best text is in Krebs-Rott, pp. 528-29.

[34] *TE*, Second Preface, p. VII.

brotherhood. In this respect, Marpeck is definitely not an individualist.[35] He is receptive to further knowledge and truth. In his *Confession* he says: "I have not come to pose as the light, but rather place myself before it and testify to it" (*Conf.*, 171). To Schwenckfeld's reproach that he ought to study a little more, he replies that he does desire sincerely to learn more from the Master (V, 230; cf. V, 88). This attitude of teachability comes out even more clearly in the introduction to the *Vermanung*, where the writers say that with this testimony to the covenant they offer themselves to the judgment of their readers, and that they desire to submit humbly to obedience of the saints and the Holy Spirit, in the hope that each one related to the covenant (*puntsverwandte*) with a pure conscience before God will judge them with lenience and in the unity of the faith in Christ;[36] if God the Father through Christ gives someone something clearer and better, they hope that it will not be in contradiction to their confession, but rather bring it more clearly to daylight.[37] This desire to be corrected can be seen also in his letter to the Swiss (1541), where he says,

> If I err, I desire to be shown by God through his Holy Spirit and Biblical Scriptures, if through grace I

[35] Krebs-Rott, p. 351. The contrast with Luther is striking. When criticized for the insertion of the word "alone" in Romans 3:28 he defended himself in an angry letter on translation: "It is my NT, and my version, and I will not let the Papists judge it. If the word 'alone' is not found in the Latin and the Greek, yet the passage has that meaning, and must be so rendered to make it clear and strong in German" (Preserved Smith, "The Methods of Reformation Interpreters on the Bible," *The Biblical World*, Vol. 38, New Series [1911], p. 241). Yet Luther also valued group work on the Bible, especially a translation, and cited Matthew 18:20 in support (*Tischreden*, I, 961).

[36] *TB*, 189:8ff. The Marpeck brotherhood was critical of those who refused to submit to the judgment of others, and Helen von Freyberg's Confession written for the brotherhood (*KB*, No. 28) indicates that her sin was that "I wanted to instruct and punish my brother, but was not teachable or punishable myself" (fol. 244b). At the conclusion she says: "So I submit to the discipline and punishment of God my heavenly Father, of his holy community (*Gemein*) and Christian church as long and often as it pleases the Holy Spirit" (fol. 246).

[37] A similar sentiment, but not expressed as strongly, occurs in the the *Bekentnisse*, p. 2 (cf. also p. 56). The Preface as such is not translated by Marpeck, just the opening lines.

confess to the truth, then I desire to have a testimony of
the truth from the ones belonging to the truth.[38]

In the same epistle he says,

> There is no lack of Spirit that there should be divisions
> among us, the only lack that exists is in our weak con-
> science and dullness of understanding, from which divi-
> sion has originated. All lack of understanding I will
> attribute to myself, that I might through my lack of
> understanding liberate and recognize your understand-
> ing, through laying before you the Gospel in creatures,[39]
> for my sake and yours, insofar as God gives grace, that
> we might meet and find one another in our hearts with
> God in Christ Jesus, our Lord. It is my heartfelt re-
> quest of you, that you read the following parables in
> Christ with attentiveness and patience, for perhaps I am
> more concerned about you than you are about me.[40]

[38] *KB*, fol. 28. The position of the Marpeck brotherhood was that
they desired correction where they were wrong, and "Mitzeugnis" where
they were right. Much stress was placed upon this "Mitzeugnis." When
the Swiss would not give this to the Bilgramites, Marpeck became concerned about their attitude to them.

[39] The phrase "predigt das Evangelium allen Creaturen" is taken
by a number of Anabaptists to mean "durch allen Creaturen." They
say that Jesus used all kinds of analogies from nature to preach, so
that all levels of society would be reached with the gospel. Where
this originated is not easy to say. It appears in Hans Hut (*LM*, I,
15ff.), who passed it on to Ambrosius Spittelmayer (Karl Schornbaum,
Bayern I, p. 48) and no doubt also to Hans Schlaffer (*LM*, I, 85ff.).
It does not, as far as the present writer can determine, appear in Hans
Denck. That it does not occur often in Marpeck (*TB*, p. 245) is accepted by Schwenckfeld (*CS*, VI, 61; XIV, 773). The effort of Grete
Mecenseffy ("Die Herkunft des oberösterreichischen Täufertums," *ARG*,
47 [1956], 252-58) to trace a genetic connection between Thomas
Müntzer's use of "Kreaturen" and this usage does not appear to have
succeeded. A comparison of the two usages shows that Müntzer never
uses the term in the same way as do the later Anabaptists. It may be
that Hut derived the term from Müntzer, but that he used it in the
same way simply is not the case. This is not changing the dative into
the genitive (so Fast, *op. cit.*, p. 218) but giving it an instrumental force
(cf. Col. 1:23). See also G. Rupp, "Thomas Müntzer, Hans Huth, and
the 'Gospel of All Creatures,'" *Bulletin of John Rylands Library*, 43
(1961), 492-519.

[40] *KB*, fol. 55b f. On the date of this epistle see Fast, *op. cit.*, p. 227,
footnote 63. The same willingness to blame himself appears in an
epistle to the church at St. Gall and Appenzell, dated August 9, 1551,
"Ich will mir aber gern selbst die Schuld geben, viel lieber weder euch

Likewise in the Second Preface to the *Testamenterleutterung* the writer requests more precise understanding and exposition in the event that he has not found the right meaning in his appended notes (*TE*, vii; cf. *QF*, 59). He promises to yield without quarreling at all times and not to retain any discrepancy between the text of the Bible and his appended summary. He knows that the more thoroughly Holy Scripture is interpreted the more clearly it will concur with the summary, for the Holy Scripture does not contradict itself. He begs the reader not to reject the whole book if he does not agree with some things in it.

Jan J. Kiwiet defines theology for Marpeck as the systematic exposition of Scripture.[41] One could suggest that it is the corporate exposition of Scripture by the band of believers, or what we today might call *Gemeindetheologie*.[42] Marpeck believed that the Holy Spirit illuminates the writings of Scripture as the two or three gather together in Christ's name. When Schwenckfeld attacked the *Vermanung* in his *Judicium*, the *Judicium* was read in the meeting of the brotherhood and discussed by them.[43]

Marpeck's desire to establish relations and mutual respect with the Swiss Brethren was frustrated by the tendency of the

---

zu beschuldigen, dass ich vielleicht von Gott nicht wert geachtet oder geschaetzt bin, in solchem eurem beklagten grossem . . . Anliegen zu dienen . . ." (*KB*, fol. 272b). At the beginning of No. 7 he admits his own lack of knowledge and understanding of Christ and his concern about it (fol. 27) and expresses his desire to submit his understanding of Christian freedom to the least of Christ's saints (fol. 28).

[41] *Op. cit.*, p. 84.

[42] Cf. Horst Quiring, "Die Anthropologie Pilgram Marpecks," *Menn. Geschbl.*, II (1937), 12, bearing in mind the difference as it is used with reference to the early church.

[43] *QF*, p. 59. Apparently Schwenckfeld had accused them of being afraid to read it in their meeting, because the leaders did not wish the others to see the truth. Or is Marpeck here confusing the point that Schwenckfeld did not wish the *Judicium* to be circulated beyond the Anabaptists? See *QF*, p. 65. Writing to the Swiss, Marpeck says: "The true saints of God and children of Christ have as their ruler the Holy Spirit in the Word of Truth. And wherever two or three are gathered together in His name, He is in their midst, and rules alone in Faith through patience, in genuine love among His own. I pray to God my heavenly Father that He may never separate me from such a gathering and communion of the Holy Spirit. Whoever they may be, wherever they may have gathered, I hope to be in their fellowship and I submit to such a rule of the Holy Spirit of Christ unto obedience in faith" (*KB*, fol. 41).

Swiss to deny the value of written and oral communication
with each other. Protesting against this attitude, Marpeck
asserts that the Lord's Word is brought to us in several manners for salvation. Whether it comes through writings or oral
discussions it behooves us to accept out of them the witness
and truth (as Christ himself), even though this may require
some exertion of the mind, because of our human weakness.[44]
The Holy Spirit is sovereign and works at his own time and
place. He gives his gift as it pleases him, through writings,
talks, discipline, suffering, and punishment, through lofty or
simple understanding. He is Lord over all, even over writings
and oral talks. "Therefore whoever rejects and despises written
and oral vehicles of the Holy Spirit, as though more harm
than good would result from them and matters would proceed
better if not so much were written or spoken, accuses the Holy
Spirit and the vehicles of his gifts . . . and desires to instruct
the Holy Spirit rather than be instructed by him."[45]

The Swiss give evidence of a type of spiritualism here that
if it does not entirely reject, at least minimizes the value of
external means to build up the unity of the church and shows
some reluctance to share in them. Apparently the issue did
not deal with the sacraments (as with Bucer) nor with
the necessity of suffering or church discipline (as with
Schwenckfeld).

Marpeck's vigorous critique of the Swiss approach is easily
understood in the light of his strong belief in the continuity of
apostolic teaching and his stress on the unity of the written
and the spoken Word.[46] Pressed to its logical conclusion,
Marpeck's position means that the word preached and written
by him, to the extent that it agreed with apostolic doctrine,
was the same as that of the New Testament. Because of his
awareness of the danger of substituting his own views for the

[44] *KB*, fol. 275f.

[45] *KB*, fol. 277f. He continues: "Dann es wäre ein greulicher Irrtum
schriftliche und mündliche Gaben des hl. Geist zu verachten, das fern
von uns sei. Das schreib ich darum, weil ihr mir noch nie kein Mit-
zeugnis in h. Geist über mein vielfältiges Zuschreiben, noch Danksagung
Gottes (die uns um seiner Gaben willen gebühren) getan, ist mich
Furcht und Sorg angestossen und verursacht worden (mein getreue
Fürsorg für euch) zuschreiben, unsere Seelen vor dem betrug und
List des Feindes unsers Heils zu verraten und zu verhüten."

[46] *V*, pp. 404f., 522.

views of the Holy Spirit, and his own impulses for the leading of the Holy Spirit, he rejects any blanket assertion that wherever the external means are used, the external ceremonies practiced, there the Holy Spirit works. The Spirit is sovereign (*KB*, 295b) and works in the brotherhood to exercise this sovereignty.

Moreover, he is critical of the tendency of some of his contemporaries to separate the apostolic services of the church (*apostolische Dienstbarkeit der Kirchen*) from the movement of the Holy Spirit. The Spirit has been sent to remind us and to teach us all truth, but his starting point is the "physical spoken Word, injunction and command of Christ" (*leiblichen geredten Wort, Befehl und Gebot Christi*). Separating them is driving a wedge between Christ and the Holy Spirit.[47] Furthermore, those deceive themselves who think that when they serve, teach, and baptize it must follow that the Holy Spirit moves and teaches because the apostolic service runs its course and that because of the externals alone there must be a church. Not at all, says Marpeck, for wherever the internal (*inwendig*) does not through the Holy Spirit testify with the external through faith, all is in vain.[48]

The external gifts of the Spirit that form a part of the church's life are given for the common good, and to possess the gifts of faith for the common good is a test of belonging to Christ (*KU*, B iiib). To the argument of the spiritualists that they had the gifts of the Holy Spirit for their own private good but no command to exercise these gifts among others,[49] Marpeck replies with a battery of New Testament Scriptures showing that Paul sees the gifts of the Spirit only for the good of the Body and for the exercise of love to the neighbor. "So the gifts of the spirit reveal themselves to be not only for one's own good but for the common good, service and improve-

---

[47] *KB*, fol. 296.

[48] *Ibid.*

[49] Bünderlin in *Erklärung durch vergleichung* (1530) said that one should baptize only where there is a direct command (*Befehl*) from above (p. 48) and that the Holy Spirit was experienced by the eunuch not "under vil volck, sond' uff den weg uff den er heim reiset" (p. 68). According to Bünderlin John is warned in the Apocalypse (a book very dear to him) by the Spirit of Christ of the decline of the external church and its change into a beast, therefore he warns the believers "yedermann für sich selb bleiben zelassen" (p. 91).

ment" (*CV*, b ib).[50] This impels the Christian not only to
share the gospel with those who do not believe but also to
have fellowship with believers so that mutual edification,
exhortation, and admonition may occur.

Little is known about the actual worship service of the
Marpeck group. While the natural talents of leadership possessed by such men as Leupold Scharnschlager were developed and strengthened in the church, no one person became a dictator of the group. Pilgram's letter to Leupold
indicates that amity and good will existed between these two
leaders. It is quite probable that Marpeck was not considered
the formal head of his brotherhood since he nowhere signs his
letters   as   anything   but   "Your   servant   and   comrade
(*mitgenoss*) in the tribulation of Christ," while Scharnschlager twice signs them as "Mitältester." Marpeck signs his
letter to Scharnschlager, "Your comrade and fellow soldier in
the truth in tribulation" (*KB*, fol. 240b).

What is described above as *"Gemeindetheologie"* is not to
be confused with modern "group dynamics" where leadership
often does not exist. In the Marpeck brotherhood leadership is
considered as much a gift of God as the Scriptures themselves, but authoritarianism could not get a foothold because
fellowship was real to all members. Marpeck did not use his
group to enhance his own prestige, but within the group gave
and took counsel as the Scriptures were studied in the context
of the covenant community. The glimpses allowed us into the
group through the *Kunstbuch* indicate that both the joys and
the tribulations of being in Christ were shared. Protestantism
could learn much from this corporate approach to the Scriptures where the Holy Spirit opens up the Word of God to
those committed to obey it under the banner of Christ.
Those who would accuse Anabaptism of being individualistic
might well note this feature of the Marpeck brotherhood.[51]

[50] Again it would seem that Marpeck may be indebted to Schiemer.
Talking about sharing with fellow Christians the latter says: "For
these are his neighbors, so he must have in common with them all
gifts which he has received from God, be it teaching, talent (*kunst*),
goods, money, etc. What God has entrusted him with he must offer up,
for the common good (*zu aim gemainen nutz*), as we have it in our
articles of faith, and everywhere in Scripture, especially in the work
of the twelve apostles" (Lydia Müller, *Glaubenszeugnisse*, I, 67).
I Corinthians 12:7 is the common source.

[51] In view of the above it is lamentable to note the continuing confusion that exists between "spiritualists and Anabaptists" in some

The place that is here assigned to the church as an instru-
ment of the Holy Spirit in the process of interpretation, assures
a balance to the extremes of individualism and its accompanying subjectivism. It guards also against pure spiritualism
because it insists on the union of the work of the Holy Spirit
with external forms. These external forms (he lists external
preaching, teaching, admonitions, miracles, footwashing, discipline, punishment, ban, excommunication, separation from the
body of Christ, and the Lord's Supper) are an assistance and
preparation for the Holy Spirit.[52] But throughout the sovereignty of the Holy Spirit is maintained. He alone decides if and
when he desires to work, and no mere mechanical conduct or
ritual can bring his working to pass.[53] But this does not
justify speaking of a spiritualistic tendency in Marpeck, for
the evidence is overwhelmingly in the opposite direction.
Several passages seem to be equivocal. One of these is the
passage in the *Confession* where Marpeck is discussing the
role of the state:

---

modern writing. Thus George S. Hendry (*The Holy Spirit in Christian Theology* [Philadelphia, 1956], p. 68) speaks of "spiritualism, enthusiasm, Schwärmerei: it is the view represented in its extreme form
by the Anabaptists of the Reformation period. . . ." It is patently false
to say of Marpeck, e.g., that he "exalts the sovereign freedom of the
Spirit . . . in such a way as virtually to sever the connection between
the mission of the Spirit and the historical Christ" (*ibid.*). It is equally
erroneous to say that it is individualistic religious experience (*ibid.*) or
not at all interested in media (p. 70). This section vitiates an otherwise helpful book by relying apparently exclusively on Karl Holl. The
reader is given no hint of the possibility of any other interpretation of
the whole left wing of the Reformation and left with the statement:
"Enthusiasm presents no serious challenge to Protestantism . . ." (p.
71). Furthermore the very definite spiritualistic strain in Luther (see
Karl Gerhard Steck, *Luther und die Schwärmer* [Zollikon-Zürich, 1955],
Chapter I) and Calvin (Walter Kreck, "Wort und Geist bei Calvin,"
Festschrift für Günther Dehn [Neukirchen, Kreis Moers, 1957], pp. 167-
181) is totally ignored. This fundamental misreading of Anabaptism
occurs also in Hendry's Weber memorial lectures on the Holy Spirit
when he says that "the Anabaptists reduced the church to a more or less
instrumental role, its function being that of assisting and promoting the
vitality of the Spirit in the individual" (*Moravian Theological Seminary
Bulletin*, Fall, 1962, p. 4).

[52] "Ein Behilf und Wegbereitung" (*KB*, fol. 294b).

[53] The phrase "er geistet wo er will" is used often by Marpeck (cf.
KB, fol. 296).

> Such true believers are sustained, ruled, and led by the Spirit of God, without human assistance and addition, those who are driven by the spirit of God are the sons of God, he who shares in the tribulation of Christ is also heir in his kingdom (*Conf.*, 170).[54]

Another is Marpeck's statement in the *Testamenterleutterung* that through the Holy Spirit the children of the kingdom of God are born by Christ through the office of the apostle and the proclamation of Christ's gospel as a service of the New Testament

> (*neben*) with which service God gives his love through the Holy Spirit and pours it into the hearts of men, which Spirit is the instrument of our rebirth (*TE*, fol. 234a).

The preposition *neben* has been interpreted as contradicting the view of the relation of spirit to form that has been depicted above as characteristic of Marpeck.[55] In view of the total overwhelming evidence, however, these statements should be considered as an emphasis on the sovereignty of God's Spirit. Such an interpretation agrees with Marpeck's insistence that the office is not effectual without faith, and faith is always *donum Dei*. This is not a clever logical circle, but the expression of Marpeck's position is determined by consistent opposition to all forms of spiritualism.[56] More con-

---

[54] "Solh warglaubigen werden erhallten, geregirt, vnd gefuert durch den geist gottes, on ainige Menschliche hilff, und zuthun, die der geist gottes treibt, seind gottes kinder. . . ."

[55] Bergsten is correct in seeing in the preposition "neben" merely a "warning not to conceive of Marpeck's conception of the relationship of Spirit and office too mechanically" (*op. cit.*, p. 99). "Neben" here means "with," not "alongside of," or "in addition to."

[56] While Bergsten speaks of a spiritualistic tendency in Marpeck he notes that such is also present in Luther's statement: "Denn es mag niemand Gott noch Gottes Wort recht verstehen, er habs denn ohn Mittel von den Heiligen Geist" (*op. cit.*, p. 100). Hermeneutically Luther's statement is more dangerous than Marpeck's, although he expresses a germ of truth. On this point Marpeck is not opposing Luther as much as the spiritualists including Denck (*Schriften*, II, 21f.). Equally dangerous is Luther's spiritualistic distinction between a visible and invisible church, which explains why the fact "dass das fleischgewordene Wort in einem realen Sinne sich in der Kirche inkarniert" appears to be totally lacking in Luther's theology (Steck, *op. cit.*, p. 52, quoting Torrance).

sistently than Luther he demanded that the use of God's ceremonies, be they sacraments or the Scriptures or church office, be accompanied by faith. Where this is not the case a serious abuse has crept into the church, which is bound to have devastating consequences.

Marpeck holds at the same time both to the free, spontaneous working of the Spirit and the historical channels within which he works. Freedom and form in the reality of the historical situation can complement each other and do not rule each other out. In this connection he appeals to the experience of Paul; though he had received a direct revelation from Christ, he did not trust his own understanding but feared that it might become confused with divine revelation; hence he went up to Jerusalem to submit his gospel to the chief apostles (*KB*, fol. 27f.). In this account of Paul's experience one sees the peculiar slant Marpeck gives to it, viz., the distrust of human intelligence, for which one looks in vain in Galatians.

Not only does the brotherhood contribute toward completion of human understanding, but it also finds its correction there. When Luther's Reformation was born, a rugged individualism, a "Here I Stand," was desperately needed. Whereas Luther never lost this individualism, the Marpeck Anabaptists at least tried to arrive at the leading of the Holy Spirit through his action within the covenant community.

E. TENSION OF THE SPIRIT AND THE LETTER[57]

After 1540 Marpeck found himself in the peculiar position of being accused by Schwenckfeld of being too legalistic,[58] and by the Swiss Brethren of being too free.[59] This ambiguity was the result of his view of the relationship between the

[57] The contrast between letter and spirit is often restricted primarily to the matter of allegory (so R. M. Grant, *The Letter and the Spirit* [London, 1957]). Here it is used in a more inclusive sense, referring to allegory, to legalism, and the problem of the inner word and its relation to Biblical authority. To some extent these problems are already present in the Biblical writings although it is easy to see neoplatonic distinctions in the Bible even where they are not present (as A. W. Argyle does in "'Outward' and 'Inward' in Biblical Thought," *ET*, LXVIII [1957], pp. 196-99). On the problem of literal versus intentional meaning, see Boaz Cohen, "Note on Letter and Spirit in the New Testament," *HTR*, 47 (1954), 197-203. The question of "the inner word" has been studied in detail by J. H. Maronier, *Het Inwendig Woord* (Amsterdam, 1890); R. H. Grützmacher, *Wort und Geist*

spirit and the letter. To discuss this problem it will be necessary to state the views of the Swiss Brethren.

It has been common practice to consider Pilgram Marpeck a
leader of peaceful Anabaptists in South Germany, a group
genetically and organizationally related to the Swiss Brethren.[60] Prior to Horsch, Hulshof had in general noted the
differences between the South Germans and the Swiss, noting
mainly the differences in personalities rather than regional and
theological differences.[61] In his research in South German
Anabaptism, Jan J. Kiwiet has proposed a rehabilitation of
Hans Denck as an Anabaptist in good standing and has
stressed the individual character of the South German Anabaptists as over against the Swiss. He portrays the South Germans as a free type of Anabaptism, which did not practice rig-
orous close communion and in other matters was more tolerant
than the Swiss, the Swiss being more biblicistic than the South
Germans.[62] Kiwiet's thesis, however, overstates the case. It is
not true that *all* of the early Swiss Brethren were legalists,[63]
nor is there any evidence that the Marpeck brotherhood

(Leipzig, 1902), and by Wilhelm Wiswedel, "Zum Problem 'Inneres
und aüsseres Wort' bei den Täufern des 16. Jahrhunderts," *ARG*, 46
(1955), 1-19 (also in *MQR*). Only Wiswedel treats Marpeck. See also
Eric Gritsch, "The Authority of the 'Inner Word,'" Yale Dissertation,
1959.

[58] *CS*, III (1530), 832f.; VIII (1542), 91, 93.

[59] In an epistle to the Swiss he says: "Wie ich beschuldigt bin, ich
streck die Freiheit Christi zu weit" (*KB*, fol. 34b); "wie ich vor vielen
beschuldigt bin, ich brauch die Freiheit Christi zu einem Deckmantel
der Bosheit" (*KB*, fol. 44); "als sollten wir Freiheit (so wir in Christo
haben) zuweit wider sein Wort fuehren und halten, so ihr uns solche
erweisen moechten" (*KB*, fol. 66).

[60] So John Horsch, *The Mennonites of Europe* (Scottdale, Penna.,
1942), p. 135; John Wenger, *op. cit.; et al.* The line of distinction between Swiss Brethren and South German Evangelicals is not very clear
in Horsch. Hut is the only one of the major leaders treated in the
three pages he devotes to South Germany (*op. cit.*, pp. 141-43).

[61] *Op. cit.*, p. 24. Compare also A. Nicoladoni, *op. cit.*, p. 114.

[62] *Op. cit.*, p. 69.

[63] Compare the little tract, "Von zweyerley gehorsam" in the Sammelband, *Concordantz und Zeiger der Namhafftigen Sprueche* (no date,
no place). This book, which dates from the sixteenth century, comes
from an unknown provenance; but the presence of the Schleitheim
Confession and Sattler's Epistle indicates Swiss Brethren influence if not
origin. The tract is published in English in *MQR*, XXI (1947), 18-22.
Cf. also *MQR*, XVII (1942), 82-98. It is similar to *KB*, No. 15.

allowed unbaptized believers to share in the Lord's Supper.[64]

It will be necessary therefore to redefine the term "Swiss Brethren." In this discussion it does not include all the South German Anabaptists, nor all those who went by the name of "Swiss Brethren" irrespective of locale in the sixteenth century. It is used primarily to refer to those Anabaptists in Switzerland who were uneasy about Pilgram Marpeck and who made this uneasiness explicit by refusing his brotherhood recognition as a church.[65]

Marpeck was not the only one who had trouble with the Swiss Brethren. The first indication of tensions between them and the South German Anabaptists comes from the report at Hans Hut's trial (September 16, 1527), when Hut stated that he could not accept the strict regulations of the Swiss on the matter of bearing arms. Hut also did not accept the Swiss (*Schleitheim*) position on the oath, which he thought could be used in "community, state and civil matters" (*gemein, statt und burgerlichen sachen*). While not identifying anything but the issue of arms with the "*Ordnung*" made in Switzerland it is quite possible that Hut also refers to the Swiss when he says: "Concerning dress some had indicated that clothing must be simple, but he showed them that it is also not forbidden by God, for every man should be allowed to dress as he pleases."[66] The presence of one of Hut's writings in the *Kunstbuch* would appear to indicate that the Marpeck brotherhood was influenced by him, but to what extent needs to be investigated.[67]

---

[64] *Op. cit.*, p. 45. Already in the *Confession* (pp. 171, 196) Marpeck makes it clear that the Lord's Supper is not for everyone. Compare also V, pp. 445, 449, 450; *TB*, 256:38, 257 (*both taken from Bekentnisse*).

[65] Just how widely to apply the term and how precisely it was used in the sixteenth century are debatable. Johann Loserth finds evidence that even the Schwertler were called Swiss Brethren at Nicolsburg (*ME*, III, 338, 884). Cf. further, *ME*, IV, 669-671.

[66] Christian Meyer, "Die Anfänge des Wiedertäuferthums in Augsburg," *Zeitschrift des Historischen Vereins für Schwaben und Neuburg*, I (1874), 228. That the Swiss had a tendency to regulate dress questions appears possibly also from Sebastian Franck's *Chronica* (1531), fol. 446: "Etliche gerathen dahin, das sy nichts mit den Heyden gemeyn wöllen haben. . . . Dise setzen regel wie schlecht das klaid sein soll, wie ein yedes soll gehen soll, wie vil falten der schurtz. . . ." The problem recurs in Mennonite history (cf. *MQR*, VI [1932], 52).

[67] For a beginning see Herbert C. Klassen, "Some Aspects of the Teaching of Hans Hut," M. A. Thesis, University of British Columbia,

It is much the same with the second South German Anabaptist who fell into disfavor with the Swiss Brethren some
ten years later, namely, Jörg Maler, the editor and compiler of
the *Kunstbuch*. Maler lived in Switzerland for fourteen years
but left when he could no longer bear the strictness of the
Swiss. Again the issues of the oath, apparel, and force were
the dividing ones. Maler opposed the absolute rejection of
sword-bearing by the Swiss, although when the city was attacked and he was urged to fight he declined and had to
leave. He had been in St. Gall and Appenzell for fourteen
years (1534-1548) when he went to Augsburg. Specifically, he
states that he could see nothing wrong with weaving a bright-
colored coat (*gefärbt und frech*). Also the Swiss thought it
was wrong to punish one's wife and it seemed to Maler that
this was carrying nonresistance too far; a wife should be
punished just like a child if she did not behave.[68]

In any event the letters in the *Kunstbuch* show that the
tensions still existed between Maler and the Swiss in 1561 and
that he is now a "South German Anabaptist." He accepts the
oath as not forbidden in the New Testament but remains a
staunch Anabaptist until the end even though the Augsburg
preachers made every attempt to convert him.[69]

1958, published in *MQR*, XXXIII (1959), 171-205, especially p. 203.
That Schleitheim is directed against the South Germans as suggested
by Kiwiet is doubtful. The difference between South Germans and
Swiss crystallized *after* Schleitheim, not before.

[68] Roth, *ARG*, IV, 614. While this may sound a little severe to
modern ears, such a position was not uncommon then. The *Matthew's
Bible*, imprinted at London, 1549 (reprint of 1537 edition), adds the
following note at I Peter 3:7 on the words "dwelling with a wife
according to knowledge": "He dwelleth wyth his wyfe accordinge to
knowledge, that taketh her as a nesessarye healper, and not as a bonde
seruaunte or a bond slave. And if she be not obedient and helpful
unto hym, endevoureth to beate the feare of God into her heade, that
thereby she maye be compelled to learne her dutyie and do it." This
edition is also sometimes referred to as the "Wife Beater Edition."

One is tempted to identify Jörg Maler with Gregor Maler, who attended the Augsburg "Synod" in 1527. They can be considered the
same only if Gregor Maler was sent out as an apostle from the "Synod"
unbaptized, since Jörg Maler was not baptized until 1532 (Roth, *op. cit.*,
II, 419). This would seem rather unlikely, were it not for the fact that
Gregor Maler insisted at his hearing that he had never been baptized,
and was freed on that ground (see Oskar Vasella, "Von den Anfängen
der bündnerischen Täuferbewegung," *Zeitschrift für Schweizerische
Geschichte*, XIX [1939], 180f.).

[69] Compare the account of the visit of three preachers and a monk to
Maler in prison (*KB*, fol. 164), and Roth, *ARG*, IV, 640, footnote 8.

What place does Marpeck occupy in the relations of the Swiss and South Germans? The relation of the South Germans as a group to the Swiss Brethren as a group needs further investigation. As late as 1561 a complaint from the miners lists the "Bilgerer, Sattlerische, and Gabrieliter" as the various Anabaptist sects in Strasbourg.[70] Since any grouping among the Anabaptists either geographically or otherwise must be undertaken with caution,[71] and since it is not necessary for us to do so here, we will confine ourselves to the epistles that constitute the major interchange of ideas between Marpeck and the Swiss Brethren. We use the term Swiss Brethren, not as including Pilgram Marpeck, as all Anabaptist studies have done prior to Kiwiet, nor do we use it to cover the whole group of Swiss Brethren, as does Kiwiet. The question of the precise usage of that term can remain open for the purposes of this investigation.

That even the early Swiss had a Biblicism bordering on legalism, directly inherited and uncritically accepted from Zwingli, seems evident, the efforts of Grebel's biographer to prove the contrary notwithstanding.[72] In view of the fact that all the correspondence between Marpeck and Swiss Anabaptist congregations reflects differences (and since the correspondence is not restricted to St. Gall and Appenzell where in the earlier days excesses were rampant),[73] it would appear evident that Marpeck was at odds with the whole Swiss Brethren movement. That he nevertheless felt himself to be in basic harmony with the early movement is evident from the

[70] Strasbourg Akten, § 736. Does this indicate the three main groups, Swiss Brethren (Sattler), South Germans, and Gabrielites? Probably one has to be cautious with this evidence, since it comes from the mouth of people who wanted to discredit the Anabaptists. On January 14, 1556, Peter Novesianus (§ 674) said there were Hutterians, Hofmannites, Schweitzerische, and Bilgramites among the Anabaptists.

[71] Fast, op. cit., pp. 223, 225.

[72] Harold S. Bender, Conrad Grebel (Goshen, Ind., 1950), p. 175. It is not difficult to see how the approach adopted by Grebel that the NT must teach something for it to be adopted would lead to an arid Biblicism unless definite efforts were made to avert it. Who would defend the argument, "what the Scripture does not positively teach and command is forbidden" (Bender, op. cit., p. 176)? Menno, too, took this position (C. Krahn, Menno Simons [Karlsruhe, 1936], p. 135), as did Balthasar Hübmaier, according to R. Armour, Anabaptist Baptism (Scottdale, Penna., 1966), p. 28.

[73] Conrad Grebel and Manz visited St. Gall in an attempt to expunge these excesses (see Kessler, op. cit., pp. 164f.).

reference to Schleitheim in the *Kunstbuch* (by Scharn-schlager). It is nevertheless quite obvious that the answers given by the Marpeck group to ethical questions are consider-ably freer than the more simple Biblicism of the Schleitheim Confession.[74] The number of letters exchanged and the ur-gency of those extant indicate that Marpeck viewed this difference in approach to the Scriptures as a most serious problem—and well he might, for on this ground was fought the hardest battle between Biblicism and spiritualism, the letter and the spirit, law and gospel, freedom and enslave-ment. From the standpoint of Marpeck's hermeneutics this literary exchange is invaluable.

While it was necessary to begin with the spiritualists on the primacy of the Word become flesh, with the legalists within Anabaptism it was necessary to emphasize the primacy of the Spirit, while asserting the empirical union of letter and spirit. In his treatise on true faith Scharnschlager gives expression to the basic objection of the South Germans to the Swiss when he says:

> Since we have been made alive through faith and live by faith alone as it says in Romans, how then could such life come through external works as certain of the Swiss are insisting[*treiben*], as though such life, salvation, or rule of God consists in works, for it consists alone in faith. I speak of the faith that comes today after the resurrection and ascension of Christ. . . . I refer to such a righteousness before God which comes by faith in Jesus Christ to all and upon all who believe. Further, they are all made righteous without merit by his grace, by the redemption through Christ, whom God had ad-vanced as a mercyseat through faith in his blood. [After quoting Romans 5:1 he continues]: There it is clearly seen that just as eternal life, so also essential goodness [*frommigkeit*] and righteousness (valid before God) comes alone through faith. Therefore those who promote external works, cleansing the outside of the cup, saying, 'don't wear this,' 'don't bear that' and the like should desist from it and perceive that such a faith (which is not a gift of man but of God) might be planted and built up. . .(*KB*, fol. 255b).

[74] Cf. "Oath," *ME*, IV.

That the issues between the Swiss and Marpeck were primarily hermeneutical, involving both the problem of the Old
Testament and that of the spirit and the letter, is apparent.
Marpeck's most extensive discussion of the place of the Scriptures as well as the Law comes in his correspondence with the
Swiss. While the concrete issue that is repeatedly discussed is
an ethical one, namely, Christian freedom, Marpeck does not
separate systematic theology or Biblical theology from the
practical life of the church.[75]

The point at which this discussion between the Swiss and
Marpeck takes on additional importance and relevance is the
difference in conclusions drawn from the Biblical message by
separate believers, all studying the same Scriptures ostensibly
under the guidance of the same Holy Spirit. Marpeck does not
assert, as he might have, that since there was discord they
obviously did not have the Holy Spirit; but he explicitly rejects such a position and affirms that they are zealous lovers
of God and his Spirit, but lacking in the knowledge and
understanding of Christ (*KB,* fol. 27). To be sure, all knowledge on this earth is only fragmentary; and once a man
begins to think that he knows, it is certain that he does not
know.

> There is no lack of Spirit that there should be factions
> between us, but there is still a deficiency in our weak
> conscience and immature understanding and it is from
> this that divisions have come (*KB,* fol. 56b).

Marpeck's conversations with the Swiss cannot be understood
apart from his abhorrence of all sects and his deep desire to
realize the unity of Christ's body, the church (*V,* 72f., 89, 584;
TB, Preface). No aspect of Marpeck's view of the church is
more pronounced than his emphasis on its unity. At this point
too he differs radically from the spiritualists, for they insisted
that the more divisions the better; for in that way the true
members of Christ's body would be shown to exist.[76]

[75] *Vide supra,* p. 76.

[76] On the basis of I Corinthians 11:19. After having talked about
the true fellowship of believers in the presence of Christ, Marpeck says:
"Sonst entschlag ich mich aller Sekten, Rottierungen, und Versammlung-
en . . . sonderlich deren die wider die Geduld Christi . . . das leibliche
Schwert brauchen im Reich Christi zu herrschen . . ." (*KB,* fol. 41).
In the same vein he writes: "Die rechte und wahre Gemeinschaft das

If the unity of the church formed the theoretical theological basis for Marpeck's discussion with the Swiss, the immediate occasion was given by concrete ethical issues. We are considerably handicapped by a lack of major sources available from the Swiss side and must therefore describe the Swiss position as it comes to us from Marpeck's writings. No serious attempt will be made to evaluate whether or not this is caricature.

Evidence of the Swiss position is found in a letter by Cornelius Veh, an elder from Moravia to the church at Appenzell and Zürich, dated 1543, which describes at length the danger that Christians will not be genuine but instead counterfeit coins moved by themselves rather than by the Spirit of Christ. To test these spirits the Scriptures have to be read, for the Scriptures testify to Christ, and only as these spirits are tested by the Scriptures can their genuineness be determined. This is made more difficult because they too use the Scriptures, but according to the letter, as did Satan when he tempted Christ, and by omitting certain words or portions of Scripture. Often they distort or confuse the Scriptures. Like Pilate they use a language that means nothing to them, although sometimes it nevertheless is a witness to others (KB, fol. 219b). The touchstone is Jesus Christ, and they must be tested by this stone. Unfortunately, many are seeking Christ in the wrong places. There are still some ascetic Anabaptists who seek him in the desert, denying themselves the usual foods, drink, and clothes, hoping thereby to follow the example of John the Baptist and others of the apostolic age. Veh objects to this since John's asceticism was meant as an object lesson to the Pharisees and has no relation to us (KB, fol. 220b). Others seek him in the closet, saying, "No one can reach him there but we who have the key." After listing a number of groups who take this approach, he warns that

Leibs und Bluts Christi ist einigkeit, und Einigkeit im hl. Geist ist wahre Gemeinschaft, dann da kann und mag nicht Spaltung sein im Leib Christi, weils nur ein Glaub, ein Herr, ein Geist, ein Gott Vater unser aller ist, so ist je solche Gemeinschaft mit einem Geist, mit Wasser getauft, zu einem unzerspaltnen, ungeteilten Leib mit vereinten Gliedern" (KB, fol. 66). M. Bucer argued that the presence of many sects and heresies is a sign that the true teaching of the Holy Gospel is present (Wie Leicht unnd füglich christliche vergleichung der Religion [Strasbourg, 1545], p. LXXIII). This argument is used also by Franck, Bünderlin, and Schwenckfeld.

Christ cannot be found in the bread or any other place apart
from the human heart:

> as is the custom of the false Christians, even in part
> called Brethren, that is Baptists [*Täufer*] who would
> like to be that, of whom some say Christ is here, others
> there, once there in the Scriptures, or in other dead
> creatures like craftsmanship or other things which one
> should not or may not use. At another time they see it in
> temporal goods, as community of the same, whoever
> does not hand them over and forsake them cannot come
> to Christ, nor can he find Him, even less be saved, unless
> he sell it and give it to the other (as they say the poor)
> children of God and similar statements, as has been the
> manner of the two harmful and destructive sects called
> Swiss and Hutterian, and as even today in particular the
> Hutterians practice with regard to temporal goods (*KB*,
> fol. 221b).

Veh castigates this approach and admonishes his readers to
test themselves to see whether they have the Holy Spirit
within themselves, for:

> Whoever does not have the Holy Spirit dwelling in his
> heart is no Christian but a castaway [*Verwürfling*], nor
> can he call Christ truly a Lord because he is not ruled
> by his Spirit (which is Love) (*KB*, fol. 222).

Veh may be discussing the problem at St. Gall in a passage in
this epistle where he refers to the slothful servant who hid his
talent in a napkin. Under the guise of uncertainty they refuse
to do anything. They do not know whether they can even
trust those who baptized them, and are suspicious of those
who carry letters to them. They wish merely to stand still.
These must be left alone until the Holy Spirit punishes them
or spews them out of his mouth (*KB*, 224b f.). Apparently
some of the Swiss objected to the work of the Marpeck group
in Switzerland as though this portion of the country were not
under its mission mandate. These subterfuges are rejected by
Veh as evidence that they do not have the Spirit of Christ.
For the rest Veh says they are still in one faith, mind, and
spirit with them (*KB*, fol. 226). Similar indications are found
in the correspondence of Marpeck with the Swiss. His two

closely related criticisms of their church life are their legalistic
Biblicism and their alacrity and sharpness of judgment.

When one has become accustomed to reading Schwenckfeld's charge against the Anabaptists that they are hope-
lessly stuck in the dead letter of the Scriptures, it comes
as somewhat of a jolt to read Marpeck chiding the Swiss for
their devotion to the letter. Veh mentions such false devotion
(KB, fol. 218b) and Marpeck refers to counterfeit Christian
freedom as always adorning itself with the dead letter (KB,
fol. 34b, 35). Stressing the importance of Christian judgment
taking place in harmony with Christ, he continues:

> But the devil is using his weapons against us all places
> in part and fragmentarily [in Teil und Stückweis]
> through the dead letter (KB, fol. 37f.).

The devil confronts them with the two dangers of not judging
at all, and of prematurely judging at all times.

As we have seen above, the legalism of the Swiss came to
expression in regulations on clothes, bearing arms, etc. Veh's
correspondence also alludes to the Swiss restrictions on clothing and other matters considered adiaphorous by him (KB,
fol. 220b).

Marpeck complains that their tendency to legislate violates
the basic freedom of the Christian in Christ (KB, fol. 28);
hypocrites conceal their lack of spiritual life under human
ordinances and commandments (KB, fol. 35), and whoever
legislates, commands, or orders "usurps the office of the Holy
Spirit."[77] For Marpeck the only law in the Christian life is the
law of love (KB, fol. 49), and the only sin is the sin of
disobeying God's Word (ibid.). This adherence to the letter
and attendant legalism have in Marpeck's judgment caused the
Swiss to become victims of the malady of judging prematurely and harshly (KB, fol. 28), a malady so serious that he
refused on that ground alone to recognize them as a valid
church of Christ. He could find no evidence in either Christ or

---

[77] KB, fol. 36: "Darum wer setzt, gebeut, oder verbeut, zwingt,
treibt, straft oder richt vor der zeit der offenbarung guten oder basen
frucht, der greift dem hl. Geist des Herrn Jesu Christi (wider die lieb,
Gut und Gnad in sein herrlichkeit, Gewalt und Amt), und lauft Christo
Jesu vor." The danger of legalism is noted also in KB, fol. 37b; 40b;
44b; 48, etc.

Paul of such a censorious attitude and so could not see how they could be a church.[78]

Church discipline cannot be exercised in the flippant manner evident among the Swiss where even the elders are under the ban, some even under the double ban (*KB*, fol. 62).[79] From another source, quite unrelated to Marpeck, we are also told that among the Anabaptists of St. Gall "if anyone was guilty of a trespass, he was banned by them, for there was a daily excommunication among them."[80] Some of their bishops have prostituted their holy calling of helping and assisting the weak into an unholy desire to judge and condemn the weak and the erring. It is the function of the bishop to care for the sick, not to kick them out.[81] Leaders are tolerant of the weak and the erring just as Christ is tolerant of us and strengthens us (*KB*, fol. 57). Where all spiritual life is gone it is a different matter; but to judge the men who are not living up to a certain level because of human weakness is not in the spirit of Christ, especially when the spirit of quick condemnations rules in the church. He concludes his first letter to the Swiss with the plea:

> Above all it is my prayer for the sake of Christ that you seek judgment from Christ and exercise it there. Learn from him long-suffering, patience and tenderheartedness. May the merciful Father supplement all my shortcomings and insufficiencies which I still find daily. For it is my highest uneasiness in my conscience [*spalt in meinem Gewissen*] against you that I fail to find such quick, premature judgments and condemnations con-

---

[78] *KB*, fol. 66: "wir haben euch aber billig bisher und noch von unserer Gemeinschaft in Christo abgestellt um unbilligs grichts und bannens willen etc." Earlier he had said that even if they did recognize them as a church, God would not do so (fol. 65), and the reason they cannot be recognized is that they do not judge according to the "sündverzeihender und sündbehaltender hl. geist christi" (fol. 65b).

[79] The seriousness of church discipline is evident from Marpeck's plea that discipline follow the order prescribed in Matthew 18, and if the offender does not hear the church "so geht erst das urteil mit trübsal, angst, und trauern, und mit grossem schmerzen und leid, dann es gilt ein glied am leib christi des herrn. . . . Es wird den andern gliedern am leib christi ohn schmerzhaften grossen schmerzen und trübsal nicht zugehn" (*KB*, fol. 58b).

[80] Johannes Kessler, *Sabbata*, p. 46.

[81] "Nicht so schnell aus dem hause gottes zu stossen" (*KB*, fol. 57b).

cerning every little thing with Christ and his apostolic
church as I find among you (*KB*, fol. 61b).

In summary, it can be noted that Marpeck was caught
between the spiritualist critique of Anabaptism, which
dubbed it a heresy of the letter,[82] and a sizable proportion of
his fellow Anabaptists who were fast becoming ensnared in a
legalistic Biblicism, which picked certain issues and gave
them absolute value while the cardinal doctrines of the Christian faith were slipping from the place of central importance.
Marpeck registered a vigorous protest that human effort was
beginning to take the place of divine grace and that the
accomplishments of men were pushing the achievements and
satisfaction of Christ out of the center. In this incipient threatening change he saw a deadly foe of the Anabaptist movement, which he withstood with all the strength and vigor at
his command. Whether he ever convinced the Swiss Brethren,
no one knows; but that the foe against whom he fought was
not an imaginary one, subsequent events in Protestantism
have shown only too clearly. Where discipleship moves to the
center there is always the danger that the imitation of Christ-
ideal supplants the Pauline emphasis of God working in you
and Christ being formed within you. The one is anthropocen-
tric, the other theocentric. Even in the tension between spirit
and letter Marpeck's basic Christocentrism comes strongly to
the fore.

Marpeck had come to resolve the tension between the spirit
and the letter. The letter was important but not as a dead
standard by which to live; rather it was a vehicle used by the
Spirit to communicate its message to him, a vehicle that
would be necessary as long as man lives on the stage of
history. The letter had been infused with the Spirit and had
become "a living letter in his heart" (*KU*, C vb).

Marpeck's position is well expressed by Anna Orvena Hayer
of Holstein:

> *Aber Gottes Wort, Jesus Christ,*
> *Ist Geist und Leben, redt inwendig,*
> *Machet allein das Herz verständig,*

---

[82] Sebastian Franck, *Chronica* (1531), fol. 444b: "den buchstaben
der schrifft (den sye steiff für sich hielten)." In general it should be
remembered that Franck felt the Anabaptists were so diverse "das ich
nichts gewiss vnd endtlichs von ynen zuschreiben weiss" (fol. 445).

Aendert der Menschen Sinn und Mut,
Reicht weiter, denn der Buchstab tut,
Das äusser nur die Ohren rühret,
Das inner Wort zum Geist einführet,
Bringt mit ihm Lebenskraft und Saft,
Ohn dies das äusser wenig schafft;
Drum soll man nach dem innern trachten,
Das äusser aber nicht verachten.[83]

[83] Cited in W. Wiswedel's excellent article, "The Inner and the Outer Word," *MQR*, XXVI (1952), 190f. The footnote is in error so it was impossible to check its accuracy or study its context. On the relation of the letter and the spirit, Marpeck shows no essential deviation from the position of John Calvin. (Walter Kreck [*op. cit.*, p. 178], being unaware of Marpeck, assumes that Calvin's position is defined in relationship to his polemics against *Schwärmerei* and Rome. Marpeck had the same two opponents in mind.) G. Ebeling gives an excellent survey of this problem noting its wider reference and the influence of Augustine on the Reformation on this question. Marpeck, while not mentioned by Ebeling, appears to stand close to Luther ("Geist und Buchstabe," *RGG*, II, cols. 1290-96).

III

MARPECK'S USE OF THE OLD TESTAMENT

Ever since the second century when the awareness of a New Testament canon began to simmer in the unconscious of the church, the problem of the Old and New Covenants and their mutual relationships has been acute. As is well known Marcion gets the credit for having fanned this irritating spark, and whatever one says by way of censure or praise about Marcion there is agreement that the problem on which he placed his finger is not an imaginary one. Essentially he did not exaggerate the problem when he pictured the prophet of God in the Old Testament with his arms outstretched while the enemies of Yahweh are being murdered, while the New Testament Messiah stretched out his arms on a cross and allowed himself to be murdered in an act of unselfish love. In the Old Testament Joshua detained the sun until his wrath went down; in the New we are told not to let the sun go down on our wrath (Eph. 4:26).[1]

Marcion had several concerns. His theological concern was that the emerging moralism and legalism (seen so clearly in the First Epistle of Clement) not replace Paul's gospel of freedom and justification by faith. His hermeneutical concern was that the church should be spared the vagaries of allegory so blatantly portrayed in the Epistle of Barnabas. Neither of these concerns was heeded, partly because he overstated his case and the opposing Church Fathers threw out the baby with the bath. Whatever the precise causes, there is no doubt

---

[1] The most sympathetic and thorough study of Marcion is still the work of Adolf Harnack, *Marcion: Das Evangelium vom fremden Gott* (Leipzig, 1921). For citations on the above-mentioned points see page 105.

that allegorical interpretation ruled the day;[2] and one need only read Clement of Alexandria's lengthy description of table manners to see that at least one church father had moved several degrees from the Pauline ethic whose dominant motif is freedom.[3] To be sure there were remarkable exceptions already in the second century. Melito of Sardis approaches in his works a method of Scriptural exegesis that represents a typology less objectionable than the allegory of Barnabas.[4] The Antiochan fathers in later days, notably Theodore of Mopsuestia,[5] Diodor of Tarsus, and John Chrysostom, refused to bow at the shrine of allegory; but these men are only now returning to general favor and prominence through the efforts of modern scholars. They have caused scarcely a ripple in the exegetical stream extending from their time to our own.[6]

"In its defense against Marcion, the church by and large forgot Paul's dialectic of time, and leaned over backward placing the Old Testament and the New Testament on an equal basis."[7] One of the striking exceptions to this statement, already from the second century, is Irenaeus. In reaction to

[2] Robert M. Grant, *The Letter and the Spirit* (London, 1957), has convincingly shown to what extent Biblical studies are here indebted to pagan Greek writers (via Philo).

[3] *The Instructor*, Bk. II, ch. 1.

[4] These objections are specified by Johannes Klevinghaus, *Die theologische Stellung der apostolischen Väter zur alttestamentlichen Offenbarung* (Gütersloh, 1948). For Melito's position the best source is his homily, recently edited by B. Lohse, *Die Passa-Homilie . . .* (Leiden, 1958).

[5] Robert Devreesse has done much to restore interest and appreciation for the work of Theodore of Mopsuestia (*Essai sur Theodore de Mopsueste*, Vatican City, 1948). Ulrich Wickert has given us some excellent studies on his approach to Paul in two studies: *Studien zu den Pauluskommentaren Theodors von Mopsuestia* (Berlin, 1962) and "Die Persönlichkeit des Paulus in den Pauluskommentaren Theodors von Mopsuestia," *Zeitschrift für die neutestamentliche Wissenschaft*, 53 (1962), 51-66. Careful studies of his Christology are made by R. A. Norris in his book *Manhood and Christ* (Oxford, 1963), and by F. A. Sullivan (*The Christology of Theodore of Mopsuestia*, Rome, 1956) who declines to give him a clean bill of health.

[6] See, however, M. L. W. Laistner, "Antiochene Exegesis in Western Europe," *HTR*, XL (1947), 19-32. The wide circulation of a hermeneutical manual by Junilius Africanus is documented by Laistner. Although Junilius belongs in this school he is rarely quoted (p. 31).

[7] Krister Stendahl, "Biblical Theology," *Interpreter's Dictionary of the Bible*, I, 424.

Marcion, Irenaeus was the first to develop a rather full-fledged Biblical theology.[8] To counter Marcion's two gods, Irenaeus began with the plural "covenants" in the New Testament (Rom. 9:4; Eph. 2:12) and divided history into dispensations or economies of God's dealing with men. Here is the first developed concept of progressive revelation, and the question must remain open whether this solution to the problem is the best the church can propose. Of its widespread influence there can be no doubt.

Augustine too in his battles with the Manicheans struggled to define the relationship between the Old and New Covenants. His task was made somewhat easier by the fact that the Old Covenant could easily be relegated to a position of interest but not authority through allegory, and also through the unfortunate circumstance that Jerome seems to have been one of the few prominent Church Fathers who took the Old Testament Scriptures seriously enough to study the language in which they were written.[9]

During the Middle Ages Jewish scholars had some influence on Christian scholars, and when the Reformation was ushered in Hebrew lexicography had progressed so much that there remained no doubt about the importance of learning Hebrew.[10] Luther encouraged the young theologians to learn Hebrew. Even with respect to the Pauline letters of the New Testament he observed the importance of knowing Hebrew. "The words and concepts of Paul are taken out of the prophets and Moses. Therefore the young theologians should learn Hebrew in order that they may set (the Hebrew words) beside the Greek and note their peculiarity, their nature and their force. . . . If I were young and wished to become a famous theologian, I would compare Paul with the Old Testa-

---

[8] John Lawson, *The Biblical Theology of Saint Irenaeus* (London, 1948).

[9] On the hermeneutics of Augustine see Gerhard Strauss, *Schriftgebrauch, Schriftauslegung und Schriftbeweis bei Augustin* (Tübingen, 1959), p. 68 where Pontet is cited as designating the problem of the inner connection of the two Testaments as "le plus grave problème de la Bible" for Augustine.

[10] The myth that the Middle Ages were the dark ages for Bible study is effectively laid to rest by Beryl Smalley in her book, *The Study of the Bible in the Middle Ages* (Oxford, 1952).

ment."[11] Luther groaned because Hebrew was difficult and never claimed to have mastered it, but we can only sympathize with him on that score!

It is no cause for surprise that with the restoration of the Bible to the common man at the time of the Reformation one of the most urgent problems to emerge was the authority of the Old Testament. A host of issues including the use of images, war, usury, worship, and infant baptism, all in varying degrees, were supported by reference to the Old Testament. Two major hermeneutical issues of the Reformation were the relation of the Old and New Covenants and the relation of the Word and Spirit. On both the Anabaptists provoked the discussion and determined its course to a much greater extent than is generally recognized.[12] Harnack is surely mistaken when he asserts that the retention of the Old Testament in the church's canon at the time of the Reformation was due to an unavoidable accident.[13] It was no accident that the Reformers retained it; it was a logical result of their basic conservatism. Nor was it an accident that the Anabaptists retained it; they accepted it as God's revelation and struggled (not always successfully) to reconcile its differences with the New.

The prominence of this issue is illustrated by the way it emerges at every major disputation between Reformed and Anabaptists. At the Franckenthal Gespräch of 1571 it is obviously the most burning issue that separates the two groups.[14] Baptism, the oath, bearing of arms, and other issues continued to divide the Anabaptists and Reformers because the Old Testament was viewed differently.

[11] H. J. Kraus, *Geschichte der historisch-kritischen Forschung des Alten Testaments* (Neukirchen, Kreis Moers, 1956), p. 9.

[12] *Vide supra*, pp. 12ff.; 21ff. George Huntston Williams (*The Radical Reformation* [Philadelphia, 1962], pp. 815-832) has observed that "there was a very close connection between the way the Radicals conceived of the two Testaments and the way they conceived of the nature and the mission of the church and the solidarity and destiny of all mankind" (p. 816).

[13] *Marcion*, p. 248.

[14] In *Protocoll: Das ist/Alle handlung des gesprechs zu Franckenthal* (Heidelberg, 1571), the record of a discussion between Anabaptists and Reformed, the relation between the two Testaments is the first major item of business and appears on pp. 19, 44f., 87-90, 272f., 601f.

A. THE ANABAPTISTS AND THE OLD TESTAMENT

During the time of the Reformation the Anabaptists were sometimes accused of rejecting the Old Testament as Scripture.[15] This accusation was made because they rejected categorically the analogous position of circumcision and baptism that Zwingli,[16] Bucer,[17] Bullinger,[18] Calvin,[19] and Peter Martyr[20] used to prove the necessity of infant baptism.[21] They also rejected the ethics of the Old Testament as no longer valid for the Christian and insisted that the means of eliminating enemies and heretics used in the Old Testament could not be used by Christians.[22] The evidence that any Anabaptists rejected the Old Testament as Scripture has not yet been adduced, even though some leaders cautioned their readers to read primarily the New Testament.[23]

On the other hand the first translation of the Old Testament Prophets from the Hebrew into German was a joint effort by the Anabaptist Hans Denck,[24] and the "fringe" Anabaptist, Ludwig Hätzer.[25] The presence of Sabbatarians like

[15] So Caspar Schwenckfeld, CS, VIII, 221:10ff.; X (February 27, 1547), 926:7ff.; Jakob Andrea, op. cit., IV, 102. Bullinger compares them with Marcion (Der Widertöufferen ursprung . . . , Zürich, 1561, p. 178).

[16] In Von der Taufe (1525), ZSW, IV, 188-337.

[17] Vide infra, pp. 157ff.

[18] See Heinold Fast, Heinrich Bullinger, p. 25.

[19] H. H. Wolf, Die Einheit des Bundes (Neukirchen, Kreis Moers, 1958), pp. 88f.

[20] J. C. McClelland, The Visible Words of God (Grand Rapids, 1957), pp. 152f.

[21] According to John Howard Yoder, the distinction between the inner and the outer baptism made infant baptism possible, while the identification of the Old and New Covenants made it necessary (Die Gespräche der Täufer . . . , p. 80).

[22] The favorite illustration was the different way in which Christ treated his enemies as compared to Elijah. See Clare verantwurtung (1531), fol. C ii.

[23] So Leonhard Schiemer, in Lydia Müller, Glaubenszeugnisse, I, 45. According to the testimony of Hans Leupold the Anabaptists gathering in Augsburg about 1527 studied the Word of God, principally the Gospels and the Prophets (see ME, III, 328).

[24] On Hans Denck, see Walter Fellmann, Hans Denck, Schriften (Gütersloh, 1956); Jan J. Kiwiet, "The Life of Hans Denck," MQR, XXXI (1957), 227-259; and "The Theology of Hans Denck," MQR, XXXII (1958), 3-27. See WA, Vol. II, 2, pp. CXIII-CXXXIII.

[25] See G. Goeters, Ludwig Hätzer, Spiritualist und Antitrinitarier, Eine Randfigur der frühen Täuferbewegung (Gütersloh, 1957). On this translation, its importance, etc., see Chapter X.

Oswald Glait among the Anabaptists indicates that the early movement had not developed a "Biblical theology," but was simply going on from day to day using the Bible as a standard of life and conduct without a studied effort at relating the Old and New Covenants. The widespread use of the Old Testament in Anabaptist circles is attested to in a number of places,[26] but it was not until some rather unfortunate developments had taken place among the Anabaptists that a definite, clear, and normative position was developed.

In the development of a "Biblical" rather than a strictly New Testament theology among the Anabaptists, Pilgram Marpeck's brotherhood took a leading role. The importance of the distinction between the two covenants appears in Marpeck's debates with Bucer.[27] An important factor in Marpeck's rejection of the spiritualism of Kautz and Bünderlin was the role of the Old Testament and the definition of its purpose.[28] Furthermore, there were legalists within the Anabaptists who expressed their devotion to the Old Testament by stressing the Ten Commandments, in particular the one that appeared not to have been superseded by the New Testament, the observance of the Sabbath.[29] This devotion to the

[26] Felix Manz used the Hebrew text of the OT as a basis for group Bible study (see Emil Egli, Actensammlung zur Geschichte der Züricher Reformation, Zürich, 1879, NR. 692, 4). The recently discovered Codex Geiser (see MQR, XXX [1956], 72-75) contains a poem on the experience of Joseph which extends to sixty-four stanzas. This interest in the OT narratives is seen also in the Ausbund and in the epistolary literature. The motif of suffering was especially dear to them. Lydia Müller is certainly correct, although in a different way than she means, when she says: "Aber das Täufertum lebt an sich sehr stark im Alten Testament" (Der Kommunismus der mährischen Wiedertäufer [Leipzig, 1927], p. 25). See also Rudolf Wolkan, Die Lieder der Wiedertäufer (Berlin, 1903), p. 185. Johann Loserth ("Aus dem Liederschatz der mährischen Wiedertäufer," ZdVGMS, 27 [1925], 47) remarks: "Die meisten Lieder . . . erläutern biblische Geschichten, wobei das alte Testament den Vorzug vor dem neuen hat. . . ."

[27] Vide infra, pp. 158ff.

[28] Marpeck's relation to Hutterian Anabaptists like Ulrich Stadler of Moravia on this problem is not certain. The statements Stadler makes about the OT ("Vom lebendigen wort und geschribnen," in Lydia Müller, Glaubenszeugnisse, I, 215) do not reflect Marpeck's position.

[29] So Oswald Glait. See Wilhelm Wiswedel, "Oswald Glait von Jamnitz," in Zeitschrift für Kirchengeschichte, LVI (1937), 550-564; ME, II, 522-23; and the article "Sabbatarian Anabaptists" in ME, IV, 396. No doubt Marpeck had this group in mind when he wrote against those who attempted to reinstitute the physical Sabbath (see KB, Epistle to the Swiss, wrongly dated in KB as 1531, fol. 38b and 46b).

Old Testament, which might be called a Biblicism of the Old Testament, was present in the Münster tragedy[30] and Augustine Bader.[31] Parallel to this development from within was the pressure from outside of Anabaptism. The charge was repeatedly made that the Anabaptists, by drawing a sharp distinction between the Old and New Testaments, refused to allow Christ's atonement to be retroactive to the Old Testament. The contradictions in Schwenckfeld's equivocating position on this matter were quickly picked up by the Marpeck brotherhood.[32]

It is within this context that the revisions of the *Bekentnisse* by the Marpeck brotherhood must be seen. It was of supreme importance that the relationship between the two covenants be clearly stated and defined, or else earthly power would arrogate to itself the holy place, and Anabaptism would again be perverted into a revolutionary movement.[33] The central problem was the place of external authority in the life of faith, and in order to clarify this, Marpeck's brotherhood developed an independent position unique in Anabaptism.[34]

[30] *Vide infra*, pp. 138f.

[31] Cf. *ME*, I, 209f. These aberrations of Anabaptism have been repeatedly held up as its essential character. G. Uhlhorn (*Urbanus Rhegius* . . . [1861], p. 108) says that the Bible, especially the OT, was for the Anabaptists the law book for the life of the state and society. Jakob Andrea accused the Anabaptists of deriving the essentials of Christian piety from the Decalogue rather than from Christian faith (*op. cit.*, p. 20).

[32] See *V*, II, 409ff. While Bullinger's *Von dem einigen vnnd ewigen Testament oder Pundt Gottes* (1534) was aimed almost entirely against the Anabaptists, he does not identify the covenants as completely as Bucer and Zwingli did. On the influence and importance of Bullinger's book, see H. A. J. Lütge and G. Oorthuys, *Heinrich Bullinger. I. Het eenige en eeuwige Testament of Verbond Gods; etc.* (Groningen, 1923).

[33] The largest single addition made by the Marpeck brotherhood in the *Bekentnisse* deals with the relation of the two covenants (*TB*, pp. 226-238). See also the Preface to the *Testamenterleutterung*, which speaks of the "verruckung" of earthly power. There is little doubt that they had in mind both the Reformed union of church and state and the perversion of Münster. In *V*, p. 324 and *TB*, p. 217 the reference to Münster is explicitly made. On the revision see *infra*, pp. 166ff.

[34] That his position is unique is clear from the stress he places on an absolute distinction between the two covenants already in his *Confession* in 1532. Important leaders like Ambrosius Spittelmayer (*Bayern I*, 53:9f.) who insisted that the patriarchs had eaten Christ's flesh and drunk his blood, and Hans Hut (Lydia Müller, *Glaubenszeugnisse*, I, p. 21) who stated that the baptism by blood was from the time of Adam, did not influence Marpeck so much that he failed to develop

The simplest solution would have been to slight the Old Testament. We will examine whether Marpeck did so, whether the
Old Testament remained part of God's revealed Word for
him, and whether he ever paid more than mere lip-service to
it. More important, we will need to look at those things in the
Old Testament that are of value to him, and how he interprets
the Old Testament.

B. THE PLACE OF THE OLD TESTAMENT IN
MARPECK'S HERMENEUTICS

1. MARPECK'S USE OF THE OLD TESTAMENT: A STATISTICAL
APPROACH

It may be of some value to look briefly at some statistics
on the relative number of references in Marpeck's writings
to the Old and New Testaments.[35]

One of the striking features of Marpeck's *Confession* is his
repeated use of Scripture references, the largest number
referring to the New Testament. The statistics below refer to
obvious allusions in the text and references noted on the
margin of the *Confession* or in the text of the other books.

	KU	CV	Conf.	Verant. I	Verant. II	TE
Old Testament	20	82	53	105	264	816
New Testament	424	220	297	817	384	874
No. pages counted[36]	60	42	34	114	110	120
Ratio, OT-NT	1-21	4-11	1-6	1-8	2-3	1-1

When the books of the Bible are viewed separately it
appears that the *Confession* refers to the book of Revelation
about ten times; in two hundred pages the *Verantwortung*
refers to it only thirty-three times, while the *Testamenterleut-*

---

his own position. An evidence for this may be seen in the omission
of "Dise tauf ist nit allererst zue der zeit Christi eingesetzt sonder ist
von Anfang gwesen, darin alle auserwelten freund Gottes von Adam
bisher getauft seind worden wie Paulus anzaigt" in the *Kunstbuch*
edition of Hut's writing (compare *Glaubenszeugnisse*, I, 21 with *KB*,
fol. 23b).

[35] In doing so, we should remind ourselves that such statistics possibly
reveal very little of the underlying presuppositions. The statistical
method has limitations and an awareness of these should precede its use.

[36] The page sizes of these books are not identical.

terung refers to it six times in 120 pages. In *Verantwortung II* the apocryphal literature comes strongly to the forefront as is seen by the reference to the Wisdom of Jesus Ben Sirach thirty-five times, to the Book of Wisdom eighteen times, IV Esdras seventeen times, and Tobit once. Scattered references to these books occur in both the *Testamenterleutterung* and *Verantwortung I*. In Marpeck's earliest books (1531) the *Klarer Unterricht* cites the Wisdom of Jesus Ben Sirach three times, and the *Clare verantwurtung* cites the same book five times, I Maccabees three times, and the Book of Wisdom twice. At no point whatever is any indication given that these books are not considered part of the canon.

More significant perhaps is the fact that in the *Verantwortung* the references to the Law, the Prophets, and the poetical books are about equal in number; in the *Testamenterleutterung* 184 citations and references are taken from the Pentateuch, 146 from the historical books, 321 from the Prophets, and 165 from the poetical books, mostly from the Psalms. The prophet most often quoted is Isaiah,[37] while in the Pentateuch the book of Leviticus is most often referred to. In the New Testament the Synoptic Gospels are referred to less often than the Johannine literature. Of the epistolary literature Paul is most often cited.

These figures show that Marpeck lived in John rather than in the Synoptic Gospels and found his major theological themes in Paul,[38] and that the major source of Marpeck's ideas is the New Testament.[39] It is his ultimate court of appeal and possesses an authority that supersedes that of the Old Testament. His use of the Old Testament appears to be determined by his leisure and by his goal.[40] In the *Testamenterleutterung*, where he attempts to clarify the relationship of the Old Covenant to the New so that the Old may be used correctly, he naturally uses the Old Testament nearly as fre-

[37] According to John Lawson (*op. cit.*, p. 55) this was also Irenaeus' favorite prophet.

[38] If Robert Friedmann's theory is correct ("Conception of the Anabaptists," *ChHist*, IX [1940], 360f.), Marpeck's use of the Scripture at this point deviates from common Anabaptist practice.

[39] According to a count by Ford Battles using the *Institutes* the ratio in Calvin is roughly three to five (John T. McNeill, "The Significance of the Word of God for Calvin," *ChHist*, XXVIII [1959], 135).

[40] Both the *Confession* and *Verantwortung I*, written in haste, have a stronger majority of NT references than the other books (except the *Klarer Unterricht*), written at greater leisure.

quently as the New. And yet he believes that the Old
Covenant cannot be understood apart from the light cast on it
by the New Testament. This tabulation, however, fails to do
justice to the integral position of certain features of the Old
Testament in his thought. Therefore it is necessary to study
more closely his use of some Old Testament concepts.

2. MARPECK'S USE OF THE OLD TESTAMENT: A CONCEPTUAL APPROACH

a. The Fall of Man[41]

The Fall of man is of crucial importance for Pilgram Marpeck, and is a theme that occurs again and again in his writings. Already in his *Confession* he picks up this theme. Christ
was active in creation, and through the Word man was made
lord over all creation. Only God could rule over man, and
God initially made himself manifest to man as God in the
Word ("*als ain got im wort,*" *Conf.*, 171).[42] Through man's
selfishness he destroyed both the creatures and himself, dis-
obeyed God and his word, and was taken captive by sin,
death, and hell. This deception wrought by the serpent
brought on the knowledge of good and evil (*Conf.*, 171). The
serpent became the ruler of man through his deceit, and his
rule continues until this day. Christ defeated him on the
cross, but the knowledge of good and evil continues, concealed under the forbidden fruit (*Conf.*, 172). This knowledge is good and a form of grace.[43] The promise to Eve that
eventually her seed would overcome the serpent served as a
source of consolation for her, but did not make her righteous
or sanctified (*Conf.*, 172-73).

[41] Marpeck discusses the Fall most extensively in connection with his
treatment of original sin in *Verantwortung*, pp. 189-281. A shorter
section appears in the *Vermanung*, pp. 215f.; 241f. The theme is touched
upon in his other works but not dealt with extensively. For detailed
descriptions of his view, see Wenger, *op. cit.*, pp. 224-230; Kiwiet, *op.
cit.*, pp. 142-46; and most elaborately and lucidly, Bergsten, *op. cit.*, pp.
74-82.

[42] There appear to be some remarkable similarities in some aspects of
Marpeck's Christology to that of Theodore of Mopsuestia. It falls beyond
the scope of this work to examine these similarities as well as the
differences.

[43] *Conf.*, p. 172. The first grace is also identified with the Old
Covenant already promised to Adam and Eve (*Conf.*, p. 178). The
Holy Spirit too is already promised to Adam (*CV*, c; cf. V, 130:28f.)

Since Marpeck's rejection of the traditional view of original sin and his own unique view have been described by several scholars we will assume that it has been adequately portrayed.[44] Nevertheless certain facets of this view, which affect his use of the Scriptures, merit our attention.

Marpeck's position is this: God created the whole man good and perfect; thus it is wrong to designate "mere flesh and blood" as original sin (V, 191:38f.). Man was created immortal, an image of God and Christ; and prior to the Fall Adam and Eve dwelt in created simplicity, grace, and innocence (V, 222, 195; CV, b viii). Coincident with the Fall is the termination of the immortality of created innocence (V, 291, 266). The external act of sin was preceded by an internal yielding to sin.

The spiritualists rejected this position and asserted with the *Theologia Deutsch* that the inner desire or acceptance was what constituted the Fall;[45] indeed Schwenckfeld accused Marpeck of stressing only the external act, and Marpeck retorted that the total man, spirit, soul, and body, sinned (V, 250),[46] and that sin is a unit, the external action having been prepared by the inner attitude.

Marpeck derives the possibility of sin from his analysis of human knowledge. Adam had a "divine nature" (*göttliche art*) before the Fall, which gave him the capacity to rule over himself as well as over the rest of creation (V, 220).[47] This divine nature is also termed "natural light" or "the immortal spirit" possessed by all men.[48] Through this natural light man

---

[44] Horst Quiring, *op. cit.*, Bergsten, *op. cit.*, and *ME*, IV, *sub voce.*

[45] As quoted in the *Verantwortung*: "Aber da das annemen geschach, da war er gefallen und ob er schon nie kein apfel angebissen het" (p. 259).

[46] Already in 1527 this point was discussed by Jacob Kautz and Bucer. Kautz' seventh article asserts: "Even as the external bite into the forbidden fruit would have hurt neither him nor his progeny if the inner acceptance (the same term as in the *Theologia Deutsch*, "annemen") would have been omitted. . . ." and Bucer interpreted this as denying original sin (Krebs-Rott, pp. 110f.).

[47] Bergsten (*op. cit.*, p. 75) has correctly observed that in line seventeen in the above page reference "vom fahl" should read "vorm fahl."

[48] Bergsten, *op. cit.*, p. 75; V, pp. 197, 206, 218f., 231, 233f., 325; cf. *KB*, fol. 160a; *KU*, fol. D iiib: "Es strait ettwas im Cornelio nemlich das liecht, wort vnd naturlich gesatz, wie auch in allen menschen, Deut. 30. Mat. 6. Rom. 2."

receives a "natural knowledge of the good" (V, 231); this applies as well to the heathen who have no written law as to the people of the Old Covenant who had the Law of Moses (CV, b viib). Noah, the patriarchs, and, in the New Testament, Cornelius (V, 218, 231; TE, fol. 34b, 231a, 235b; and KU, D iib) possessed this natural piety. Through the entrance of sin into the world this light was darkened; and while before the Fall it shone without hindrance, after the Fall it shines under hindrances in those who allow these hindrances to exist (V, 219f.). Marpeck clearly presupposes the free will of man and his freedom to either hinder or assist the light in its role. Even in those who hinder the light it is not extinguished but continues as prosecuting attorney over the conscience until the end (V, 223).

The Fall, moreover, granted to man the knowledge of good and evil (TB, 242). All sin has its origin in the discernment between good and evil (KB, 45b). The knowledge of evil leads men astray to enlist on the side of the devil and hinders men from seeing that evil is sin. The knowledge of sin comes to man through the natural light awakened through the Law and must be carefully distinguished from the knowledge of evil (V, 231:8f.). Knowledge of sin is highly beneficial, for it is a means used by God to move men to Christ. The knowledge of sin safeguards against evil by frightening people (V, 232).

For Marpeck it is clear that Adam and Eve were tempted to sin by an instigation coming to them from without. Their descendants, however, have all found themselves in a more serious plight. Their knowledge of good and evil is inherited and adheres closely ("anklebischer art," adhaerens, V, 258:27). As a result of Adam's Fall all men inherit this spoiling of human nature, but this does not take place in reality until reason is awakened in youth and their created simplicity (einfalt) dies (TB, 242:15, 215; V, 194). The state of the innocent child and that of Adam in the pre-Fall state can be expressed in similar though not identical terms (TB, 216, 246; V, 199).

Marpeck always insisted that the fate of children was in the hands of God; that they are a "hidden, unrevealed creature" (Conf., 189), and that one should not say more than the Scriptures about them (TB, 250:17) but "commit them to the hidden judgment of God, who knows best how he can retain them to His honor and praise" (*TB*, 250:18).[49]

If Schwenckfeld had heeded that admonition, Marpeck would have been spared an extensive forage in a field strange to him, where his gleanings are extremely meager. In irritation Marpeck himself concludes: "What we have here written would never have happened, had not this erring spirit, Schwenckfeld caused us to do so with his false *Judicium*" (*V*, 272).[50]

The Fall of Adam is not only of anthropological interest for Marpeck but also of soteriological significance. The Fall of Adam is recapitulated (*widerbracht*) through the atoning work of Christ (*KB*, fol. 134), and its results are annulled through this recapitulation (*Wiederbringung*) of Christ (*V*, 216, 275, 288f., 380, 385; *TE*, 374a; *KB*, fol. 44b). Even Adam in some sense shared proleptically in Christ's atonement, although not in the same way as those who live after Christ (*Conf.*, 173, 184; *V*, 198f., 204f., 275; *TE*, fol. 373b).

Nevertheless, Marpeck does not entirely identify the pre-Fall condition of man with the condition of the believer in Christ.[51] The Christian is placed into a supranatural condition of grace (*übernatürlich*, *KU*, B vib). Even the tendency to do evil (*erbbrest*) inherited from Adam is atoned for and not reckoned as guilt unto condemnation to the unknowing child (*V*, 199). The descendants of Adam through God's promise received the grace of yesterday, or inherited grace, also called the "*Gegenerbe*," the counterpart to inherited sin. Inherited grace also proceeds from the loins of Adam (*V*, 130, 202, 204, 206) and invalidates the negative inherited sin. Consequently, the unknowing child is spared condemnation until he sins consciously, and the child who dies in this state is covered by Christ's grace (*V*, 242, 268). The collective sin caused by Adam's Fall is covered by Christ; only individual sin, the result of individual personal transgression, remains as imputed guilt (*V*, 275).

Marpeck refused to admit that this view is Pelagian (*V*, 190, 196ff., 209, 279) in spite of the strong rational or intellectual strain observable in it. Bergsten observes correctly that

[49] Compare Calvin's statements on this subject in *Institutes*, II, 1, VIII.

[50] Bergsten, *op. cit.*, p. 82.

[51] He comes closest to it in *KU*, B iiiib when he says: "(The Christian is restored) again into the original glory of Adam."

the counterbalance to any Pelagian optimism is found in
Marpeck's stress on the power and inescapability of sin.[52]
The main stress in Marpeck's position is that he never excuses
sin and holds each man who has come to the age of accounta-
bility without excuse, condemned before a righteous God (V,
222). The great accuser who makes man aware of this state is
the Law.

b. The Old Testament as Law

Those who are accustomed to thinking of the Anabaptists as
being primarily interested in the New Testament may be
somewhat surprised to discover that when Pilgram Marpeck
first began debating with Bucer he registered as his second
complaint against the Strasbourg preachers "that they
preached the gospel before the law, and after all no one can
come to the gospel, without first recognizing his sin through
the law."[53] In this respect Marpeck shows himself to be a
faithful follower of Luther, who also held to the position that
one should not preach the gospel without first proclaiming the
condemning Law. For Luther the Law was the vestibule to
the gospel.[54] The Law must first reprove sin before the
gospel can come with its healing. The Old Testament accordingly is given a preparatory role. The function of the Law
is to bring knowledge and conviction of sin. How can a man
come to the gospel unless he is first convicted by the Law?
asks Marpeck.[55]

Marpeck considered the consciousness of sin important as a
prelude to the acceptance of redemption. Within this context
he defined the role of the Law as increasing the sorrow of
mankind. While sorrow ruled until the time of Moses the
giving of the Law through Moses only increased sorrow and
grief, because man was forced back upon an earnest petition

[52] *Op. cit.*, p. 80.

[53] Krebs-Rott, *op. cit.*, p. 352:41.

[54] Reinhold Seeberg, *Textbook on the History of Doctrines* (Grand
Rapids, 1952), II, 228f. See also pp. 246f. Wilfried Joest, *Gesetz und
Freiheit* (Göttingen, 1956²) has compared the problem of the *tertius
usus legis* in Luther and the NT.

[55] Krebs-Rott, *loc. cit. Conf.*, p. 171, also stresses the importance of
the knowledge of sin.

to God for help.[56] The function of the Mosaic Law was to recall sin to memory that it might kill and institute wrath until the time of Christ (*TE*, 6). Before the coming of Christ man could not experience full forgiveness of sins, and he could only be comforted by using the ceremonies that God had ordained for that purpose in the Old Covenant (*Conf.*, 187). The ancients of the Old Covenant possessed a proleptic righteousness—they desired to do good, but their desires were frustrated by their lack of ability to act according to their desires (*TE*, Chapter I). These desires were as shadows pointing forward to the light that was coming in Jesus Christ (*Conf.*, 177).

Already in his complaint against the Strasbourg preachers Marpeck had defined the role of John the Baptist in terms of bringing an awareness of sins.[57] John preached repentance, revealed sin to men, and pointed them to Jesus. Marpeck refused to identify John's baptism with Christian baptism as was the vogue among the Reformers (*KU*, C; *V*, 73f.). In reply to Hübmaier's statement of the Anabaptist position, Zwingli had argued that there is no difference at all between John's baptism and Christian baptism, and that repentance was all that was necessary for Christian baptism. It was argued with fervor that the New Testament says nothing at all of rebaptism. To explain the apparent rebaptism of the disciples in Acts 19, Bucer insisted that since there is no such thing as rebaptism in the New Testament, neither by Christ, who was satisfied with John's baptism, nor by his disciples, the allegedly rebaptized disciples in Acts 19 in actuality had never received the baptism of John. Indeed, if they had been baptized with John's baptism they would have known about the Holy Spirit, according to Luke 3:16.[58] According to

---

[56] *TB*, 236:5; *Conf.*, p. 177, where the original reads: "Dann es ist die ursach aines hertzlichen gepets zu got umb hilff," and the statement on p. 181: "The law along with John is past, which brought only sorrow and tribulation, according to God's command."

[57] Krebs-Rott, *op. cit.*, p. 352.

[58] *Conf.*, p. 181; *KU*, fol. B, viiib; *V*, 244:5f. On Zwingli see *ZSW*, IV, 238ff., 258f.; on Bucer, Krebs-Rott, *op. cit.*, p. 27, December 24, 1524. For an interesting but hardly convincing solution to this problem, see Markus Barth, *Die Taufe, ein Sakrament?* (Zollikon-Zürich, 1951, pp. 165-185) and the same author, "Baptism and Evangelism," *Scottish Journal of Theology*, 12 (1959), 36f., where he asserts: "Christian baptism after the resurrection is essentially identical with John's baptism (Acts 2:38; 19:4-5; in the last passage the end quotation marks belong

Marpeck's view John the Baptist was the last of the Old Covenant who prepared the way for the New. Neither he nor his baptism was to be considered in any sense Christian (*KU*, C vi).

In Marpeck's view, the Law not only reveals sin, but also provokes sin, or at least increases the knowledge of sin; and with it grace also increases, taking the upper hand; consequently, the Old Covenant can also be called the "first grace." Affirming the pre-existence of Christ, Marpeck does not rule out the activity of Christ under the Old Covenant, but he distinguishes between Christ the pre-existent and *Jesus* Christ who took his place in history. The divine Christ existed in the Old Testament but not the human (*TE*, 399b). They are one and the same person, seen from the perspective of God; but we as humans are bound by time and space and cannot conceive of Christ's work apart from the development of history (*TE*, 401b). Until the coming of the Son of God himself, no full redemption was possible (*Conf.*, 178f.).[59] Christ is the great physician who heals those who through the Law have been "crushed, broken, and pierced" (*zerslagen, zerschnitten, und zerbrochen; Conf.*, 181. Cf. V, 234:15f.).

Not only can the Old Covenant be called the first grace, but it can also be called the first birth in contrast to the other two births in the Old and New Testaments. This first birth brings with it the dead letter in two tablets of stone, signifying the hard demands of God. Looking at himself honestly man sees that he can never meet the demands, for they are too difficult; and he cannot by his own power keep God's commands. Thus man is driven to despair and to rely on God's mercy, the only hope lying in the future, God's promise of Christ. Paul calls this first birth that of servitude (*Conf.*, 186f.).[60]

---

after verse 5, not verse 4)." Barth errs when he states that Calvin is the only one who does not see in Acts 19 a case of rebaptism (*Die Taufe*, p. 166).

[59] The Law and the Prophets are called the first grace in *KB*, fol. 285b. Marpeck in using this terminology appears to be indebted to Leonhard Schiemer; see Lydia Müller, *Glaubenszeugnisse*, I, 60f. (also found in *KB*, fol. 70bf.).

[60] Marpeck does not identify the other two births; presumably they are the second birth, regeneration, and the physical birth that all experience. In the *Kunstbuch*, No. 18, in connection with the fourth fruit of true repentance mention is made of the fact that sin "wohl in uns stecken bleibt (nach erster adamitischer Fleischgeburt," *KB*, fol. 175).

It is most important for Marpeck that the Christian live not under the Old Covenant, the first birth, but rather under the New Covenant where sonship and not servitude is the mood of all activity. He devoted an epistle to this theme in the *Kunstbuch,* entitled "Concerning the Christian and the Hagaric Church," in which he deals with the allegory of Paul on the true sons of Abraham and the children of Hagar. Already in the *Confession* reference is made to this theme; it appears in the *Vermanung* (*TB,* 234) and repeatedly in the epistles written to churches (*KB,* No. 15; *MQR,* XXXII, 208f.). In the last of these letters Marpeck does not hesitate to state that Melchior Hofmann, Schwenckfeld, Luther, Zwingli, and Sebastian Franck were motivated by servile obedience, hence were mere servants.

The work of the Law as preparation is in the main negative. Marpeck finds this to a large extent in Romans 7. His view on this aspect of the Law may have derived from his discussions with Bucer. At any rate it is most forcibly expressed in his *Confession* of 1532 where Bucer is the main addressee.

Later in his dealings within the Anabaptist group and with Schwenckfeld, the place of the Law in the Christian life took on critical importance. In part the controversy centered around the interpretation of the words of II Corinthians 3: "the letter kills, but the spirit gives life." The spiritualizers, and apparently some Anabaptists, insisted that they applied to any letter, even those of the New Testament. Both Marpeck and Scharnschlager felt that this attitude cut the motivating nerve of New Testament preaching. On the other hand, there apparently were Anabaptists who applied it only to the Old Testament but sought nevertheless to retain the Law within the Christian church. Against both of these extremes Marpeck has some telling criticisms, although both he and Scharnschlager restricted the meaning of this verse to the Old Testament.[61]

---

[61] V, II, 519. For Scharnschlager's position in particular see his "Sendschreiben an die Brüder in Mähren," which must have been written after *Verantwortung II* (published in *Menn. Geschbl.,* IV [1939], 10-12). With respect to the work of the Old Covenant he says: "Denn wer nicht durch (das Alte Testament) getötet wird, der kann durch das Amt des Neuen Testaments nicht zum Leben kommen" (p. 11). Maler (*KB,* fol. 152b) disagrees with this interpretation as does Peter Ridemann (*Confession,* p. 66). Marpeck may have been

c. The Old Testament as Promise

In the Preface to the *Testamenterleutterung* the reader is admonished to recognize the three stages (*grad*) described in the Bible; namely, events in the Old Testament (yesterday), the events during the time of the New Testament (today), and the foretelling of events in the future (tomorrow) (*QF*, 582f.). Between the first two stages there is a unifying element of promise and fulfillment. The Old Testament as Law gives us a picture of the hard demands of God, but the element of promise unites it with the New Covenant and also anticipates to some extent the joy and blessings found under the New Covenant. Not only does the Law make negative preparations for the coming of the freedom of Christ, but the Prophets also point forward positively to that coming.

One of Marpeck's basic objections to Bucer's and Schwenck-feld's (V, 325) view of the Old Testament was their identification of promise and realization, prophecy and fulfillment. The Law and the Prophets testified to the forgiveness in Christ, but this witness does not indicate that they already possessed this salvation (V, II, 400:3f.).[62] The difference between promise and fulfillment is illustrated by the promise of the loan of a certain sum of money. If someone promises to lend one a hundred gulden in two or three years, one believes that sometime in the future he will have access to the money; but that does not help him at present (V, 325:36f.).

---

aware that this verse was the great motto of the allegorists (see James Wood, *op. cit.*, p. 90). According to Wolf (*op. cit.*, p. 46), Calvin assumes that Paul is here dealing with Law which is misunderstood and thus has the effect of bringing death, but this is not the actual meaning of the Law. Walter Kreck criticizes Calvin for going beyond Paul and applying the letter to the NT (*op. cit.*, pp. 173ff., esp. p. 175). According to Schempp (cited in Wolf, *ibid.*), Luther felt that Law and gospel should be separated in the act of proclamation as in the Scriptures; however, in actual function one can fulfill that of the other, for, rightly understood, the Law is gospel (cf. W. Joest, *op. cit.*, p. 196: "das Gesetz ist die Form des Evangeliums, das Evangelium ist der Inhalt des Gesetzes"). Seen in contrast to these positions one can understand why Marpeck felt as he did about the importance of this verse. For extensive documentation that this verse should be applied only to the OT, see G. Schrenk, Kittel's *TWNT*, I, 746f.; IV, 1067:15f.

[62] One is reminded of John Chrysostom's exposition of Hebrews 9:24-26 (Homily XVII) where he asserts: "(In the OT) there was an arraignment of sins, and not a release from sins; an arraignment of weakness, not an exhibition of strength."

The patriarchs did not possess the Holy Spirit any more than a man possesses a house as soon as the owner promises to sell it to him (V, 326f.). Promise and realization are not to be identified, for possession comes only with the passing of time (*mit der zeit*, V, 332:10; V, 63).

A parallel can be drawn between the promises of the Old Testament and those of the New Testament. We are promised eternal life and bodily resurrection in the New Testament and we believe these promises in faith, but that does not mean that they are immediately fulfilled (V, 399:13f.). To equate faith with accomplishment as Schwenckfeld does is to change it to a phantom ("*gaugkelwerk*," V, 331). The nature of the Old Covenant is seen basically as promise that awaits fulfillment, and this fulfillment came in the fulness of time (*TB*, 227:28). Already in the *Confession* (174) Marpeck stressed this future aspect of the Old Covenant; but it comes most often to the fore in the *Testamenterleutterung*, which was written explicitly to help the reader understand what was reality in the Old Testament, what was fulfilled in the New, and what still remains to be fulfilled. Even the rites of the Old Covenant, like circumcision, are seen not only as a source of comfort to the patriarchs (*Conf.*, 187) but also as a promise and prophecy of something better to come (*Conf.*, 175). The figurative witness of the good deeds of the ancients and their piety pointed forward to Christ as a shadow points to its accompanying light (*Conf.*, 177; *TB*, 232f.). The faith of Abraham was partly confined to material blessings such as the inheritance of the land and partly meant to stimulate the faith of Christians in the New Covenant (V, 332:36).

The dominant theme of the *Testamenterleutterung* is this promissory character of the Old Testament. By adding a section "promised yesterday" or "longed for yesterday" Marpeck seeks to emphasize the connection between the Old and New Covenants and also the fulfillment of the Old Covenant in the New. For Marpeck the Old Covenant exists only for the purpose of the New, and he certainly does not equate them in any sense. The New Testament always forms the starting point for his interpretation of the Old, hence he insists that a clear difference must be made between promise and fulfillment. The sin of the innocent child is taken away by Christ's word of promise, but that word of promise is not to be identified with faith itself (*Conf.*, 184). In the same way as the saints of the Old Covenant, infants dedicated to God are

called children of the covenant of promise.[63] Not a letter,
however, of the Old Testament indicates that believers then
were children of God in the same way as Christians of the
New Testament are (*Conf.*, 185; *TB*, 228:6). All the patriarchs, the Law, and the Prophets join in pointing forward to
Christ; and since Christ did not come until the fulness of time
they could not share in the gifts that he brought through his
incarnation (*KB*, fol. 284b).

d. The Devotional Use of the Old Testament

The Old Covenant is Law and it is promise, but there is
also a third use of the Old Testament in the writings of
Marpeck which assures its continued relevance for the life of
the church under the New Covenant, namely, its devotional
use. In the typological or allegorical usage of the Song of
Solomon in the *Confession* of 1532, and later in two epistles of
the *Kunstbuch*, Marpeck's references to the Song of Solomon
show that his interest in this book grew with the years. The
theme of love is applied to the church, and the image of the
bride and her relationship to her lover is applied to the unity
of the church.[64] The first epistle devotes over half of the space
to a typological exposition of the Song of Solomon (Chapter
2). Marpeck is moved to write because God has approached
us in love, but our knowledge of what is God's love is only
piecemeal. "For . . . where Christ does not compel through
love, there action is dangerous and difficult" (*KB*, fol. 9b).

He writes to draw the attention of his reader beyond God's
gifts of love to the Giver himself (*KB*, fol. 10b). There is no
doubt that this tract borders on an allegorical usage of the
images used in the Canticle. Referring to the beloved looking
through the lattice (Song of Solomon 2:9), Marpeck applies
the lattice to the flesh and blood of Christ, and the friend[65]
calls to the guardian, love, within us that the winter is past
and that flowers again have come on the earth, that is, the

---

[63] *Conf.*, pp. 185f. Marpeck uses the two synonyms: "zuesagens vnd
verhaissung."

[64] No. 4, "Von der liebe," which might better be called an exposition
of the Song of Solomon. No. 5 is entitled, likely by Maler, "Dieses
Epistle meldet von der Einigkeit und der Braut Christi, samt ihrem
Schmuck, Zierd und Fruchten, aus dem Cantina gezogen . . . ." Both
are directed to the Swiss Brethren.

[65] "Fründ" is the term used for "beloved" דוד in Song of Solomon
1:13 *et passim* in the Zürich Bible.

church. The turtle dove is the Holy Spirit, who "conducts his Word and Work in the hearts of the believers" (*treibt sein Wort und Werk in den herzen der Gläubigen, KB,* fol. 10). The fig tree putting forth its figs is the breaking forth of God's goodness to his own, and the blossoms of the vine are the planting of the Father, while the vine is the true one, Jesus Christ. Those who truly believe in Christ Jesus receive eyes so that they can see the working of God in them through the implanting into Christ.[66] The dove in the clefts of the rock is the love in Christ Jesus, and the holes in the rocks are the suffering wounds, shed blood, and dying of Christ wherein the believers may have free security and peace from the devil's onslaughts.[67]

The second epistle[68] that deals with the Song of Solomon has as its theme, unity and the bride of Christ. Here the dominant note is the unity of the church. Marpeck does not go into detail in explaining various images in the Song. After citing Song of Solomon 2:10-14 he admonishes his readers to view the text "with spiritual eyes truly and well" (*mit geist-lichen Augen recht und wohl an, KB,* fol. 12b). Though the words of the text are brief, yet the understanding and knowledge of it are in the Holy Spirit, in whom is salvation; flesh and blood cannot attain unto it.

In the exposition, the stress is laid upon the change of seasons. The thunderstorm (*Ungewitter*), winter, and rain are past, that is, the period of sin, or dormancy, tribulation, and anxiety is gone. Before Christ, the true sun, came we could not flee; and even though many people before Christ were amiable (*suess*), friendly, and joyful, as the fig tree and vine, yet they had neither buds nor blossoms before summer, the coming of Christ (*KB,* fol. 12b). Even the coming of Christ did not at once bring fruit, for first the heat and wrath of the Father had to be assuaged. When the sun, Christ Jesus, appeared on earth in weakness as true man of the seed of woman and the generation of man, then man began to blossom. When the sun went down, the heat of the day (the wrath of the Father) became cool. Up till the time of the

---

[66] *KB,* fol. 10b f. Commenting on "die wynstock haben ougen gewuenen" (Song of Solomon 2:13, in Zürich Bible of 1525).

[67] *KB,* fol. 10. Bernard (*ad loc.*) says: "The literal meaning does not yield us much; but someone has interpreted 'the clefts of the rock' as meaning the Wounds of Christ, and fitly too . . . ."

[68] No. 5, *KB,* fol. 11-14b.

resurrection and ascension of Christ, the bridegroom with the bride nourished other flowers and buds as a foretaste and a shadow, until spring and the turtle dove came. Again the turtle dove is said to be the Holy Spirit, which is sealed in the forgiveness of sin with the cool dew of grace. Marpeck concludes this tract with a fervent admonition for the church to adorn itself with love, the most precious of all ornaments and adornments.

Here Marpeck's usage of typology clearly borders on allegory.[69] But a comparison with Bernard of Clairvaux's famous sermons on this book shows an important difference in method.[70] For Bernard the historical line is gone; for Marpeck the Song of Solomon is used to accentuate the historical continuum, especially the place that the incarnation has on that continuum. As far as the present writer can tell, Bernard never uses the winter-summer image to refer to the Old and New Testaments, while for Marpeck it is very important.[71]

Furthermore, the Old Testament characters are used as

[69] On the difference between typology and allegory Torm says: "The difference between typological exposition (or consideration) and allegorical is: The allegorical exposition goes its own independent way apart from the literal interpretation while typological exposition proceeds from the literal interpretation" (op. cit., p. 223, footnote). Allegorical interpretation finds something different than the words mean, typological extends the meaning of the words beyond their immediate application. Allegorical interpretation is ably treated in RGG³, I, 238f. and R. M. Grant, op. cit.

[70] A modern abridged translation of Bernard's sermons is given in Saint Bernard on the Song of Solomon: Sermones in Cantica Canticorum (London, 1952). Claude Tresmontant (St. Paul and the Mystery of Christ [New York, 1958], p. 148) states: "It is the agelong tradition of Jewish mysticism, as of Christian mysticism, that the . . . Song of Songs is the key to all Scriptures, for it enshrines the secret of secrets—God's bridal love for his bride." For a history of the interpretation of this Biblical book see F. Ohly, Hohelied-Studien (Wiesbaden, 1958) and H. Riedlinger, Die Makellosigkeit der Kirche in den lateinischen Hoheliedkommentaren des Mittelalters (Münster, 1958).

[71] Bernard does state that the change from winter to summer took place at the resurrection and that the disciples did not have the Holy Spirit before that time (ad loc.), a view with which Marpeck would have agreed. It is quite possible that Marpeck's interest in the Canticles instigated the Streicher request (1550) that Schwenckfeld write on the subject (CS, XII, 361). For Schwenckfeld the spiritual Christ is the bridegroom not of the church, but of the individual soul (CS, IV, 134; VII, 442). On this view, missing in Marpeck, Denney says: ". . . there is no Scripture authority for using this metaphor of His relation to the individual soul" (Expositor's Greek New Testament, II, 638).

illustrations for behavior. Marpeck refers to the tragic results
of Michal's premature judgment when she saw David dancing
before the ark of the Lord (KB, 53b). The way in which God
blessed the reforms in the total sweep of the Old Testament is
used in one of Marpeck's earliest writings (CV, Ch. 1) to
illustrate that God plans that his people do something about
abuses that creep into their midst.

His sharp differentiation between the Old and New Testaments safeguarded the danger of making the Old Testament a
rule book for Christians, and his refusal to admit the patriarchs
to the rank of the Christian church made it much easier for
him to deal with the immoralities and lower ethical standards
of the Old Testament.[72] Consequently, what God did through
them has abiding value in Marpeck's hermeneutics, but it
never becomes a standard for the Christian who is guided by
the brilliant light of Christ's incarnation. Incidents of the Old
Testament history instruct New Testament believers primarily in a negative sense; for instance, the incident of Korah
teaches that resistance to God through rebellion ends in de-
struction. Such rebellion Marpeck calls the abomination of
desolation mentioned in Daniel and referred to by the Lord
(TB, 218:2; 244:36). In the first-mentioned passage Marpeck
is referring directly to the kingdom of Münster. On the other
hand, Abraham, for example, also gives the Christian a positive
lesson by his willingness to suffer persecution as the father of
believers (KB, fol. 250b; 253, both by Scharnschlager).

In conclusion, it should be noted that differences of ethical
standards between the two covenants do not imply for Marpeck that God has changed his nature, or that a God of wrath
rules in the Old Covenant while a God of love rules in the
New. The reason, as Marpeck sees it, for the change in the
matter of revenge is that after the incarnation of Christ a
stricter criterion of judgment is used, for now one can know

---

[72] The problem caused by these immoralities to exegetes and the
rather ridiculous extremes used to defend them find abundant documentation in Roland Bainton's essay: "The Immoralities of the Patriarchs
according to the Exegesis of the Late Middle Ages and of the Reformation" (HTR, XXIII [1930], 39-49). Faustus, the Manichaean, was
particularly keen in capitalizing on these immoralities (see Augustine's
incisive retort in Contra Faustum Manichaeum, XXII, 25). The Mani-
chaeans were mainly responsible for making the inner connection of
the two Testaments "the most grave problem of the Bible" for Augustine
(so Pontet as cited in Gerhard Strauss, op. cit., p. 68).

Christ better and his power can more mightily transform us. Revenge is ruled out because now the Spirit is mightier in us to overcome through patience (*CV*, c ii; *V*, 393).

3. THE DISTINCTION BETWEEN THE OLD AND NEW TESTAMENTS

An important principle in Marpeck's hermeneutics is his thoroughgoing distinction between the Old and New Testaments. The difference between the two covenants as he defined it had important consequences for his study of the Bible. The Old Testament was yesterday, the New today. In this respect Marpeck stood virtually alone, a factor that contributed no doubt to the absolute way in which he stated this difference.[73] He admits in the Preface of the *Testamenterleutterung* that the arguments of the one side are not new, "but known to everyone and been circulated in print to a large extent, therefore, for the sake of brevity they have been omitted, and only the position of the one side is presented herein in the end because it is still less known" (*QF*, 581: 39ff.).

While there is no doubt that Pilgram Marpeck's convictions against infant baptism caused him to stress this distinction between the covenants, it would be misleading to assume that this was the major determining factor in his thinking throughout his life. The reasons why this distinction is important to him are stated in the Preface to the *Testamenterleutterung*.

The first is the claim of some people that the suffering of Christ was retroactive in the Old Testament and therefore the same benefits of his passion are present there, only a little more dark, restricted, childish, less complete. Among them the sword was used; so we may also use it. On his side Marpeck says that such an approach denies the article of common faith "descended into hell," minimizes the place of Christ's suffering, and ignores the fact that only today has essential redemption taken place (*QF*, 579-80). Furthermore, the suffering, death, resurrection, and ascension of Christ are thereby "grievously slandered and disgraced, trampled under feet, made suspect and caused to be mocked"

---

[73] Biblical theology in reaction to Harnack's idealism has also stressed the continuity of the two Testaments disproportionately. J. K. S. Reid (*The Authority of Scripture* [London, 1957], pp. 186ff.) in some respects takes the same position as Marpeck in stressing a categorical difference (p. 187).

(*QF*, 580:4-6; cf. *Conf.*, 176; *TE*, 406). Thirdly, the position of the first group is against all holy, clear, Biblical Scriptures, especially the New Testament, which clearly shows that essential salvation did not exist yesterday. Fourth, through such a position worldly power is deranged out of the place assigned to it by God and set into the holy place (Dan. 9; Matt. 24). The space allotted to this final reason seems to indicate that it looms rather large in Marpeck's thinking.[74]

Only one of these reasons is directly ethical; two are concerned with the status of Christ's work, and one with the preservation of the trustworthiness of Scripture. Marpeck takes these reasons seriously. He treats them in the *Testamenterleutterung*, not as a peripheral problem, but as a problem central to his understanding of the Christian faith. His solution to the problem is not now under judgment. But it is clear that he thought he saw a vital problem in clear focus.

Since Marpeck differed consistently from his opponents on the problem of the relationship of the two covenants, it becomes necessary to consider Marpeck's unique position. His arguments with Bucer and Schwenckfeld can be placed under two headings, i.e., the salvation of the patriarchs (which included the idea of a church in the Old Testament) and the validity of the analogy of the Old Testament rites to the New Testament sacraments, in particular infant baptism.

The basic distinction that Marpeck makes between the Old Testament and New Testament is "yesterday and today." Each one of the themes treated in the *Testamenterleutterung* is treated under these two divisions, and at times a third section is added on the verses that indicate that something was longed for yesterday.[75] The point in time that marks the line between yesterday and today is the life and death of Christ. Speaking in general terms, Marpeck asserts that it is simply Christ; but when specific points come up for discussion and he is forced to be more precise, he says that forgiveness and the work of Christ were completed with the resurrection, while his ascent to the Father is to be seen together

---

[74] *QF*, p. 580. He is undoubtedly thinking both of the Strasbourg Council's authority of deciding issues of faith, as well as the Münsterite perversion of power.

[75] The first 114 chapters have the "yesterday/today" contrast, while the last ten chapters deal primarily with describing the way things took place yesterday. Most often he adds a section on "Gestern verhaissen," so in ninety-eight chapters.

with the coming of the Holy Spirit, which really ushered in "today." He uses a number of terms to show that the difference between the Old and New Testaments is one of history. First there is the contrast "summer and winter," taken from the Song of Solomon (*KB,* fol. 13). The Old Testament is a time of dormancy, a time when no flowers are available. The New introduces the church and other signs of life.

Related also is the contrast of day and night (V, II, 347), which Marpeck, however, does not use in the sense that Bucer did, namely, that God revealed himself a little less clearly in the Old Testament than in the New. For Marpeck the difference between day and night is quite pronounced, but night does gradually change into day. Here also the reference to the coming of the New Year in the sense of new aeon needs to be mentioned. The Old Year is gone, and as Christians we now live in the New Year (*KB,* fol. 283b, 284, 286, 291, 300, alluding to Luke 4:19 in an epistle dated February 1, 1547). Related to this is the contrast between temporal and eternal, which Marpeck used to take the place of Schwenckfeld's distinction between inner and outer.[76] To answer any apparent contradiction between the Old Testament and the New, Marpeck could say that the patriarchs of the Old Covenant had realized some benefits of salvation and some of the promises of God, but only the temporal ones and not the eternal ones.[77]

Also referring to the revelation of God in history is Mar-

---

[76] Kiwiet lists "äusserlich und innerlich" as a pair of terms that Marpeck uses. The examples he cites, however, must be seen in the light of the total argument. Marpeck is not arguing for the differentiation, but insisting that the inner lust and the outer act must be kept together. Marpeck does not say that Hebrews 11 contains a whole row of examples "rein äusserlichen Religion" (so Kiwiet, *op. cit.,* p. 119). He does say they are "leiblich" and not "geistlich" (V, p. 370), but this is quite another matter.

[77] In direct contrast to Calvin who argued that the patriarchs obtained spiritual rewards only in the future life, and trial and tribulations in this life. For Noah the building of the ark involved "excessive fatigue," and his escape from death was attended with greater distress than if he had died a hundred times. The ark was as it were a sepulchre and nothing could have been more disagreeable than to be detained for so long a period almost immersed in the ordure of animals. Marpeck argues that they received only physical benefits such as the land, and the spiritual promises apply to their spiritual descendants. Calvin called this "the principal point on which this controversy turns" (*Institutes,* II, X, 10).

peck's pair of terms, "promised/accomplished" (*verhaissen/ gelaistet*). Many things were promised or prophesied yesterday, but only accomplished today. Again in the Preface to the *Testamenterleutterung* the writers state that they wish to show what in the Old Testament refers to the captivity of the children of Israel, and which promises refer to the New Testament release from the captivity of sin (*QF*, 587). Often the word *"verhaissen"* is placed on the margins of the *Testamenterleuttterung* to indicate that the subject discussed has been promised in the Old Testament and has been realized in the New.

Some of Marpeck's terms do not seem to be related to time. His terms "figure/essence" (*figur/wesen*) are not basic, but are used in his polemics against Schwenckfeld. Since they are derived from the Bible (Col. 2 and Heb. 10)[78] no Platonic ideas of essence and form should be read into them. He explicitly states that the term "essence" is used in the way Paul used it, namely, to indicate that only that is essential (*wesenlich*) which has become present, not something that is still hoped for or expected. What was in the Old Testament was shadow, what has come now is essence (*wesen*).[79]

He also holds that there are two kinds of truth, one in the New Testament and another in the Old. They are not contradictory. The first type of truth is that expected of a witness, who promises not to lie or to deceive. It is the result of faithfulness and is seen in both Testaments. The other kind of truth comes to us in symbols, when something in the future is shown to us by means of external matters, or through parables. God used this means yesterday when by means of the tabernacle or temple he pointed toward things that only today have come into being. Hence, whoever says that these symbols were already in the Old Testament identical with what they signified is not speaking the truth (*TE*, 291).

The evidence of the New Testament is clear. Peter says that the grace of today is the true grace of God (I Peter 5); Christ says his blood is the true drink; Paul speaks of the true tabernacle in Hebrews 8, and of Jesus not entering into the sanctuary made with hands (Heb. 9), which is an antitype (*gegenbild*) of the true; and Christ the Man as real high priest himself said: "I am the truth" (John 14). Nor should

---

[78] In Froschauer Bible (Zürich) after the edition of 1531.
[79] Preface to the *TE*, *QF*, p. 582. Compare also *TE*, 288b and 291-92.

one say that the type or symbol is false simply because it is
not identical with the essence to which it points. The essence
has come only with Christ, and it is through the Son of God
that we can see the truth (John 16; I John 5; *TE*, 291b-
292).

This distinction of time is supported by what Marpeck
calls the *"ordnung Gottes,"* a concept found in all of Marpeck's writings. The order of God is a result of God's nature;
he could not allow the confusion of having the dispensation of
the Holy Spirit already in the Old Testament (*V*, 394; *KB*,
fol. 47b). Though the concept of *"ordnung"* is most fully
expressed in the time relationship between the two covenants, Marpeck finds his strongest support for it in the
difference between Creator and creature. God, of course, is
not bound to time or space; but when God's dealings with
man are under discussion it makes no sense to wipe out the
lines of time. All creatures are bound to time and space, and
can only realize themselves within the restrictions of person,
time, and place (*V*, 321; *TB*, 233). In this way God has
ordered all things in number and weight (Wisdom 11:20) and
has weighed the world and measured the times (II Esdras
4:36f.). Therefore all of God's creatures have these limitations,

> and none can attain to the accomplishment of the will of
> God without means, who also for the sake of his crea-
> tures has disclosed his will in order of time and measure
> according to his word which remains forever (I Peter 2)
> and will not pass away (Matthew 24) and according to
> Holy Scripture which cannot be broken (John 10)...(*V*,
> 322).

Marpeck returns to the incarnation and insists that the participation in Christ is also a part of God's order. Only today in
the fulness of time is Christ available to us; and while it is
true that he existed before his incarnation and that in the
foreknowledge of God even his atonement may have been
accomplished, yet as far as man is concerned it is a "great
calumniation of God," and "against divine order" to place all
the stress on the divine working and power of Christ, and not
reckon with his work in the order of time (*V*, 322).

In order to explain this point to Schwenckfeld so clearly
that even a first-grader could understand it, Marpeck used

the illustration of the building foreman. The foreman and his creation must be kept separate, for they are not the same. The foreman has a definite plan for seeing the building through from blueprint to completion in a specified sequence. First the foreman must exist, then he must consider the work, then prepare, then form the goal, outline, time, order, measurements, and all characteristics of the work, then finish and use the work, and finally he must be able to view his work in peace and use it with satisfaction (V, 312). God's order is seen throughout the world and in the Scriptures, and must be in the church. Whoever ignores this order of God puts God to shame and shows that he despises God thereby.[80]

When the Scripture says that Christians are first to make disciples, then baptize, then to teach, this order must be observed with scrupulous care. Much trouble has come into the church because this order has been ignored. Luther's continuing in infant baptism and the mass is outside of the realm of God's Word.

> For God in his word, and through his word, i.e., Jesus Christ, his firstborn from eternity, is Himself the wisest Order, and whoever uses the power of God outside of the order of God is a deceiver and a seducer.[81]

The heathen have rejected God's order and created and used their own, having by their actions denied God and made themselves into gods (KB, fol. 48).

The importance of this concept to Marpeck may be seen in the fact that he calls it the order of God, the order of Christ (KB, fol. 295b, margin), or the order of the Holy Spirit (KB, fol. 246f., Scharnschlager). This order is observed by following the admonitions (V, 376). To those who argued that God could grant faith to an infant Marpeck replied that this was indeed possible, just as it was possible for God to raise up children to Abraham from stones. The important fact was not the theoretical power of God, but the means he has revealed in his Word, for

> God has enclosed His power in the order of His word, and whoever ascribes another power to God reviles His

---

[80] It is apparent that this is not a mere mechanical order but a teleological one ("Got handelt nach ordenung mit fürgeding," CV, cib).

[81] KB, fol. 48. On Maler's view of Ordnung compare KB, fol. 150f.

order and power, as though He had not sufficiently revealed His power and glory through the order of His
words (*TB*, 249:8f., not in Rothmann).

He refused to accept the argument of the dialecticians that
just because a thing is possible it is so in reality.

4. THE DECISIVENESS OF THE "LIFE OF CHRIST"[82]

The most decisive event for Marpeck in the redemption of
the world is the life of Christ. He severely criticized any
discounting of this event. The coming of Christ was the
culmination of centuries of waiting and earnest expectation,
and his suffering assured complete redemption for all who
received the benefits of his atoning death.

In a vital sense all the elements of Marpeck's hermeneutics
and theology converge in his Christology.[83] The relation of
inner and outer, external means and internal experience, finds
its clue in the incarnation, in God taking upon himself human
flesh. One of his favorite terms for Christ was *"das ver-
menschte wort"* (*KB*, fol. 134, 134b; *V*, 311), and upon
occasion he used the vivid term "enfleshed word" (*einge-
fleischtes Wort*, *V*, 496:25). He criticized Schwenckfeld for
not making enough of Christ's incarnation and being interested
only in the glorified Christ,[84] which in fact is honoring only a
half-Christ (*V*, 471). The humanity of Christ is the key to the
treasure chest of the Scriptures, without which they remain a
closed book (*KU*, A 6b).

Marpeck does not, of course, ignore the reigning, victorious Christ. But, says Marpeck, Christ is not entirely glorified
until his church, his suffering body, has ceased to suffer and
been glorified.[85] Christ is victorious inasmuch as he has al-

---

[82] The term "life of Christ" is here used to designate what Marpeck
refers to as "das leiden, todt, auferstehung und himmelfart Christi."

[83] Seen especially in his writing "Von der Tieffe Christi," No. 35 in
the *Kunstbuch*.

[84] *V*, pp. 244 and 160: "Er leert nur das innerlich und den verklerten
herlichen unleidenden Christum im hymel und nit den leydenden auf
erden, ja nur das wort von seiner glori und herligkeit und nit von seinem
kreuz und trüebsal, wie ers als haubt vor der verklerung und hymelfart
hat tragen und noch heut seinem unverklerten leib zu tragen gebürt."
According to Lang (*op. cit.*, pp. 110-13) Bucer too is interested primarily in the exalted Christ.

[85] Compare Hans Hut's stress on "der ganz Christus" in *KB*, fol. 18
(L. Müller, *Glaubenszeugnisse*, I, 16).

ready conquered the serpent (*Conf.*, 172). His victory over sin
and death is the culmination of the incarnation, and was a
part of his mission as the restoration of the Fall of Adam,
which only the humanity of Jesus Christ could accomplish (*V*,
380; *Conf.*, 173, 174). Only he can understand the true evil of
sin, who has gone down into the depths of hell with Christ,
for the soul of Christ had to lead sin out of hell (*V*, 265). The
one who suffers with Christ can more easily understand this
than he who approaches the Scriptures with the desire to
learn it "out of the letter and artistry of Scripture" (*aus dem
buchstaben und kunst der schrift, V*, 265).

For this reason also, Marpeck rejects the view that Christ's
coming was simply to reveal more plainly something already
existent in the past. To say so is a "calumnious defamation" of
Christ and does not give him the honor due to him for his
suffering on our behalf (*Conf.*, 176; *V*, 399, 403).

Because Marpeck wished to honor Christ's suffering, two
closely related themes, the faith of the patriarchs and the
descensus ad inferos, occur repeatedly. The second part of the
Verantwortung especially stressed the problem of the faith of
the saints of the Old Covenant in the debate between Marpeck and Schwenckfeld.[86]

The discussion is touched off by Schwenckfeld's irritation
that the writers of the *Vermanung* do not allow Abraham and
the other patriarchs to be considered as having the Holy
Spirit. In the reply the writers of the *Verantwortung* point out
that Schwenckfeld is misquoting them, for they do not say
that *now* these patriarchs are not Christians or have the Holy
Spirit, they only insist that they did not have salvation before
Christ (*V*, 317, 319). They go on to say that the men of the
Old Testament did have forgiveness, but this forgiveness covered only the temporal punishment that was forthcoming.
After all, the eternal, valid sacrifice for the atonement of sin
has only been offered by Christ, therefore it is impossible to
say that the saints of the Old Testament already had that (*V*,
318; *TB*, 235).

Also they admit that the Holy Spirit was already available
to them in the Old Testament, but his working was quite

---

[86] The section 317-426 is taken up with a discussion of this point,
although it continues to turn up in other sections also. The discussion
of this point causes the writers of the *Verantwortung* to point out the
many contradictions in Schwenckfeld's writings, pp. 409-427. It is also
discussed in *TB*, p. 235.

different, i.e., he worked only for the physical Exodus from
Egypt and a physical salvation from a life of physical bondage. Also it was his work to institute the Law and the Old
Testament, to institute and preserve the figure (that is, the
figurative tabernacle and people of Israel), and to promise
things that only today have come to fulfillment, and thus
prepare the way for Jesus Christ. This Spirit of God worked
yesterday through the Law and the services of the Old
Testament in the hand and mouth of Moses in order to
preach damnation. It was given unto servitude, and not unto
sonship, and was a Spirit of fear (V, 318). The Spirit of the
New Testament was not available until Christ's ascension.

Schwenckfeld is critical of the Anabaptists for judging the
New Testament "as for us alone" according to the revelation
of time and not as it was before God.[87] To this the Anabaptists reply that they admit that according to the foreknowledge
of God the New Testament did exist before Christ, but they
wish to allow the counsel, purpose, and foreknowledge of God
to remain in their proper place (V, 321:19ff.). The important
thing is not whether the New Testament existed as far as God
is concerned, but rather whether man had access to it and
could live by it. They wish to keep the creation and the
Creator separate, or as they also state it, they wish to observe
carefully the order of God (V, 322).

To the argument used by Schwenckfeld that God worked
in a more hidden way in the Old Testament, the Anabaptists
reply that it was hidden to such an extent that no one
received the promised New Testament as Christianity, for
even though in, before, and with God it was decided or
ordered, yet it was not in the hearts of men, irrespective of
their faith of yesterday.[88]

The argument that the sufferings of Christ retroacted into
the Old Testament is also turned aside with the rebuttal that
it is of no profit to speak of things that are in the providence
of God alone, which things are alone in God and not in the
knowledge of men, and are not yet realized among men. For

[87] V, p. 320. Cf. V, p. 417, where words are quoted from Schwenckfeld's polemics against Bucer that are exactly the opposite.

[88] V, pp. 323f. Note again the quotation the Anabaptists refer to in a
book written by Schwenckfeld against Bucer in which he says exactly
the opposite. Cf. V, p. 333.

such people cannot be called Christians.[89] Marpeck concludes his argument on this point by saying that the position of
Schwenckfeld appears similar to that of Sebastian Franck in
the *Paradoxa*, who states that the church was invisible before
Christ. Marpeck expressed his grave reservations about such
an attitude because soon one begins to justify his actions on
the basis of the actions of the men of the Old Covenant, and
the result is the Peasant's Revolt, Zwingli taking the sword,
or the Münsterite insurrection in the name of the gospel. No
doubt all of these believed that men were Christians before
the advent of Christ, and as Christians used the sword.[90]

Both the faith and the salvation of the patriarchs were
proleptic, not yet accomplished in the reality of historical
experience even though treated as such. When Marpeck says
in the Preface of the *Testamenterleutterung* that he is concerned about the article of common faith "he descended into
hell," he refers to an idea that is quite important to him.
Already in the *Confession* the *descensus ad inferos* appears,[91]
and one finds it recurring several times in his writings. He
takes the preaching aspect of Christ's descent seriously, for
through it the patriarchs were told of the redemption that
Christ accomplished and for which they had waited so long
(*Conf.*, 176). The *descensus* also has a victorious aspect
(*Conf.*, 180, taken from Ephesians 4). When Schwenckfeld
stressed the victorious aspect of the *descensus* and stated that
Christ's mission was to announce his victory Marpeck reacted
to this as but another illustration of Schwenckfeld's tendency
to stress the glorified Christ, and therefore rejected this interpretation.[92] The *descensus* is like Jonah's three days in the
belly of the fish. It is an example of the depths of Christ's suffering (*tieffe Christi*), and one should not minimize the horror

[89] *V*, pp. 323f. Compare also the extended discussion of this point in
TE, Chapter 125, pp. 399b-406b.

[90] *V*, p. 324. Will-Erich Peuckert (*op. cit.*, pp. 480, 562) is obviously
confused in his description of the relation of Marpeck to Franck and
Schwenckfeld.

[91] *Conf.*, pp. 176, 180. Bucer reacts to its being called "hell" in
Krebs-Rott, p. 411, and says there is no talk even of a "vorhelle." In
the later reference he replies that Christ did not preach to those who
had pleasure in the gospel before, but otherwise does not argue against
the *descensus* (Krebs-Rott, pp. 447f.).

[92] A conspectus of Schwenckfeld's view on this matter can be seen in
CS, IV, 522, 543, 544, 547; V, 420f.; VI, 144, 146f., 626ff.; X, 16, 347f.,
363-65; XI, 297, 802; XII, 557; XIII, 597.

of it, for Christ cried: "My God, my God, why hast thou for-
saken me?" The other side is the ascent into the heavens, but
this can only be stressed if the descent is given its full due.
"And as Jonah experienced it for a little while in the fish, so
Christ also in death and hell until the debt of sin had received
full payment on our account through Jesus Christ."[93] Only he
who has gone down with Christ into the depths (through baptism) can really understand the nature of sin. For this cannot
be learned from the letter and *kunst* of Scripture.[94]

We need not attempt to trace the origin of this view in
Marpeck, but it is clear that it is of some importance to him.
It may surprise some to find that an Anabaptist (who are
often considered noncreedal, not to say anticreedal) wrote his
magnum opus partly because he was concerned about a sentence in the Apostles' Creed. Indeed it is surprising to have
Marpeck appeal not to Scripture, but to raise the question:
"Where would the belief of the ancient teachers and of many
people with them who through their understanding and testimony of holy and apostolic scripture have held and still hold
to the article of Christ's journey to hell be . . ." if the distinction between the two Testaments is not observed?[95]

Of course it should be pointed out that he is concerned
about the article of faith only because he thinks that it is in

[93] *KB,* fol. 280b ff., where the error of "etliche irrige Geister" is referred to, and the name Schwenckfeld stands on the margin. The similarities of certain sections of "Von der Tieffe Christi" on these pages to
V, p. 265, are striking.

[94] V, p. 265. References to the status of the patriarchs after death and
the *descensus* are found also in V, pp. 202, 317. Kiwiet (*op. cit.,* p. 106,
footnote 210), referring to *TE,* Chapters 5, 60, and 115, shows that Marpeck uses the terms "bosom of Abraham" and "hell" synonymously.
Bergsten asserts that this is not true of the *Verantwortung* but does not
indicate what this argument *e silentio* signifies (*op. cit.,* p. 86). No
doubt Schwenckfeld's statement that Marpeck asserted Christ's suffering
in hell has a grain of truth in it, which would indicate that Marpeck
is not dependent on the Gospel of Nicodemus, which stresses primarily
the victory of Christ. Marpeck's view of the *descensus* appears to be
much more similar than dissimilar to that of Luther (see Erich Vogelsang, "Weltbild und Kreuzestheologie in den Höllenfahrtsstreitigkeiten
der Reformationszeit," *ARG,* 38 [1941], 90-133; on Luther's view see
pp. 96-100). Williams (*op. cit.,* p. 820) does not support his statement
that Marpeck cited this apocryphal Gospel and seems to have confused Anabaptist usage of OT apocrypha with usage of pseudepi-
graphical writings of the New Testament (*op. cit.,* p. 819).

[95] Preface to the *TE, QF,* pp. 579-580.

accord with Scripture.[96] Certainly Marpeck had no inclination toward placing a degree of authority upon tradition apart from Scripture, but nevertheless tradition must be taken into consideration. Tradition, for him, was always to be judged in the light of Scripture.

As Bergsten remarks, this discussion of the salvation of the patriarchs may seem rather fruitless to us, but for Marpeck and Schwenckfeld it contained essential, practical, and theological consequences.[97] Marpeck would have agreed that the subject is not of great importance *per se*. But he was not a theoretical theologian who retreated to his study to determine relevant issues. His theology is eristic, and the discussion of these points results from the effect that the other position had in the church. His concern is always practical. If it is recalled that the *Vermanung* is a confession, meant to unify the Anabaptists and give them a rallying point, then it will be easy to understand why Marpeck could not allow the *Judicium* to go unanswered, even though Schwenckfeld had never published it and did not want it to circulate beyond the pale of the Anabaptists around Augsburg. Furthermore, the writers of the *Verantwortung* leave us in no doubt as to their lack of enthusiasm for writing in such a way against Schwenckfeld (*V*, 429:45f.). The whole affair seemed distasteful to them, but because of the threat to the church, they felt they could not evade their responsibility.

In conclusion, it should be said that Marpeck does not press either the point that Christ must have suffered in the *descensus* or that the patriarchs suffered in the intermediate state. He is using the term "hell" in the way that it stands in the Apostles' Creed, and relates it to the Old Testament term

[96] Whether the Bible teaches an explicit doctrine of the *descensus* is debated (see Bo Reicke, *The Disobedient Spirits and Christian Baptism* [Kobenhavn, 1946] and Karl Gschwind, *Die Niederfahrt Christi in die Unterwelt* [Münster, 1911] to mention only two books from a vast number of treatments of this theme). Particularly relevant for our period is Erich Vogelsang, *op. cit.* Serious objection was taken to Marpeck's inclusion of the believing patriarchs of the Old Covenant among the "spirits" and also to the aspect of Christ's suffering in Hades. Obviously Marpeck's view of baptism colors his view of the *descensus*. Other Anabaptists who dealt with this theme are Hans Hut (*Glaubenszeugnisse*, I, 35) and Leonhard Schiemer (*ibid.*, p. 53), both of whom are commenting on the Apostles' Creed, and Hans Schlaffer (*ibid.*, p. 96).

[97] *Op. cit.*, p. 87.

"Grube," as well as the New Testament term, "the bosom of Abraham."[98]

Bucer already found that Marpeck insisted that the patriarchs of the Old Testament be placed on a different level than the saints of the New. No doubt the apparent shift that Schwenckfeld made on this point,[99] and the result it had in his view of the church, caused Marpeck to be even more reluctant to yield this point. Only thus, he felt, could the Christian ethic retain its distinctiveness and the Christian revelation retain its individual character. His reference to Franck would seem to indicate that he was afraid that Schwenckfeld's position would inevitably result in a generalization of revelation, which would move from the revelation in Jesus Christ to a general revelation not only in the whole Bible, but even beyond the Bible into the realm of the pagan philosophers and nature itself. He saw these extremes in Bünderlin and Franck, and wished to avoid them at all costs. In doing so he overstated his case. But one can hardly deny the relevance of his concern.

5. The Revision of the Bekentnisse of Bernhard Rothmann

One of the most startling discoveries in the field of Anabaptist studies in recent times was made by Frank J. Wray, who discovered that Marpeck's *Vermanung* is actually a translation and revision of Bernhard Rothmann's *Bekentnisse*.[100] Wray does not stress enough the corporate authorship of both of these documents, and if that is borne in mind, we will need to see both of these statements as group confessions. Even in pre-copyright days it is apparent that documents of this nature with corporate authorship were considered as belonging to a group. To speak of the individual authorship of

[98] The absence of these terms in the *Verantwortung* should not cause one to conclude anything. Bergsten unduly stresses this difference and thus comes to the conclusion that the two ways in which Marpeck discusses the state of the patriarchs before Christ result in two irreconcilable contradictions (*op. cit.*, p. 50). For a summary of Vogelsang's description of the place of the *descensus* in the Reformation see Excursus at the end of Chapter IV.

[99] *Vide supra*, p. 131 and *infra*, p. 165.

[100] *ARG*, 47 (1956), 243-251. The latter was edited by Heinrich Detmer and Robert Krumbholtz, *Zwei Schriften des Münsterschen Wiedertäufers, Bernhard Rothmann* (Dortmund, 1904), pp. 1-85.

either of these confessions would be similar to talking about individual authorship of the Apostles' Creed.[101]

By the time the Marpeck brotherhood translated the Münster *Bekentnisse* the fiasco of Münster in 1535 was familiar throughout Europe. No doubt all the ingredients that combined to precipitate this debacle will never be known, but from the Marpeck revision it is clear that the South German Brethren felt the Münsterites did not reject the use of force decisively enough. Closely related to this, they did not stress enough the necessity for the Christian to suffer. The Hofmannite view of the incarnation, although not present in the *Bekentnisse,* is repudiated by the Marpeck brotherhood, as well as the idea of community of goods. On this point there is no apparent polemic against the Münsterites; and no doubt we will need to view this addition in the light of the discussions the Pilgramites had with the Hutterites. As Wray says, "For Marpeck community of goods was a matter of individual conscience and should not be used as a basis for admission to or exclusion from the Christian fellowship."[102] To use Marpeck's own terms, it is a matter of the freedom of love, and not of force or compulsion (*TB*, 265).

The most striking change of all is the increased attention given by the Marpeck brotherhood to the difference between the Old and New Testaments. Again this must be seen against the background of the Münster tragedy. For at Münster the

[101] The individual authorship of neither of these documents has been established. Apart from the signature of the six Münster men, the testimony of Kloprys needs only a shift of a comma to indicate the authorship of the six. See Joseph Niesert, *Muensterische Urkundensammlung,* I (Coesfeld, 1826), 110. That the Marpeck brotherhood exercised the right to change a document to suit their theology is seen in Hut's "Ein Anfang eins rechten christlichen Lebens" as it appears in the *Kunstbuch.* The differences between the version published by Lydia Müller (*Glaubenszeugnisse,* I, 12ff.) and the *Kunstbuch* version are too striking to be explained merely on the basis of sixteenth-century or modern editors' mistakes. The other epistles published by Lydia Müller that occur also in the *Kunstbuch* do not appear to show any marked changes, but the textual history of most of these documents lies shrouded in darkness, so one should not conjecture too much about the presence of a "Gemeindetheologie" at work here. For further illustrations of literary "borrowing" in the sixteenth century see *MQR,* XXXII (1958), 215.

[102] *Op. cit.,* p. 247.

Old Testament alone was read,[103] polygamy was justified on the basis of a strict legalistic Biblicism of the Old Testament, especially the "command" in Genesis 1:28 to be fruitful and multiply.[104] The fanatical Jan Matthys followed an asinine inspiration to disperse the besieging army as had been done in the days of the Old Testament, and fell in the attempt. Hille Feicken, moved by the gallant example of Judith who beheaded Holofernes, decided to emulate her, but was captured and put to death.[105]

Finally, even the Lutheran theologians criticized the Münsterites for going to the Old Testament for their ethics and inspiration.[106] Is it any wonder that the *Vermanung* attempts to make the Anabaptist position clear on this point by showing that a radical difference is an essential feature of Anabaptist theology?

For an understanding of Marpeck's position we cannot ignore the events at Münster. The *Bekentnisse* of Rothmann's group was for the most part acceptable as far as it went, but its fatal weakness was a lack of clarity on the place of the Old Testament.[107] This left the door wide open to a perversion (*verruckung*) of earthly power from its God-ordained place and station to the holy place, and the justification of the use of the sword.[108] To prevent a repetition of such a despicable event, Marpeck insisted with consistent clarity that a decisive line be drawn between the Old and New Testaments.

Marpeck did not explicate what it was in the Münster group's attitude toward the Old Testament that the South Germans did not find palatable, but it is clear from the revision and the open polemic cited above that they were critical of its approach to the Old Testament.

Before looking at some of the changes made in revising the

---

[103] See Heinrich Gresbeck's report in C. A. Cornelius, *Berichte der Augenzeugen ueber das muensterische Wiedertäuferreich* (Münster, 1853): "Wan et aver middagh was, dat sie setten und etten, so stunt dair ein iungh und las ein capittel uth dat olde testament oft uth den propheten" (pp. 34ff.).

[104] Cornelius, *op. cit.*, pp. 59ff.

[105] See *ME*, III, 778.

[106] Antonius Corvinus, *Acta . . .* (Wittenberg, 1536), fol. G.

[107] That the question of the Old Testament becomes a fork in the road between Rothmann and Marpeck is clear from the one major omission from the *Bekentnisse* (43-46) and the largest single addition by Marpeck in its place (*TB*, 226:32-238:22).

[108] See the Preface to *TE*, and V, II, 324; *TB*, p. 217.

Bekentnisse we should look at the introduction of the *Vermanung*. As the title indicates it is an exhortation to the true Christian, covenantal union against all supposedly Christian unions that are carried on under the name of Christ (*TB*, 185). The editors promise to speak what the Lord says, against all false prophets (I Kings 18), especially those who have joined with the regents and powers of this world against the Lord. All are crying "covenant, covenant" and yet denying God according to the truth, and becoming apostate (*TB*, 185).[109]

After the table of contents the translators wrote a lengthy introduction giving the reasons for their treatise, and telling somewhat of their sources and purpose.[110] This is introduced by a reference to the way in which Satan has splintered the believers into a multitude of sects and divisions, for the last twelve years (even as in the beginning of the church), through false messengers of Satan placed among the true members of the covenant.[111] The first reason for writing the *Vermanung* then is to attempt to do something about the false apostles that are within the covenanters themselves, and to strengthen the true covenanters (*TB*, 187).

The second purpose is to encourage those who are getting weary of the battle, and who are beginning to despair over the outcome of the struggle against the powers of darkness. It is meant to be somewhat of a battle cry to strengthen the weak, and help them to rally around the banner of their Master, Jesus Christ, who uses only spiritual weapons of warfare (*TB*, 187-88).

The third reason given is that they wish to purify their confession, for there is nothing so dangerous as truth mixed with falsehood. They have used a number of other confessions

---

[109] Lowell Zuck fails to take adequate note of the fact that men like Marpeck were acutely aware of the perversion of the covenant idea into a revolutionary token ("Anabaptism: Abortive Counter-Revolt within the Reformation," *ChHist*, XXVI [1957], 211-226; also in his Yale dissertation [1954] entitled "Anabaptist Revolution through the Covenant in Sixteenth Century Continental Protestantism").

[110] This covers three-and-a-half pages in *TB*, while the *Bekentnisse* had a Preface of only about a page. Only a few phrases of this Preface are translated by the editors of *TB*.

[111] The reference to "twelve years" must refer to 1530, and a parting of the ways there among the Brethren. No doubt the spiritualists like Bünderlin are meant, as well as Schwenckfeld.

and have purified them, corrected them, and omitted the errors contained in them.[112]

In the actual translation comparatively little is omitted from the *Bekentnisse*. At times the enthusiasm of the writers of the *Bekentnisse* is tempered,[113] and at other times their pessimism is softened.[114] An omission easily explainable is the phrase *"uith der fonteyn des doepsals"* after the words *"denen so wider geboren seind"* since baptismal regeneration as well as immersion is thereby rejected.[115]

A rather striking omission is the quote from I Corinthians 10, *"Se syn alle in Mosen gedoept,"* found in the *Bekentnisse* but omitted in the *Vermanung*, and instead changed to *"auff Mosen vertroestet!"*[116] This omission of the exact words found in the *Bekentnisse* and then the substitution of an explanation considerably different from what the Bible text says, is an interesting example of Marpeck's reworking of the *Bekentnisse* and indicates the desire he had to fit all the

[112] "We are moved, according to our obligation and covenant in Christ to publish this our testimony, along with other testimonies contained herein published by others, and tested by us . . . and cleansed, corrected, and the deletion of errors (which in part we have found therein, such as do not agree or accord with our faith, love, and patience in Christ, so that we may give free witness only to the good and to the pure truth without mixture of error). In this way the truth will not be slandered through mixture with its counterpart, by those slanderers and impure critics who are accustomed continually to slander good with evil and to discard the good and the truth without discrimination or protection" (*TB*, 188).

[113] The omission of "Myt Goddes hulpe" (p. 85; *TB*, p. 282) comes in this class. So also the omission of "morderysshes" in *TB*, p. 269:7.

[114] The omission of "also oick, dat schyr geyne erkenntnusse Gades mer is averbleven up erden" (*Bekentnisse*, p. 37), *TB*, p. 220:23 after "worden" is an example of this.

[115] *TB*, p. 210:31 (compare *Bekentnisse*, p. 27). The addition of "ueberguss" or its cognate is almost universal where the form of baptism is alluded to (not added in *TB*, p. 192:4; in *TB*, p. 192:37 it is in Rothmann. Marpeck [*TB*, p. 196:11] omits: "dan yeder mennichlick weet wael, dat doepen heth underducken oft int water steken" from *Bekentnisse*, p. 10, and adds sprinkling terminology in *TB*, pp. 201:8, 19; 202:23, 41, 42; 203:8; 206:31, 37; 207:17; 209:6, 25; 210:24; 214: 35, where it is lacking in Rothmann). Cf. Wray, *op. cit.*, p. 250.

[116] While it is true that the translators do not very often give the Scriptural reference, the difference in translation here is too striking to explain it simply as a lack of precise knowledge of the Westphalian dialect. Marpeck was always in a difficult position as far as I Corinthians 10 was concerned (cf. *TE*, 247-283; 285; 400, and *V*, pp. 348-354).

evidence into his theology. He left to a later time to deal with I Corinthians 10 in detail, and it is surprising indeed that Schwenckfeld did not score him on this point more than he did.[117]

Further, there are two omissions that look suspiciously like errors caused by homoioteleuton. The omission of the phrase "*versoent unde van sunden gereynigeth voertan in Godt durch Christum*"[118] is best explained in such a way, as well as the omission, "*thom derden dat hoichwerdige nacht-mal. Hyrmedde sal die hillige kerke in eynicheit bewareth werden.*"[119]

In contrast to his age in general, Marpeck did not seek to find Christ everywhere in the Old Testament. This is especially clear in the *Vermanung* where the translators reject Rothmann's line of argument on the analogy of circumcision to infant baptism and substitute their own.[120] At the beginning of this section, the *Vermanung* omits the sentence: "*Abraham is eyn vorbelde up Godt dem vader, ghelyck als Isaac up Christum.*"[121] Furthermore Rothmann's line of argument focuses on his statement:

Want Abraham is hyr nicht eyne figur up de Chris-tenolderen, dan eyn belde up Godt den vader, desghe-lycken de kynder Abrahe synt geyn evebelden up de kinder der Christen, dan up de gheloevighen unde wed-dergeborne kinder Gades, ja, unde up de Christen sul-ven.[122]

---

[117] Since we are dealing with modern editions of these texts, a word of caution is in order. The edition of the *TB* has been checked with the British Museum copy (photostat), and has revealed only a small number of differences from the edition by Hege. On p. 203:41 it inserts the important word "nicht" after "seligkeyt" and thus brings it into harmony with the *Bekentnisse*, which has "verneynet" where Marpeck has "vermeynet" (203:40, *Bekentnisse*, p. 19). No doubt this error is either Hege's or the printer's.

[118] *TB*, p. 195:17 after "durch Christum" (*Bekentnisse*, p. 8).

[119] *TB*, p. 278:20, after "vereiniget werden" (*Bekentnisse*, p. 84).

[120] In the *Bekentnisse* Rothmann deals with this argument in four pages, 42-46. In the *Vermanung* it is dealt with in pages 225-238, with most of *Bekentnisse* 43-46 omitted. The pages in the *Vermanung* are a little larger, but Rothmann's Westphalian dialect is less verbose.

[121] *Bekentnisse*, p. 43; *TB*, p. 226:30, where the sentence would come at the place of the comma, if it had not been omitted. In *KB*, fol. 226b "der rechte wesentlich Abraham," father of Christians, is God the Father; and in *TB*, p. 237:36, the true Isaac is Jesus Christ.

[122] *Bekentnisse*, p. 44.

Using this typology, Rothmann argues that in the church, the circumcision of the Old Testament becomes the baptism of the New, and applies only to the true children of Abraham, the believers. The eight-day period before circumcision is applied to baptism thus:

> also alle rechtgeloevige und weddergeborne kynder Gades soellen und moethen up den geystliken achteden daghe, dat is der upverstentnisse ofte wanner se der upverstentnisse gelickfoermich werden unde den sabbath myt Christo gestorven und begraven vullenbracht hebben. . . .

To this argument is added that since only *children* of Abraham were circumcised, so only believers can be baptized.[123] Rothmann argues from the command of the Old Testament that since circumcision should take place on the eighth day and not before, so also infant baptism, especially baptism of the foetus, is rejected.[124] Marpeck changes this Biblicism of the Old Testament and comes to the same conclusion via a different route.[125]

A comparison of both of these confessions indicates that they are in substantial agreement in their conclusions. But the manner by which these conclusions are reached is significantly different. The *Vermanung* rejects the allegory of the *Bekentnisse* and its devotion to the literal command of the letter of the Old Testament. This confusion of Biblicism and allegory later became evident in the Münster episode and undoubtedly contributed to the revision of the *Bekentnisse*.[126]

This departure from Rothmann's line of reasoning throws considerable light on Marpeck's approach to the problem of infant baptism. It was no arid Biblicism that moved him in

[123] Page 45. The reason why the revisers of the *Bekentnisse* omitted this line of reasoning would appear obvious. The servants of Abraham's house also were circumcised, and Bucer used this argument to support infant baptism. Cf. *TB*, p. 226:26, where the editors add "knecht," even though the *Bekentnisse* has "gesinne." Compare also p. 236:23f. and *Conf.*, p. 175.

[124] *Op. cit.*, p. 46.

[125] *TB*, p. 238.

[126] Another factor that may have contributed to the translated revision is the reply that the Strasbourg ministers wrote to the Rothmann confession (*vide supra*, pp. 45f.). According to Herbert C. Klassen (*op. cit.*, p. 276) this confusion goes back to Thomas Müntzer.

the direction of adult baptism but rather his emphasis on the freedom of the Christian man. Because this freedom was abused in the Lutheran circles in which he moved he submitted voluntarily to baptism, and the reality of this experience as well as the abuses of infant baptism enforced his conviction. The church is built on the individual confession of faith (*TB*, 228), Peter's being the foundation.[127] Infant baptism meant for him the compulsion of the Old Testament, in which the choice of the individual was not given its rightful place. Bucer called infant baptism an "offering of children to God," and for Marpeck this could only be seen as a reversion to the Old Testament, for in the New Testament a man offers himself as a sacrifice to God (*TB*, 227:14). Offering one's children to God in the rite of infant baptism was nothing but a Molochite offering (*Conf.*, 191, 200). If we were Jews then we would baptize infants indiscriminately as they circumcised all, sons and servants, but since we are Christians we are under no law or compulsion. "Now in the revealed kingdom of our Lord Christ there is no, 'Thou shalt,' but rather, 'Whoever wills,' let him come and permit himself to be baptized in the name of Jesus Christ" (*TB*, 236).[128] In a carefully wrought piece of argument Marpeck tries to show that infant baptism is merely an imitation of external circumcision, while Paul is speaking (in Col. 2) about a spiritual circumcision of the heart which only Christ can perform and which finds logical expression only as a part of believers' baptism (*TB*, 236f.).

At the heart of this argument stands Marpeck's view of the covenant; and whether this view coincides with the view found in the Bible or not, it is clear that he drew it from both

[127] Compare the statement: "Und wer sich nit selbs willig, selbs wissend, selbs glaubend, selbs bekennend tauffen lasset zu vergebung der sünde, dem werden sie behalten" (*TB*, p. 231:17f.). To the accusation that a literal Biblicism had moved him to baptism he replied that he had allowed himself to be baptized "because it is written . . . and that the faith in Christ's resurrection and his own is a living letter in his heart" (*KU*, C vb). The principle of voluntary participation in the sacraments is also expressed in *KU*, D ii and *CV*, a vib; c iib.

[128] *Conf.*, p. 171, expresses it similarly thus: "(In the kingdom of Christ) there is no compulsion but rather a voluntary spirit . . . whosoever wills, let him come, and let him drink freely and without price. All external power may not rule, profit or reign in the kingdom of Christ." R. Armour (*op. cit.*) has ably and accurately represented Marpeck's unique position on baptism.

the Old and the New Testaments. Schwenckfeld criticized Marpeck for using the term "covenant" in view of the associations of the term at that time. Marpeck admits these negative associations but insists that the term needs to be redefined instead of abandoned. One can find poison wherever one seeks it (V, 86). For Marpeck the term has meaning because it is used in I Peter 3 to describe baptism and has a long history in God's dealing with his people. Two things comprise a covenant, promise and commitment, the promise being of God, the commitment being the part that man plays. God promises forgiveness of sins, peace, and to be our God; we commit ourselves to be his people, taking upon ourselves the vows that are a part of being united with Christ through baptism (ibid.). Marpeck is fond of the image of marriage to describe the relationship of the church to Christ because in that way the word "sacrament" can be seen in its original meaning of vow or oath of commitment (V, 94:48ff.).

It lies beyond the scope of this study to examine in how far Marpeck remained true to the deeper meaning of baptism as portrayed in the New Testament in this development of his position.[129] It should only be observed that his argument

---

[129] Whether Luther's translation (Bund) for ἐπερώτημα in I Peter 3: 21 is theologically correct is still debated. G. C. Richards renders it as "a pledge to God proceeding from a clear conscience" (E. G. Selwyn, The First Epistle of St. Peter, London, 1952, ad loc.). Selwyn cites a papyrus occurrence where the word corresponds to the Latin stipulatio and was used for "the clause in a contract containing the formal question and consent (homologia) of the contracting parties" (ibid.). The rendering of Windisch, "prayer for a good conscience," lacks linguistic support. The assertion by Otto Schmitz (RGG[2], I, 1362f.) defining the covenant as a "one-sided disposition" can be seriously challenged in the light of the Biblical evidence (compare now Hempel's references to "Zweiseitigkeit" in RGG[3], I, 1515f.). Marpeck's insistence on making the covenant a mutual relationship would seem to have Biblical support although Marpeck seeks to guard God's initiative. It is God who makes the covenant (Conf., p. 170), and it is essentially God's (Conf., p. 174). In another connection he says: "Christ has established the covenant of a good conscience (which we owe to God) in our hearts through his resurrection. . . . Thus Christ the man is the covenant of God with us, through forgiveness of sins. . . . And he is also our covenant with God, in the fulfilling of God's commands, through the love and spirit poured out today as He [the spirit] is God and Christ himself (II Corinthians 3, I John 4). Thus Christ is the covenant, which God promised yesterday to inscribe in our hearts, Jeremiah 31" (TE, fol. 138). On the source of some of these terms, see Excursus I at the end of this chapter.

moves on a theological level rarely attained in Anabaptism and is determined more by his understanding of the Christian as portrayed in the Bible than it is by isolated proof-texts. At the heart of this position lies a radical difference between the Old and New Covenants.

Conclusion

Jan J. Kiwiet has made the observation that the organizing principle of Marpeck's theology is the concept of *order*. The concretization of God's order Marpeck sees in the covenant. Nothing is more basic to Marpeck's total position than the idea of the covenant. Baptism is a covenant, the church is a covenant community, a confession is a testimony to the covenant, etc. This being the case, it is of interest for our purpose to ask whether the concept of the covenant is derived from the Old Testament. An examination shows that the concept of the covenant is almost entirely derived from the Old Testament (V, 86). As a covenantal commitment, Christian baptism finds its antecedent in the seal of circumcision in the experience of Abraham (V, 94).

Having noted one central point at which Marpeck was strongly Biblical,[130] one question remains. It would appear as if Marpeck does not stress enough the revelatory aspect of the Old Testament. While it has been shown that he uses the Old Testament as Scripture in the same way that he uses the New Testament, his statements pertaining to the redemption of the people of the Old Testament appear to indicate that he does not differentiate sharply enough between them and pagans prior to the coming of Christ. Has Marpeck in his attempt to stand against the stream been forced to depreciate God's acts in history prior to the coming of Christ? There is certainly some evidence that this is the case, but perhaps it is a necessary concomitant of noting the full splendor of the incarnation and seeing all of God's acts in the glorious light of Christ.[131]

---

[130] "Biblical" is used here in contrast to testamental, not necessarily as in harmony with the Bible. The statement by Leonhard von Muralt, "For the Anabaptists only the writings of the New Testament are God's Word in a full and unrestricted sense" (*Glaube und Lehre der Schweizerischen Wiedertäufer* [Zürich, 1938], p. 30), is obviously not applicable to Marpeck.

[131] The awareness of this problem prompted chapter 119 in the *Testamenterleutterung*, which deals with the advantages of the Jews over the heathen in the period of the Old Covenant.

Excursus I: Marpeck's Bible

Apart from the work of Hans Denck and Ludwig Hätzer, Anabaptists did not do any work in the area of Bible translation. They used the German Bible of Luther extensively and at times critically,[132] but the most popular Bible among the Anabaptists was the Froschauer, or Zürich Bible (see *ME*, II, 415f. and *RGG*, I, 1207f.). After 1588 it was repeatedly reprinted in Basel for the Anabaptists and received the name *Täufertestamente*. As late as 1787 a reprint of the Froschauer New Testament was made at Ephrata, Pennsylvania, for the Mennonites.

Marpeck used three versions of the Bible. For the Old Testament Prophets he used the Worms edition; at times he quotes only this version (*TE*, fol. 83b and 87b). It is not evident which of the twelve editions of the Worms Prophets he used (cf. *ME*, IV, 983).

The Worms edition is most often compared with the Zürich Bible (*TE*, fol. 147b, 157, 185b, 193, 197, 198, 205, 205b, 206, 220, 239, 252, 264b, 283, 284, 288, 296b, 303b, 306b, 309b, 310, *et passim*). A comparison of the quotes in the *Confession* (1532) with the Froschauer Bible of 1525 would seem to indicate that Marpeck used this version at that time, but when he wrote the *Testamenterleutterung* it is clear that he was using the Froschauer Bible of 1531. When Marpeck quotes Genesis 17:1 in the *Testamenterleutterung*, fol. 129, he follows the 1531 rendering: "*Wandle vor mir vn biss steyff vnd getreüw an mir,*" whereas the 1525 version reads: "*wandel vor mir / vnd biss uffrecht.*" In Genesis 17:2b he follows the Zürich Bible against Luther.

In quoting Ezekiel 16:62 where both the 1525 and 1531 Zürich Bibles have "*Ich will meinen Bund mit dir erneueren,*" Marpeck understandably prefers the Worms and Luther renderings, which instead of *erneueren* have "*aufrichten.*" (According to Koehler-Baumgartner's Lexicon the word קום here means "carry out, or keep.") Marpeck prefers "establish" be-

---

[132] The most interesting case is that of Leonhard Schiemer, who criticized Luther's rendering of John 1. After the sharp words, "Here Luther translated wrongly" the reader is urged to consult "all the Latin and Hebrew Bibles!" (Lydia Müller, *Glaubenszeugnisse*, I, 61). Marpeck simply attributes the "wrong" translation of the Zürich Bible to "mangel an Verständnis!"

cause in this way one can speak of more than one covenant.[133]

At one point he clearly rejected all other versions and accepted the Luther version, namely, on the rendering of I Peter 3:21. Here, according to Luther's version, baptism is defined as a covenant; this immediately struck a sympathetic ear among the Anabaptists.[134] It would be an interesting study to multiply cases where the Anabaptists selected renderings that agreed with their theology. More often than has been realized in the past, the mold in which Anabaptist thought-patterns come to us is decisively conditioned by the translation of the Bible they used. When confronted with more than one version they chose the one that most closely approximated their position.

[133] For Marpeck the New Covenant was essentially different; and while there was continuity, he stressed the difference. With respect to the New Covenant of Jeremiah two modern OT doctoral dissertations have reached opposite conclusions. Heinz Ortmann ("Der Alte und der Neue Bund bei Jeremia," Berlin, 1940) concluded that there was no essential difference, that Jeremiah merely prophesied the renewal of the Old Covenant; while Walter Lempp ("Bund und Bundeserneuerung bei Jeremia," Tübingen, 1955) stresses more the difference. See *ThLtzg*, Vol. 80 (1955), col. 238f.

[134] The Froschauer Bibles of 1524, 1531, 1534, and 1536 render this verse: "sonder die gewüesse kundtschafft eines guten gewuessens mit Gott."

IV

THE DEVELOPMENT OF MARPECK'S
HERMENEUTICS

A. THE TWO CENTRAL PROBLEMS DEFINED

The study of Marpeck's hermeneutics has revealed that two problems remain in the forefront, namely, the problem of the Old and New Covenants, and the problem of spirit and letter. These problems are not defined by Marpeck but are a part of the culture into which he was born and of the times in which he lived. As an Anabaptist he took an active part in the discussion of both problems. Since both were primarily ethical problems, perhaps Marpeck does not have a hermeneutic in the strictest sense of that word. At least, his hermeneutic is not of the reflective type. A comparison with Augustine, for example, whose philosophical roots are clearly traceable and who wrote at some length on hermeneutical issues, makes a difference immediately observable.[1] Somewhat the same latitude in the use of the term "hermeneutics" exists as with the term "theology." We do not hesitate to speak of the theology of the New Testament and the theology of Thomas Aquinas, though they are worlds apart.

To show the place of these two problems in Marpeck's theology, an attempt will now be made to isolate some major strands that were woven into Marpeck's thought in the course of his life.[2]

---

[1] A recognition of this difference facilitates describing them under the same rubric. For this reason the excellent monograph by Gerhard Strauss, *Schriftgebrauch, Schriftauslegung und Schriftbeweis bei Augustin* (Tübingen, 1959), has little to contribute to this study, not even in the area of method.

[2] Some of the men to be named played a much greater role in Marpeck's development than the paucity of references to them in Marpeck's writings would lead one to believe. For that reason we will not restrict ourselves merely to checking on the sources used by Marpeck.

B. SOLUTIONS ENCOUNTERED AND REJECTED

1. RADICAL SPIRITUALISM: SEBASTIAN FRANCK AND
JOHANNES BÜNDERLIN

We take these two men together because they represent an
almost identical position, Bünderlin being the leader, with
Franck having nothing but highest praise for him.[3] Franck
was always concerned about the hopeless confusion in the
churches because of the inveterate mixture of the Old and
New Testaments and had come to a clear decision about the
place of the Old Testament. In his *Chronik* or *Geschichtsbibel*
his evaluation of the Old Testament is clearly expressed.[4] The
Old Testament is seen as history pure and simple without any
stress on its revelatory character. History has didactic value for
Franck; he goes so far as to say that if Adam had had some
historical illustrations to serve him as examples the Fall might
have been averted and we might still be in Paradise. Instruction is a dead letter, but examples have a tremendous
teaching power.[5]

Franck is quite free with the historical narrative of the Old
Testament, especially when issues are at stake which do not
suit his world view. Describing the building of the temple he
remarks:

> In my opinion it would have been much better if never
> a stone or a board had been laid on the temple. Rea-
> son: the people adhered in their worship only to the
> temple and thought that the temple should make good
> all of their evil.[6]

[3] Franck's letter to Campanus of 1531 contains phrases describing
Bünderlin, such as "he is a learned man, wonderfully God-fearing and
utterly dead to worldly things," "profoundly grounded in the Scriptures and with uncommon clarity of mind to judge all matters" (*Spiritual
and Anabaptist Writers*, pp. 156f.).

[4] The 1531 edition is here used. On this aspect see Kuno Räber,
Studien zur Geschichtsbibel Sebastian Francks (Basel, 1952), Ch. II,
"Die Geschichtsbibel und das Alte Testament."

[5] *Chronica* (1531), fol. a 4b. Modern idealism, too, seemed to assume that we learn from the mistakes of the past. The view is too
shallow. Modern man still repeats Adam's mistakes in spite of a knowledge of the consequences.

[6] *Ibid.*, fol. 48a.

His continual critique of the cultus is in apparent conflict with his acceptance of the enduring character of God's Word, since the cultus was a result of God's command. He solves this dilemma with the idea that "The temple, the Sabbath, the whole Moses are not actually God's word, but are that which they symbolize or mean."[7] Only that which is timeless is God's Word, "therefore everything that is external and temporal, having its beginning in time," is not God's Word.[8] The external aspects of the Old Testament were given to the people as a doll (*puppe*) to play with so that in time God could show them the opposite and introduce the truth.

> The fools wanted it that way and the child wanted to play with the doll, so God imposed it upon them, in order that they might not do worse things and even become apostate. . . . For when Cain began to sacrifice, God also had to begin to sacrifice through his Abel and reject Cain's sacrifice, showing therewith that Abel was in the right and not Cain, so that he too could be converted to the God of Abel.[9]

Nevertheless, Franck the moralist can draw illustrations from the Old Testament and thus follow the example of the Middle Ages, especially the *Divine Comedy* of Dante, with this difference that for Franck the line between secular and sacred history is not only minimized (as with Dante) but almost entirely erased.[10]

Most important, the Old Testament is for Franck not a period in history, but an attitude that man can have at any time in history, characterized by service of the letter rather than the spirit. For this reason Franck's praise of Old Testament religion is never unqualified.[11]

The position of Johannes Bünderlin is much the same.[12]

---

[7] *Paradoxa*, p. 82.
[8] *Ibid.*
[9] *Ibid.*, p. 115.
[10] Räber, *op. cit.*, p. 38.
[11] *Ibid.*, p. 29.
[12] Still the standard work on Bünderlin is that of Nicoladoni, *op. cit.* In addition, the article "Johannes Bünderlin," in *ME*, I, 469-470, and Rufus Jones, *Spiritual Reformers in the 16th and 17th Centuries* (Boston, 1959[2]), Ch. III, should be consulted. The four works identified as his by Nicoladoni were used for this study through the courtesy of the librarian at Dresden. The *Clare verantwurtung* ascribed to him by

While Bünderlin used the Old Testament to some extent (especially the book of Daniel) he saw it primarily as a concession to man's dullness in opening his life to the influence of the inner light. God sent the external Word to "shake the world up a little" (*wollte die welt widerumb auffshüttlen*),[13] because the world would **not** heed the internal. As sin increased and people moved farther away from God the letter came to remind them of God and their sin.[14] Since everything in the Old Testament was external and everything in the New Testament internal,[15] Bünderlin does not hesitate to speak of a contradiction between the two Testaments, though affirming that the same God works in both.[16] God made a concession to the carnal nature of the children of Israel,[17] the majority in Israel being carnal and sluggish and unconcerned about spiritual matters.[18] In doing so God accommodated himself to man's weakness;[19] because the flesh desires creaturely things so avidly, God in his patience tolerates the people's stress on earthly things.[20] Furthermore the external Law served to hold the children of Israel together.[21]

Positively, Bünderlin asserted that the saints of the Old Testament may have had the spirit but served God unto wrath, not unto grace;[22] and that the Old Testament is a time of servitude while the New Testament is a time of sonship. That is not to say that the Old Testament from Moses to Christ is a period of Law alone. "As the law even today fulfills its role in us, so also the Gospel was in the hearts of the believing patriarchs, however concealed in the mystery under the letter of the law."[23]

Nicoladoni and by G. H. Williams and A. Mergal (*op. cit.*, p. 156) is more likely by Marpeck (*vide supra*, pp. 40ff.), certainly not by Bünderlin. On the relation between Bünderlin and Denck, cf. C. R. Foster, *op. cit.*

[13] *Eine gemayne Einlayttung*, p. 16.
[14] *Ibid.*, p. 10.
[15] *Ibid.*, p. 12.
[16] *Ibid.*, p. 14.
[17] *Ibid.*, p. 31.
[18] *Ibid.*, p. 24.
[19] *Erklärung*, p. 21.
[20] *Ibid.*, p. 22.
[21] *Ibid.*, p. 66.
[22] *Ibid.*, p. 93.
[23] *Aus was ursach*, p. 26.

> Even the ancients were saved before Christ came be-
> cause they received the true word of God in their
> hearts. This served for their salvation just as if the true
> Word of God, the inner light, already had been external-
> ly uncovered, revealed or accomplished. For they also
> desired the glory of God and the salvation of their
> neighbor.[24]

Like Franck, Bünderlin also rejects the Old Testament as
an unconditional revelation of God's will. Rather, it is a means
to the education or training of mankind, which has strayed
from the true inner spiritual religion. It has a general application to the world and a more specific one to the Jews. All of
the Old Testament is a figure that has a hidden deeper
meaning; the Exodus, e.g., is simply a symbolic portrayal of
man being led out of the fleshly sinful world into a spiritual
Christianity.[25] The Scriptures are not God's will for his people, they are only a witness to what God wanted from his
people at a definite time, and are applicable to us only in so
far as they agree with the inner word.[26]

For both Bünderlin and Franck the Old Testament is of
little more than antiquarian interest. It possesses historical
and instructional, but not revelational value. Franck places
Moses alongside the great minds of Greek philosophy[27] without any indication that he rates him higher, and Bünderlin
speaks freely of the possibility that some of the Gentiles and
Jews alike saw the inner light clearly at the time of the Old
Testament.

Marpeck refers only once to Franck's *Paradoxa*, expressing
concern about his position that "yesterday there was a hidden
church,"[28] which Franck had discussed at some length,

[24] *Ibid.*, pp. 27f.
[25] Nicoladoni, *op. cit.*, p. 154.
[26] *Ibid.*, p. 136.
[27] In *Das verbütschiert mit siben sigeln verschlossen Buch* (1539) the
title page has Christ and Moses along with the philosophers, thus making
a union between culture and theology. Often in listing the saints of
history who did not recognize Christ in a historical sense, he puts Abel,
Job, Noah, Abraham, and Hermes Trismegistos into the same class
(*Paradoxa*, pp. 111, 272). Zwingli expected to meet a number of noble
heathen in heaven. See R. Seeberg, *op. cit.*, II, 315.
[28] V, p. 324. Only a lack of knowledge of Marpeck's position can explain Peuckert's statement that Marpeck used Franck's texts against
Schwenckfeld (*op. cit.*, pp. 480, 562).

dealing with the position of "many who assert that there was
no Christ, no faith, no grace, no forgiveness of sin, no Holy
Spirit in the Old Testament."[29] Franck's position is that all
these things existed in actuality but not according to revelation; even though the ancients had them they did not know
they had them since Christ had not yet been revealed. The
purpose of Christ's incarnation was merely to reveal that
which had already taken place in the counsels of God. Like a
city dimly visible through the mists, like a sum of money that
one possesses hidden in a pocket, so was redemption for the
ancients.[30] The New Testament, since it is not letter but the
Holy Spirit himself, must be learned from God himself; this
some of the ancients had done, although there were only a
few.[31] On the other hand he says, "I do not know whether
the apostles had a true faith in Christ before Pentecost or
knew him in the Spirit according to his heavenly essence."[32]

In view of the uniqueness of Marpeck's position with respect to the Old Testament there is little doubt that this is a
debate between Marpeck and Franck. There is adequate
evidence that Marpeck refused to accept Franck's position.[33]
As to Bünderlin, Marpeck does not specifically mention his
position on the Old Testament, but comes to grips with his
position in the *Clare verantwurtung*, where reference is made
to the erring spirits who draw so many of their arguments from
the Old Testament. Marpeck answers from the Old Testament, asserting that God was at work there renewing and
reforming his people, and in like manner he was at work
among his people under the New Covenant. There is no
doubt that Marpeck's position on the Old Testament was
greatly determined by these spiritualists for whom the Old
Testament became an almost irrelevant book.[34]

For both Bünderlin and Franck religion in the New Testament is an inner experience, a spiritual thing that wells up
from within and is not fostered by the externals such as

[29] *Paradoxa,* p. 106.
[30] *Ibid.,* pp. 108f.
[31] *Ibid.,* p. 108.
[32] *Ibid.,* p. 163.
[33] Peuckert, *op. cit.,* pp. 308f. Peuckert's assertion to the contrary,
there is no evidence that Franck and Marpeck agreed on the value they
ascribed to the OT.
[34] *CV,* Chapter I.

Scripture, sacraments, etc. Since the letter is the weapon of the antichrist to conquer the saints,[35] and the Anabaptists are the heretics who are enslaved by the letter,[36] Franck considers it a marvel of the Reformation that there is a fourth party

> well underway which considers all external preaching, ceremonies, sacraments, ban, calling [of ministers] as unnecessary and seeks to put them aside and to gather directly an invisible, spiritual church in the unity of Spirit and faith among all the nations, and to rule it directly with God's eternal invisible Word, without any external medium.[37]

Scripture according to Franck was the eternal allegory, whose letter should not be taken seriously. The letter belonged to the infancy, not only of the human race, but also of the church. Bünderlin spoke out strongly and explicitly against the Antiochan school of interpretation, which stressed so much the letter that it lost the spirit.[38] The letter was an introduction into the secret of the mystery of Christ but has now served its purpose.[39] "In Christ all that is old and literal (*buchstabisch*) has its end and the spiritual begins."[40] The New Testament speaks primarily in a spiritual manner although it makes some concessions to the carnal nature of man.[41] The letter kills the spirit even in the New Testament.[42] The external commands and practices of the apostolic church were a concession to the carnal people of Christ's day and especially to the Jewish Christians who would have been offended at such a radical change from their religion.[43] Even the Council of Jerusalem was a clear concession to those who had not made the transition to a spiritual

---

[35] *Paradoxa*, p. 6.

[36] *Chronica*, fol. 445.

[37] Sebastian Franck in the Preface to his *Türkenchronik* (1531), cited in Nicoladoni, *op. cit.*, p. 123.

[38] *Erklärung*, pp. 10, 73 (cf. Nicoladoni, *op. cit.*, p. 145).

[39] *Eine gemayne Einlayttung*, p. 20.

[40] *Ibid.*, p. 42.

[41] *Ibid.*, p. 74.

[42] *Erklärung*, p. 41.

[43] *Ibid.*, p. 51.

religion.[44] Time had changed since then, age is always an
indication of less value; "the Spirit does not stand still but
always moves forward with speed."[45] The bishops in the
postapostolic age were legalistic and enforced adherence to
these outward practices, when in fact they had served their
purpose when the apostles died.

Marpeck rejected this view because in effect it placed the
authority of the spiritualist above the Word of God. Who was
to tell the church what had become obsolete and what was
still valid? Accordingly, Marpeck pressed the question repeatedly, both of the radical spiritualists (Franck and Bünderlin, *KU*, A viii; *CV*, a v), and also of Schwenckfeld (*V*,
99, 105:1f.): On what authority were they writing all their
books? What was the source of this "*sendung*"? The spiritualists insisted that justifying baptism and the organization of a
fellowship in the name of Christ necessitated a direct commission from God accompanied by miracles and signs. In thus
taking a criterion of Luther they tried to cut away the validity
of much Anabaptist activity, but also committed themselves to
a quietism that made their efforts a clear contradiction of
their position. Marpeck insisted instead on the continuity of
apostolic doctrine, witness, and commission and saw the external means as an abiding avenue or medium through which
the Spirit works. Thus the encounter with Franck and Bünderlin accounts to a large extent for the development of the
strong antispiritualist strain in Marpeck's hermeneutics.

2. SPIRITUALISTIC TENDENCY: MARTIN BUCER

The figure of Martin Bucer looms as one of the greatest of
the Reformation period. Modern scholarship has, however,
been slow to appreciate his genius because of the inacces-
sibility of his works, and because he was overshadowed by
his pupil, John Calvin.[46] No Reformer of any stature dis-

[44] *Ibid.*, p. 99.
[45] *Erklärung*, pp. 52, 54.
[46] On Bucer research see Robert Stupperich, *Bibliographia Bucerana*:
Schriften des Vereins für Reformationsgeschichte, Vol. 58, No. 169
(1952), pp. 37-96; *idem*, "Stand und Aufgabe der Butzer-Forschung,"
ARG, 42 (1951), 244-259; and the article by Bard Thompson, "Bucer
Study Since 1918," *ChHist*, XXV (1956), 63-82. Still of lasting value

played Bucer's ideals of religious tolerance, and Anabaptists owe more to him on this score than to any other single Reformer.[47]

The relations between Marpeck and Bucer were extensive and cordial. Mutual respect and admiration permeate their dealings with each other from beginning to end. The disagreements, at times sharp, and the accusations, at times impulsive, lack the acrimony typical of an age not particularly noted for its tolerance or restraint in name-calling. The culmination of Marpeck's relationship with Bucer came in the drawing up of Marpeck's *Confession* in January 1532, and Bucer's reply in February of the same year, both of which are fortunately found in the minutes of the City Council.[48]

This material shows that the two major areas of disagreement between Marpeck and Bucer are again the place of the Old Testament and the problem of spirit and letter. On December 9, 1531 (*vide supra*, p. 27), Marpeck indicated to the City Council that he was dissatisfied with the lack of preaching of the Law in Strasbourg, and several days later requested that the ministers bring for discussion a short statement of their views on the relation between the Old and New Testaments.[49] The rebuttal to Marpeck's *Confession* and the accompanying documents clearly show that Bucer did not accept Marpeck's distinction between the Old and New Covenants. In the following pages his position will be mainly described on the basis of his rebuttal of Marpeck, without

---

is A. Lang, *Der Evangelienkommentar Martin Butzers und die Grundzüge seiner Theologie* (Leipzig, 1900). Bucer's writings are slowly being published. One work of 1584 appeared in the *Revue d'histoire et de philosophie religieuses*, 31 (1951), 12-100 and another in the series *Cahiers de la Revue d'histoire et de philosophie religieuses*, No. 32 (Paris, 1951). Max Lenz edited the *Briefwechsel Landgraf Philipps des Grosmüthigen von Hessen mit Bucer* in three volumes (Leipzig, 1880, 1887, 1891) but this does not begin to tap the materials for Bucer study (see further *ARG*, 1959, pp. 111f.; *RGG*, I, 1453-57). Fundamental for our study but published too late to be fully utilized is J. Mueller, *Martin Bucers Hermeneutik* (Gütersloh, 1965).

[47] On at least three occasions Bucer pressed the City Council for discussions with Anabaptists, March 15, 1529; October 31, 1530; and February 25, 1531 (see Krebs-Rott).

[48] Krebs-Rott, pp. 416-527.

[49] Whether he ever received this is not stated; at any rate it apparently has not been preserved.

assuming that this is necessarily a complete description of Bucer's theology.[50]

In debate with Caspar Schwenckfeld, Bucer made the statement: "Those who believe Moses, believe also Christ."[51] This was not an exaggeration of his position but expresses his equation of the Old and New Testaments. Particularly on the issue of infant baptism Bucer stressed the similarity, stating that Saint Paul recognized circumcision and baptism to be "*so gar ein ding*" that whoever is baptized, that person is also circumcised. Thus, Bucer argued, it would seem even more imperative that our infants be baptized than that the children of the ancients be circumcised, since the grace of Christ has been given to us so much more clearly.[52] Since circumcision is the initial and authentic sign of the covenant and our children belong no less to the covenant of God than did the children of the ancients, we ought also to give them the sign of the covenant for which the ancients received circumcision.[53] Bucer argues against the "spiritual" understanding of Capito and Cellarius, who would view circumcision as spiritual in this passage,[54] and against the "figurative" application of circumcision. Circumcision is not a figure but a mark of the covenant, and the same covenant and the same people exist today as in the Old Testament.

According to Bucer circumcision had three distinct values in the Old Covenant, which are equally applicable to infant

[50] Methodologically something can be said for the procedure adopted by John Howard Yoder to study the disputations for an Anabaptist theology because they evidence the greatest degree of reflective thinking. On the other hand, such literature may magnify the differences. In the case of Bucer, however, where there were significant shifts (Lang has shown this to be the case even in his Gospel commentaries), it is important that we study a document that represents Bucer's thinking in 1532.

[51] *CS*, IV, 796:31.

[52] Krebs-Rott, pp. 419, 422. The same expression "so gar ein ding" occurs in *TB*, p. 227:18f. In the *Bericht* (1534) he asserts, "der heylig Paulus dise zwey sacrament in dem selbigen so gleich haltet" (fol. K iv). Bucer is fond of this *a fortiori* argument for infant baptism (*Bericht*, K iiib). He will not concede that the New Covenant is more restrictive than the Old but insists that it also includes offspring (*Bericht*, fol. P iiib). These arguments are still used (Harry Hutchinson, *Why Baptize Infants?*, New York, 1957).

[53] Krebs-Rott, p. 422.

[54] Lang, *op. cit.*, p. 234. The Christian's baptism corresponds to Christ's circumcision, not to his baptism (*Bericht*, q iiib).

baptism: (1) It verified that God was also a God of children. (2) It solicited the parents to train their children in a God-fearing manner. (3) Children knew from early youth that they belonged to the people of God, and thus imbibed the fear of the Lord along with the milk of their mother. Without infant baptism (as in Greece and under the pressure of the Mohammedans in the west), Bucer thought, the light of the gospel might have been entirely extinguished through the ungodliness of the past few centuries.[55] Apart from the analogy between circumcision and baptism Bucer supports his position that the two Testaments are basically one. Bucer takes issue with Marpeck's assertion that the patriarchs of the Old Testament did not have the same faith as Christians have,[56] for it is precisely the unity of the same faith that unites the Christians of the New Testament with the children of Abraham, so that we can be called children of Abraham. Over against this basic unity all the figures and meanings adduced from the Old People of God that no longer exist in the New, cannot disrupt the unity of the two peoples.[57]

The basic difference between the Old and New People is that the former had a more childish faith, since Christ was preached to them in a more hidden way than to us, and they had more external ceremonies and practices. Also after the exaltation of Christ the fruit of his incarnation is better recognized and the gospel is preached to the whole world, rather than merely to the people of Israel.[58] Bucer, however, notes various ways in which the Old and New Testaments are differentiated.[59] He would agree with Marpeck in making the Old Testament a grace of the knowledge of sin, the New Testament forgiveness of sin, as long as the people of the Old Covenant are also granted forgiveness of sins in the same way as we have it today. The main difference between the two is that the New Covenant is according to the revelation of

[55]Lang, op. cit., pp. 234-245.
[56] Krebs-Rott, p. 427.
[57] Ibid., p. 399.
[58] Ibid., p. 400. In Bericht Bucer indicates that Paul refers to the people of the Old Covenant as a young boy who only grew up in the New Covenant (m iib). In his writing against Hofmann in 1533 Bucer says Israel had more ceremonies because the warmer climate made them more lively! See also Krebs-Rott, p. 432. For Calvin's views, see Wolf, op. cit., pp. 69ff.
[59] Krebs-Rott, p. 429.

Christ, and will not be erected as a covenant with the Jews, but will endure eternally. Pilgram's error is that he does not realize that with God the future is the same as the past; it is already present. Hence Abraham could have partaken of the sufferings of Christ.[60] Children born according to the flesh are accepted into the Christian church because they are also children according to God's promise. His promise is that in a particular sense he will be their God. Bucer claims to have shown in his first writing that Ishmaels and Esaus are born of Christians[61] (thus baptism is no guarantee of salvation), for circumcision is the same as baptism and designates the same as does baptism, namely, the removal of the body of sin.[62] Regeneration was also experienced among those of old. Moreover, it is Christ who worked in them and with infants begins his work even in the womb of the mother. For through him vessels both of grace and of wrath are made out of nothing.[63] Accordingly, it is Bucer's respect for the example of the ancients, as well as his respect for tradition, that caused him to retain infant baptism in an effort to promote Christian harmony.[64] His view of the relation of the two covenants must be seen as defined in a polemical context, which did not allow him to define it freely. The relation of the covenants held an appeal for him, and he expressed a desire in 1528 to pursue the study of the prophecies of Christ in the Old Testament more fully.[65]

For Bucer the contrast between the Law working wrath and the gospel assuring salvation is changed into a contrast *"zwischen äussern, statuarischen, nur für eine Zeit geschaffenen Geboten und dem ihnen zugrunde liegenden ewigen Willen Gottes; auch dieses Lehrstück wird in den Kreis des Dualismus zwischen Geist und Fleisch hinein-*

[60] *Ibid.*, p. 435.
[61] *Ibid.*, p. 477.
[62] *Ibid.*, pp. 481f.
[63] *Ibid.*, p. 499.
[64] In *Bericht* (r iiib) the "universal practice" argument is used to retain infant baptism (cf. also Krebs-Rott, p. 398). Paul Althaus maintains that in Luther the same argument comes strongly to the fore. "Dass ist gewiss nicht sein letztes Wort zur Sache, aber sein erstes" ("Martin Luther über die Kindertaufe," *ThLtzg*, Vol. 73 (1948), col. 705). Bucer even advocated baptizing infants against the parents' wishes: "Plato hatt doch dz erkennet, das wyr meer der gemein, do wir leben, dann unseren elteren, geporen werden, vnd eigen sind" (*Bericht*, y 4b).
[65] Lang, *op. cit.*, p. 68.

gezogen."[66] The Old and New Testaments are, therefore, *"idem in substantia, quia eodem in utroque Deus spectat, nimirum ut ipse sit, per suma bonitatem Deus noster, et nos eius per fidem populus."*[67] But in the New Covenant the redemption of Christ is more clearly revealed, more universally extended, and is freed from the external ceremonies, the *"elementa mundi"* in the Law, and the *"umbrae veri testamenti et beneficii Christi."*[68] Even though the ancients stood under the spirit of servitude, and did not yet know the purely spiritual nature of the Kingdom of Heaven, *"tam revelate atque potenter"* as the *"sancti recentiores, qui post meritum Christi fuerunt,"* they were nevertheless citizens of the Kingdom of Heaven.[69]

Bucer's lack of clarity on the distinction between the two covenants testifies to the individuality of his concept of God, which does not allow any part of God's revelation to appear of less value than another. It also testifies to Bucer's strong ethical drive. Later in his life this valuation of the Old Testament was strengthened.[70] He consistently contrasts the two as being particularism versus universal invitation to salvation, and the freer attitude in the New Covenant toward ceremonies and rites. Circumcision, however, he did not regard as merely a sign of the covenant, but as the covenant itself, just as the *est* in the sacramental bread and wine indicates identity of the symbols with the covenant itself.[71] The covenant that God makes with his own, be they Jews or Gentiles, alongside the external things that are promised, basically means that God promises them that he desires to be their God, that he extends to them eternal life; and the covenant effects that those who accept him in faith dedicate themselves entirely to his will and sanctification.[72]

There is apparent in Bucer's thinking a dimming (*verwischung*) of the distinction between the two Testaments, seen in his generalizing tendency concerning salvation, which

[66] *Ibid.,* p. 144.
[67] *Ibid.,* p. 145 (quoting from Gospel Commentary, I, 150b [1536, 120]).
[68] *Ibid.,* p. 145.
[69] *Ibid.*
[70] So *ibid.,* p. 147.
[71] *Ibid.,* p. 239.
[72] Krebs-Rott, p. 431. Lang, *op. cit.,* p. 258, where Lang notes that the idea of the covenant does not loom very large in Bucer's thinking.

led Bucer to stress that *"in substantia"* the covenants are the same.[73] Especially is this true in Bucer's polemics against the Anabaptists (and those influenced by their ideas, as Capito and Cellarius). A theoretical differentiation does, however, exist, which comes to expression in a favorite theme of his, the *acta dei*.[74] It recedes most sharply when ethical issues like the oath or the sword are involved. The problem most irritating to Bucer in his conversations with Marpeck was the union of church and state, again a point at which Bucer is greatly indebted to the Old Testament.[75]

If spiritualism is defined as the separation of Word and Spirit, it is possibly correct to speak of a measure of "spiritualism" in Bucer.[76] Like all great men, Bucer changed his position in the course of time; there is evidence that after 1536 the earlier spiritualist strain receded. On December 26, 1524, he writes: "Turn where you will, you must allow freedom in baptism as an external rite, which God has not joined to any particular time."[77] Since God did not command it to be carried out at any particular time and it is a comfort to the parents, baptism in infancy is to be preferred. Bucer is afraid that the devil is trying to separate the Christians about mere externals. Baptism is not so important, love and patience are

[73] Lang, *op. cit.*, p. 260.

[74] On the basis of a hitherto unpublished letter by Bucer the claim has been made that Lang has not fairly represented Bucer's position on the difference of the two Testaments. See Scherding and Wendel, "Un Traite d'exégèse pratique de Bucer," *Revue d'histoire et de philo. religi.*, 26 (1946), 37. The criticism is justified only in a limited sense, since it must be admitted that Bucer was an intuitive rather than a logical or systematic thinker. In this Lang is correct, for Bucer was a churchman, not a scholar.

[75] When Hans Wolff von Benfeld said that a Christian governor could not bear a sword Bucer tried to show that he was not understanding the Scriptures correctly "and that the pious ancients, King David, Josiah, and also Samuel and others carried the sword and were priests, and that Christ has been from the beginning and will be until eternity" (Krebs-Rott, p. 53). The gift of administration (I Cor. 12:28) Bucer applied to government (Krebs-Rott, p. 424).

[76] "Man pflegt doch gemeinhin unter Spiritualismus die Distanzierung von Wort und Geist zu verstehen im Gegensatz zu ihrer Verbundenheit bei Luther . . ." (Walter Köhler, "Die Spiritualisten," *ARG*, 41 (1948), 181). Müller (*op. cit.*, p. 199) prefers not to speak of "spiritualism" but of "einem pneumatischen Bewusstsein."

[77] "Du wendest dich wohin du wilt, so mustu mir den tauff als ein eusserlich ding frey lassen, das gott an kein zeit bunden hat" (Krebs-Rott, p. 28:24f., cf. 421).

what matter. If anyone wishes to postpone baptism and can do so and retain the peace of the community in which he lives, let him do so; the Strasbourg ministers promise not to condemn him or disagree with him, only let him be sure of himself.[78] The Lord's Supper and baptism are external matters and not to be confused with the spiritual realities they represent. Since they are external, Christian freedom should govern our attitude toward them.[79]

On the other hand, in reply to Denck and Kautz, Bucer is explicitly clear about the value of the external Word and ceremonies.[80] According to John Martin Usteri, Bucer makes the following assertion in that writing:

> That we still have these two ceremonies is something legal, as we are still in part, in so far as we are clothed with our sinful bodies, under the law. What actually belongs to the New Testament, witnessed to in the law and the prophets, is pure spiritual essence (*Ding*), as the baptism of Christ through the Spirit and fire and the spiritual nourishment of the flesh and blood of Christ.

Bucer redefines the meaning of baptism to coincide with the Anabaptist practice of infant dedication, which was practiced in the assembly of the believers and consisted of a service of thanksgiving to God for the new life he had granted and a committal on the part of the parents to do all in their power to give this life back to God.[82] Since in this service the minister laid his hands upon the infant, Bucer argues that for the Christian whether one's hands were dry or wet made no difference.[83]

[78] Krebs-Rott, p. 29, taken from *Grund und Ursach* (1525), written by Bucer even though it bears the name of all Strasbourg ministers.

[79] *Ibid.*, p. 26.

[80] *Ibid.*, pp. 97f.

[81] "Die Stellung der Strassburger Reformatoren Bucer und Capito zur Tauffrage" (*Theologische Studien und Kritiken* [Gotha, 1884], p. 474).

[82] The practice of infant dedication widely practiced among Mennonites appears to go back at least to Hübmaier, from whom Marpeck no doubt learned about it (see "Consecration of Children," *ME*, I, 699f.).

[83] Krebs-Rott, p. 405 (his refutation of the arguments against infant baptism).

This depreciation of the external rite of baptism subtly called into question the whole Anabaptist movement, tacitly labeling it as based on a few foolish externals instead of seeing it as a radical response to God's call for a church that displays the character of a divine society, a covenant people serving the God who had redeemed them. From the start Zwingli, Oecolampadius, and Bucer argued that if the Anabaptists would pay more attention to love than to these "externals" all would take care of itself. Marpeck caught this strain of spiritualism not only in Denck, but also in Bucer. Its detection contributed in no small measure to Marpeck's consistent and stubborn opposition to all forms of spiritualism.[84]

One final point that emerged in the debates between Bucer and Marpeck deserves some attention, namely, the place of the consensus of the church in solving problems of interpretation. It has been demonstrated that Bucer became increasingly more dependent upon the tradition of the church, insisting that it was impossible for so many Church Fathers to have erred. Marpeck also placed much emphasis on the church, but apart from the basic creeds of the church he selected only those things from the Church Fathers with which he agreed. The emphasis for Marpeck was placed upon the church in the present which studied the Word under the direction of the Spirit to find solutions for the problems facing it. Whether this is a better hermeneutical approach than allowing tradition to help determine the meaning of the text is a moot question, but one should not ignore the problem that is raised once the consensus of interpreters becomes a hermeneutical principle. Perhaps it was an advantage for the development of Marpeck's hermeneutics that he did not read the Church Fathers very intensively.

[84] John Howard Yoder has supplied the evidence of this spiritualism among the Swiss Reformers expressed in the debates with the Anabaptists (op. cit.). Some of it is already gathered by John Horsch, "The Faith of the Swiss Brethren," MQR, V (1931), 7ff. It is not correct merely to say that Bucer is a spiritualist; but it is clear that as far as his arguments with Marpeck are concerned he used definite spiritualist arguments, such as the separation of the inner and outer baptism. J. Müller, although clear in his judgment that Bucer goes beyond Biblical evidence in his definition of the relation of the covenants (p. 202), notes that for Bucer the cross is not an historical event, not "Heilstat, als vielmehr Offenbarungsereignis" (p. 206). He gives no attention to Bucer's debates with Marpeck.

3. Pietist and Spiritualist: Caspar Schwenckfeld[85]

Whereas Bucer apparently moved from a neglect of the Old Testament in his preaching to an emphasis on it in political and social ethics, Schwenckfeld at first opposed Bucer's identification of the Old and New Testaments only to make a virtual about-face in his discussion with the Anabaptists. Since Marpeck had access to Schwenckfeld's earlier writings to Bucer he reminded Schwenckfeld of the latter's change a number of times. Whatever the precise change and the reasons for it may have been, the Anabaptists rightly or wrongly saw this only as another instance in which Schwenckfeld bowed to the pressure in order that he might be spared some persecution.

During his earlier life Schwenckfeld was dominated by Luther, but later as a result of the Eucharistic controversy he separated himself more and more from Wittenberg.[86] In his later life the Eucharistic controversy receded somewhat into

[85] Schwenckfeld studies have suffered much the same fate as Anabaptist studies. His opponents were used as sources for Schwenckfeld's views, and often no attempt was made to portray the Silesian's own theology. In an attempt to overcome this, the American church that bears his name began to publish the *Corpus Schwenckfeldianorum* (Leipzig: Breitkopf and Härtel) in 1907. The final volume (XVIII) was published in 1961. The *Corpus* fittingly honors the man who himself was no mean scholar, and is a tribute to the comparatively small group that could undertake and complete such an ambitious undertaking. The Associate and Managing Editor of the *Corpus,* Selina Gerhard Schultz, has also written a complete factual biography (*Caspar Schwenckfeld von Ossig,* Norristown, Penna., 1946). Prior to her work, the standard treatment was that of Karl Ecke, *Schwenckfeld, Luther und der Gedanke einer apostolischen Reformation* (Berlin, 1911). The most reliable interpretations of his theology are: Emanuel Hirsch, "Zum Verständnis Schwenckfelds," pp. 145-170 in *Festgabe für Karl Müller* (Tübingen, 1922); Joachim Wach, *Types of Religious Experience* (Chicago, 1951), pp. 135-170; Hans Urner, "Die Taufe bei Caspar Schwenckfeld," *ThLtzg,* 1948, col. 332f. His Christology has been treated especially by Hans Joachim Schoeps, *Vom himmlischen Fleisch Christi* (Tübingen, 1951). Rufus Jones, *op. cit.,* Ch. V, was one of the first sympathetic treatments of Schwenckfeld. For some recent attempts at evaluation, see *ME,* IV (suppl.) and Bergsten, *op. cit.* The fact that Marpeck disagreed so extensively with Schwenckfeld should not obfuscate the latter's greatness. He is called a Pietist here in the good sense of the term. Urner (*op. cit.,* col. 331) says Schwenckfeld was not a forerunner of Pietism, but its founder.

[86] Shown especially convincingly by Hirsch, *op. cit.,* and repeatedly acknowledged by Schwenckfeld.

the background. Concerning the Old Testament, Luther and Schwenckfeld were at first very close, as can be seen by Schwenckfeld's republication of Luther's book on the Mosaic Law, to which he wrote an appreciative introduction.[87] In the introduction Schwenckfeld notes that it is not in vain that Moses had such a mysterious death, the meaning of it being that he should not be made into an idol while in the grave. In spite of this there is daily strife about Moses' grave, and many seek perforce to resurrect him.[88] In the hope that this book by Luther would restore some perspective to the scene and help his readers to see the place Moses occupies in the Christian church, Schwenckfeld republished it.

On the other hand two of Schwenckfeld's biographers have observed that his basic criticism of the Reformed churches centered in his opinion that the basic mistake of the Reformers was a lack of clear differentiation between the Old and New Testaments, which resulted in Jewish legalism and an intolerance applied with the use of force.[89] One of the constant refrains in the earlier writings of Schwenckfeld is the importance of differentiating between the Old and New Testaments, the basis of much trouble in the church being this lack of differentiation.[90] Unless we observe this difference we cannot see why Christ came in the flesh, what benefits he gives us, or what a true Christian is. In a writing entitled "On the Difference Between the Old and New Testaments, the Symbol and the Truth," written approximately 1531, Schwenckfeld begins with a complaint about the trouble that has resulted in the past from a confusion (*Vermischung*) of the two Testaments (*CS*, IV, 417). Those who do not make a difference clearly enough come to the point where Moses is preferred to Christ (*CS*, IV, 418). Such an attitude brings them to the place where Christian piety is not valued higher than that of the heathen guided by natural law (to say nothing of the Jews in their works and ceremonies) and the church is considered little higher than the synagogue of Moses. Schwenckfeld's argument is this: even some learned writers say that they are the same in substance. All of this is to act as if Christ had died in vain, as if in his suffering and

[87] First published by Luther in 1527, and reprinted by Schwenckfeld in 1538 (*CS*, VI, 290-305).

[88] An idea that occurs also in Franck.

[89] Karl Ecke, *op. cit.*, p. 199 and Schultz, *op. cit.*, pp. 190-91.

[90] *CS*, IV, 470ff. Cf. also V, 133, 135; X, 159; XII, 849.

death he had accomplished nothing more than that the world should be slightly reformed, the Spirit multiplied somewhat, and the people in the old skin (*haut*) given a new name. Thus Christianity is created out of Judaism simply by the change of ceremonies. Some say that Christ is merely a preacher of the word of God in whom the prophetic spirit dwelt more fully than in the prophets, and thus he was able to declare God's will more fully. Others say that the gospel was present already in the Old Testament. This new Judaism has Christ on its lips, but Moses in its heart (CS, IV, 155), and Moses is called both a law-giver and an evangelist. Such confusion results from a mixture of the two Testaments, and Schwenck-feld will have no part in it (CS, IV, 419). Other groups that are guilty of a confusion of figure and truth, of Old and New Testaments, are the radicals and the enthusiasts, who also lack faith in Christ's work. Those who stress an essential difference between the two Testaments, like Irenaeus, fortunately are growing strongly today. They do not, like the enthusiasts, imagine that God merely renewed the Old Covenant. The enthusiasts speak of degrees of recognizing Christ, and hence the ancients did not know Christ as clearly as we do today. Abraham and the rest of the ancients had a hidden faith which is only revealed with Christ's coming (CS, IV, 434-39).

In a letter written to the brotherhood at Strasbourg on February 13, 1532, Schwenckfeld attempts to refute those who teach that in the Old Testament the suffering and merits of Christ and the benefits of salvation were proclaimed in the Jewish church order and preached openly as in the New Testament (CS, IV, 519-20). Such he seeks to refute with Scripture and show to be dangerous and false, for on this one article (i.e., differentiation of the two Testaments) nearly the whole ground of our salvation lies (CS, IV, 521). Schwenckfeld is also certain that without the merit of Christ's suffering and prior to it no man entered into heaven or was able to receive salvation. All holy fathers, patriarchs, and prophets waited for Christ and were, through faith, preserved for this realization of the promises in the bosom of Abraham (CS, IV, 522). Hence it is incontrovertible that they were not perfect before that nor could they see God or enter into heaven, their flesh being still covered with sin. They had a bad conscience; before God they were nothing and devoid of goodness until the Son of God cleansed them through his blood (*CS*, IV, 523). Not one of the ancients ascended into heaven before Christ but they all waited for the coming and redemption of Christ and could in no wise enter heaven before Christ.[91]

The importance of this point is that the suffering of Christ is thus put in its proper perspective (*CS*, IV, 548). People who mar the distinction between the two Testaments make invalid the suffering of our Lord Jesus Christ (*CS*, IV, 549), and the problem of the fall of the church (Schwenckfeld, like Franck, dates it 1400 years ago) can be partly accounted for by the mixture of the Law of Moses with the gospel. Some critics of Schwenckfeld rate the Old Testament too high and the New Testament too low, and confuse the issues with the problem of predestination (*CS*, IV, 550). If the redemptive work of Christ is not stressed, then Christ becomes little more than a prophet (*CS*, IV, 551).[92]

Again, in a letter to Leo Jud, written March 3, 1533, Schwenckfeld stressed the importance of this distinction.[93] Whoever is not able to discriminate between these two manners of dealing with God's people cannot walk with certainty in the Scriptures. He beclouds Christ and his rule, despises the grace of God, mixes Law and gospel, confuses the conscience, and destroys the incipient light, stumbling everywhere (*CS*, IV, 758). There are two vantage points from which God's dealings with man are to be judged. First of all, they must be seen from God's viewpoint. Here it is true that there is only one Testament, as only one Christ, and there is no Old Testament, for a distinction of time has no relevance with God. This way of dealing is too deep to fathom (*CS*, IV, 759). Secondly, there is man's viewpoint. God has only spo-

---

[91] *CS*, IV, 543, 544, 547. It was likely one of these writings that Marpeck showed to Musculus in 1542 as a result of which Musculus was "grimmig" toward Schwenckfeld (*CS*, VIII, 289).

[92] Schwenckfeld considers this subject most necessary, most beneficial, and worthy of much time (*CS*, IV, 555).

[93] *CS*, IV, 750-771. Heinold Fast in his dissertation, *Heinrich Bullinger und die Täufer* (Heidelberg, 1957), notes that this was an issue between Bullinger and Leo Jud (pp. 125, 266f.). Possibly in Bullinger's estimation Schwenckfeld was a negative influence for Jud. The argument of the unity of the covenants and of circumcision and baptism first stated by Zwingli received support by Bullinger's discovery of two passages in Tertullian and Lactantius. Both Zwingli and Leo Jud were informed of these passages (see Heinold Fast, "On the Beginnings of Bernese Anabaptism," *MQR*, XXXI [1957], 293).

ken once, so as far as he is concerned there is only one Testament; but we who are limited by human flesh heard it twice.[94]

There are three dangers for those who consider only one Testament. First, they are misled by the *providentia*, or choice of God. They consider too much God's revelation outside of Christ and think in too lofty terms, in eternal rather than temporal dealings. Because there were a few believers among the old Jewish people they view the Old Testament too highly (CS, V, 66). The second danger is that the hidden counsels of God are not allowed to remain figures or symbols of Christ. Whoever cannot judge the figures of the Old Testament in their order and attempts to reject allegories,[95] will remain with the Jew forever in the letter and derive little benefit from the Scriptures. The third and final danger is that these people who consider only one covenant do not know Jesus Christ. Later in a letter to Helene Streicher on March 15, 1536, Schwenckfeld states that the reason the teaching of the preachers has improved so little is that they mix in Moses too much with their teaching (CS, V, 660; cf. also CS, IV, 155). Indeed it would seem that this was a factor in Schwenckfeld's arrival at a policy of "*Stillstand*" (CS, IV, 818).

The above evidence leads to the conclusion that the importance of the distinction between the two covenants in Schwenckfeld's opinion cannot be overemphasized. This has led to the opinion of Karl Ecke, and also that of Schwenckfeld's most recent biographer, that Schwenckfeld insisted on this differentiation in opposition to the Reformed groups.[96]

However, this is but one side of the coin. While it is true that Schwenckfeld is aware of the importance of this distinction in his writings it became a point of contention between him and Marpeck after 1540. Schwenckfeld's starting point in the differentiation of the Old and New Testaments was the sacramental controversy. In 1531 he wrote an epistle in which

[94] The basis for this interpretation is Psalm 62:12 (Heb.), which he quotes: "Gott hatt ein mall geredt, zowej mall hab Ich das gehoret" (CS, IV, 760).

[95] On the importance of allegory see CS, IV, 762; VIII, 91: "The literal meaning is not the correct one of the Holy Spirit in the OT." His own use of allegory is constant and uninhibited (cf. CS, V, 460, 474ff.; VIII, 361ff.; X, 472, 543, 648, 944 [NT exposition]; XII, 149, 345ff., 462).

[96] *Vide supra,* p. 166.

he has shown that the sacrament of Christ does not come out of the Law of Moses and that it cannot be compared with the ceremonies and sacraments of the Old Testament. The sacraments of Christ have a much more wonderful understanding and usage than the ceremonies of the Old Testament.[97] What then were the ceremonies of the Old Testament? They were merely symbols and pointers that pointed to Christ, to his people, and to the New Testament, as a picture points to the reality (Heb. 10.1; Col. 2:17). As a figure ceases when the essence comes, so also the ceremonies of the Law have passed away with the appearance of the rule of Christ. For when that comes which is portrayed the sign no longer has any reason for existence. This line of reasoning Schwenckfeld follows up with a few rhetorical questions: Why should one put other signs in the place of those of the Old Covenant when the usefulness of the sign is past, as those who stress the sacraments assert about the sacraments of Christ? Schwenckfeld would pay attention to that which is symbolized and not to the useless symbol (CS, IV, 151).

This leads Schwenckfeld into an extended polemic against the position of Luther that Jesus began with the old ceremonies of Moses.[98] Does not such a position come close to taking from Christ the position of ground and rock? If one says that Christ began with Judaism and the Law of Moses and laid there the beginning and basis of his people one perpetuates an error that Schwenckfeld felt was held in his time almost universally with regard to the sacrament of baptism. If they would say that Christ transposed it from the Old, that is not said incorrectly, provided it is understood as Paul describes it in Ephesians 2:11-15. Christ truly removes man from the Old into the New; however, he does not do so through Jewish ceremonies or any external things, but through his Spirit and himself (CS, IV, 152).

Still others say that Jesus did not take the sacraments from the Law, but that he did institute new ones in place of the old legal ones. Thus circumcision would correspond to baptism, passover to the Lord's Supper. Such a thing could only happen in the old essence of the letter rather than in the newness

[97] CS, IV, 150. Later he argued against Luther's view of the real presence on the basis that the patriarchs could not have shared this physical eating (CS, IX, 231).
[98] WA, IV, 285, 305.

of the spirit of faith, and one ought rather to call it an evangelical Judaism than a new Christianity. It is also not correct to assume that the Lord instituted Christianity or began his reign with an outward sign, as, e.g., baptism.[99] In Schwenckfeld's opinion the identification of circumcision and baptism had been carried so far that many people did not know the basic distinction as to what was new and what was old, what was Judaism and what was Christianity.[100]

When Schwenckfeld attempts to differentiate clearly between them he asserts that the people were given a physical promise in the Old Covenant. In the New, however, they were given spiritual promises that extended into heaven and eternal life. Christian sacraments, consequently, are not signs or figures pointing forward to something yet to come, but they are mysteries, i.e., secret, obscure dealings of the spiritual Christ who lives in our hearts. The Old Testament sacraments stood in external elements and external beginnings being used by an external people in order that they might work from the externals to the internal things, to that which was future (CS, IV, 154).

In the second general epistle, "Concerning the Understanding, Use and Worthiness of the Sacrament of Christ," written May 21, 1531, it is made explicitly clear that the New Testament sacraments may in no wise be compared with the Jewish ceremonies (CS, IV, 116f.). The main point of the Jewish ceremonies is external, while the main point in the New Testament sacraments is the element of mystery. There is no element of continuity whatever; the New Testament sacraments are entirely independent of the Old (CS, IV, 149-177). While the ceremonies of the Old Testament prefigured those of the New, "it is nevertheless a unique work of God and a mystery of Jesus Christ revealed without the law" (CS, IV, 164-65).[101]

As far as the Lord's Supper is concerned, Schwenckfeld's spiritualistic approach led him to say that the real Lord's

---

[99] As Bucer asserted (Bericht, q iiib).

[100] CS, IV, 153. He also opposes the identification of circumcision with baptism in the section, De collatione circumcisionis & baptismi Christiani, in his Questiones de baptismi sacramento, written about 1530, CS, III, 846-858; and also VIII, 98; IX, 214-17.

[101] The whole discussion of external rites was distasteful to Schwenckfeld, as Hans Urner has shown (op. cit., col. 334, citing CS, XIV, 147f.).

Supper is not partaking of the external bread and the wine, but rather the inner fellowship with the Lord. When the question was raised whether the saints of the Old Testament held the Lord's Supper with Christ, he answered, "Yes." He held it also with the Canaanite woman and with Martha (CS, X, 404-07).

Furthermore, when the Anabaptists practiced baptism he accused them of basing baptism on the rite of circumcision (CS, XI, 850; XII, 676).[102] In view of such an irregular accusation one must remember that Schwenckfeld calls every form or externalization of religious experience "Judaism." It is at this point that his understanding of the Old Testament has relevance for every phase of his theology and particularly his view of church reform. Everything which builds and trusts in external things is "Judenthumb" (CS, V, 727).

In the church Christ works from the internal to the external not looking back to the Mosaic Law (CS, IV, 155). He does not direct himself according to the external, but desires much more that all externals direct themselves according to him and his Spirit. Where the internal mystery is lacking, the external act is in vain, indeed, is done unto judgment. Jesus could not have been called a perfect mediator of a New Testament if he would have had to get it from Moses or the old Jewish Law.

In the refutation of Oswald Glait[103] the Sabbatarian, written in 1532, Schwenckfeld lists eighteen differences between the Old and New Testaments.[104] The basic difference is that the Old Testament is promise, the New is fulfillment. Furthermore the Old Testament preceded and applies to sinners under the yoke of servitude, and the New follows and applies

---

[102] Hans Klöpfer von Feuerbach (CS, XII, 777). His charges against the Anabaptists sometimes lack consistency. For example, he congratulates them on distinguishing so clearly between John's and Christian baptism (CS, V, 438f.; VIII, 176) but soon thereafter has apparently forgotten their distinction (CS, XII, 736).

[103] On Glait see ME, II, 522-23, and also the article by W. Wiswedel, "Oswald Glait von Jamnitz," in Zeitschrift für Kirchengeschichte, LVI (1937), 550-564.

[104] The various titles of this book are given in CS, IV, 446ff. It is actually a letter to Leonard von Liechtenstein; and while it deals with the Christian Sabbath, it also treats the wider problem of the relation of the Old and New Testaments. It is printed in CS, IV, 453-518. Capito also wrote a refutation to it, in part reproduced by Krebs-Rott, pp. 363-385.

to the righteous in the freedom of the children of God. The Old has a bitter spirit, a spirit of compulsion; the New has a spirit of sonship, of power, joy, and love. The Old brings with it an outward knowledge according to the letter, outward signs, etc. The New brings with it a spiritual and true knowledge of God through which God himself lives, dwells, and rules in believing hearts. The Old has had physical, transient goods and promises; those of the New are spiritual. A study of these eighteen differences shows clearly that the external-internal, outer-inner contrast is most important for Schwenckfeld. The true use of the Law is that the old man through it would recognize his sin, wretchedness, and impotence and would then learn to seek Christ, the true Sabbath.[105]

The very same theme motivates another pamphlet written about 1531: "On the Difference Between the Old and New Testaments, the Symbol and the Truth" (*CS*, IV, 414-443). Here the Old Testament is defined as being composed completely of external transient deeds; hence it also had a temporal mediator, Moses, the faithful servant in the symbolic house of God. It had external people, Israel according to the flesh; an external unerasable mark of the covenant in the flesh; an external tabernacle, tent or temple; and externally prescribed worship service, customs, and ceremonies. It also had an external, written law (Paul's *mandatum carnale*).

Schwenckfeld distinguishes between two types of people in the Old Testament, for even Paul in Romans 4:11, 12; 9:7, 8, speaks of Abraham as being the father of two peoples, the external and the internal (*CS*, V, 67). God dealt with Abraham in two manners, "one the external figurative way and the other the internal spiritual, hidden way" (*ibid.*). Whenever one interprets the Old Testament, especially verses like Genesis 17:7, one must remember this. One must not confuse these two kinds of covenants. David, according to the flesh, was a Jew, subject to the same covenant as the Jews; but, according to the spirit of faith, according to the inner man, he was an heir of the faith, which was secretly hidden in his heart (*CS*, V, 68; cf. also VII, 195ff.).

Even though the difference between the two Testaments is observed, Schwenckfeld warns that this is not to be inter-

---

[105] *CS*, IV, 509. In V, 438:35 the OT is called a time of wrath while the NT is a time of grace.

preted as though "there were no members of the New
Covenant in the Old Testament; for all the saints already had
faith in the same way as the Christians, for faith made everything promised a present reality for them" (CS, V, 66; cf. also
VII, 193). Acts 15:10, a verse he already used to show that
Christians could be such without the use of the sacraments
when he was arguing against the Augsburg Confession, is
cited as evidence (CS, III, 915). For

> although Peter speaks in Acts 15:10 of the ceremonies of
> the law nevertheless he clearly asserts that both the
> Christians in the Old Testament (when there were no
> sacraments yet) and the Christians of the New in the
> same manner, through the grace of the Lord Jesus
> Christ are made righteous.[106]

When John Bader raised the question how the patriarchs
could have partaken of the body of Christ, he answered that
before God time means nothing; it all depends upon the
"living faith."[107] This faith was sufficient to make them
righteous and give them salvation, but it took place in a
hidden secret manner (CS, IV, 421). Hence it is to be noted
that the believers of the Old Testament, "to be sure in a hidden dark manner, just as much as we have shared in the sufferings of Christ. Through faith in the promise the Lamb was
slain for them from the foundation of the world" (CS, VI,
30f.).

In his pamphlet on rebirth written in 1538 he states that the
evidence that the saints of the Old Testament give of rebirth
is so overwhelming that it would be too much to write down;
even if he were to confine it to Isaiah, he would need to
transcribe the major share of his prophecies (CS, VII, 69).
One reason he refuses to insist on uniting external baptism
with salvation is that then "I would have to damn all the believing Fathers of the Old Testament, as well as now all unbaptized children" (CS, VII, 69).

Of special interest is the critique Schwenckfeld writes of
the Marpeck edition of Rothmann's *Bekentnisse*. He criticizes
their lack of comprehension of the faith of the patriarchs (CS,
VIII, 199). For true faith brings with it that which is still to

---

[106] CS, III, 881; cf. also V, 496; VI, 169; VII, 443; IX, 428.
[107] CS, IV, 26, 442; cf. also VII, 358, 578.

come in the future, "and so the ancient believers partook of Christ just as well as we who live after the incarnation." Grace ruled among the believers even under the Law, since the office of the Law was to point to Christ (*CS*, VIII, 206). This passage in Schwenckfeld's *Judicium* formed a major battleground between Marpeck's view of the Old Testament and Schwenckfeld's. This theme recurs throughout their controversy. As Bergsten has observed, while the subject may seem somewhat theoretical to us, it had practical consequences for both Schwenckfeld and Marpeck.[108]

Schwenckfeld's identification of the two Testaments reached its apex when he asserted that Christianity is older than Judaism (*CS*, IX, 670), and that Abraham was a Christian before he was a Jew (*CS*, VIII, 199).

In conclusion, Marpeck found two things objectionable in Schwenckfeld. With reference to the Old Testament he did not accept the position that everything relating to salvation was already accomplished in the Old Testament and that Christ came merely to reveal. Christ, insisted Marpeck, was more than a prophet who came to uncover something already there in a hidden manner. Christ's coming affected the salvation of mankind in a real and definitive way. Secondly, Marpeck refused to admit that Christ's commission to his church was now invalid. He fused the inner and outer and decisively rejected the neoplatonic streams that Schwenckfeld sought to inject into the life of the church.[109] The difference between Schwenckfeld and Franck and Bünderlin, Marpeck saw only

[108] *CS*, VIII, 221, 282, 283. Bergsten, *op. cit.*, pp. 83-87. On the relation of the *descensus ad inferos* to this view, see Vogelsang, *op. cit.* Jean Danièlou (*Holy Pagans of the Old Testament* [London, 1957]) widens the problem to include even non-Jews of the OT and notes some implications.

[109] Hans Urner (*op. cit.*, col. 335, footnote 3) has shown that the distinction between outer and inner so dear to the spiritualists came through Franciscan theology from neoplatonism, Augustine being the key person. The Picard, Peter Kanisch, expresses the position well when he says, "Spirit can only act on spirit, body only on body." A. W. Argyle ("'Outward' and 'Inward' in Biblical Thought," *ET*, LXVIII [1957], 196-99) views the distinction as a basically Hebraic category. Marpeck's missionary interest stems ultimately from his refusal to "spiritualize" any of the mandates of the New Testament or to relegate them to the apostolic age. On this missionary drive which characterizes all Anabaptists, see Wolfgang Schäufele, *Das missionarische Bewusstsein und Wirken der Täufer* (Neukirchen-Vluyn, 1966).

as one of degree. In the practical life of the church Schwenck-feld was more pietistic, but the effect was practically the same.

4. HANS DENCK, MELCHIOR HOFMANN, ET AL.

In addition to the above, a variety of other people left a deep imprint on the development of Marpeck's hermeneutics. Because of the nature of the case their impact is more difficult to analyze. Nevertheless certain traits that Marpeck has in common with these men he may well owe to them.

Through the work of Jan J. Kiwiet, Hans Denck has received a certain degree of prominence, which he merits, in the discussion of South German Anabaptism.[110] It is doubtful, however, that Kiwiet is correct in seeing Denck as the leader of South German Anabaptism, and even more doubtful that he can support his position that Marpeck was definitely indebted to Denck. Denck's name never occurs in Marpeck's writings, nor do any of his writings find a place in the *Kunstbuch*. Conceivably they were omitted from this collection of manuscripts because most of Denck's writings were already available in print, but it is likely that there is a more basic reason for the omission, namely, that he did not represent the Marpeck position.

Denck's nature was such that he did not get vitally involved in Anabaptist church life. He baptized only Hans Hut and appears to have had some misgivings about that, even if his "Recantation" was not actually such, as G. G. Röhrich and others have held.[111] Whether genuine or not this "Recantation" became the pattern for others like it, and the publicity it received would inevitably have prejudiced the Marpeck Anabaptists against claiming Denck as one of their leaders.[112]

---

[110] Jan J. Kiwiet, "The Life and Theology of Hans Denck," *loc. cit.*

[111] Georg Andreas Will (*Nürnbergisches Gelehrten-Lexicon*, I [Nürnberg and Altdorf, 1755], 245) says: "wiewol auf seine an Oecolampadium überschriebene Revocation nicht viel zu bauen ist." G. G. Röhrich, *Essai sur la vie, les écrits, et la doctrine de l'Anabaptiste Jean Denk* (Strasbourg, 1853), p. 31. Ludwig Keller (*Ein Apostel der Wiedertäufer* [Leipzig, 1882], pp. 321f.) supports this with some evidence contained in a letter by Oecolampadius to a friend.

[112] One clear case of another "Recantation" is that of Jörg Propst Rothenfelder, who signed a document (manuscript copy in SL) given to him by his interrogators at Augsburg in 1533. It contains some phrases that are identical to Denck's "Recantation."

More serious than what may be called the public-relations aspect of Denck's life is the decided spiritualistic strain that runs throughout his writings. Even in Marpeck's Strasbourg period there is no evidence of the depreciation of ceremonies seen in Denck, and they part ways decisively in their views of the Word of God. Even if it cannot be shown that Marpeck was dependent upon Denck in his view of the covenant or order, there does appear dependence on him at the point of asserting a great freedom in the ethical sphere, particularly such matters as the oath and participation in the state. Apart from that the influence of Denck on Marpeck does not seem to have been great.

Melchior Hofmann was in Strasbourg about the same time that Marpeck was, but there is no clear evidence of their meeting. Marpeck's friend Scharnschlager opposed Hofmann's Christology, and later Marpeck has only depreciatory words for Hofmann.[113] Nevertheless, it seems that Hofmann exerted considerable influence on Marpeck, especially in the area of hermeneutics. One of the emphases Marpeck may have taken from Hofmann is his sharp differentiation between Old and New Testaments.[114] If so, he changed its point considerably in making the difference more of a historical one than Hofmann did.

For Hofmann the difference between the Old and New Testaments was basically that of figure and essence. While Marpeck uses this, we have noted above that this is not the most frequent or most important distinction. The *Figur* is not a basic category for Marpeck, while it is the central category for Hofmann.[115]

Since modern scholars (particularly European) generally lump the "Schwärmer" all into the same group,[116] and do not differentiate between the Anabaptists and the enthusiasts, it may be well to look at Andreas Carlstadt briefly to see how he compares with Marpeck.[117] Carlstadt was deeply inter-

[113] Humanity of Christ, p. 208.

[114] As it appears especially in *Der Leuchter des alten Testaments ussgelegt,* Strassburg, 1529.

[115] Kawerau, *op. cit.*

[116] Following Holl, "Luther und die Schwärmer," *Gesammelte Aufsätze,* I, 420-467. Hans Urner says: "Schwenckfeld verwirft die Ceremonien nicht, wie die Täufer" (*op. cit.,* col. 337; cf. also col. 341).

[117] On Carlstadt, see Hermann Barge, *Andreas Bodenstein von Karlstadt* (Leipzig, 1905), 2 vols.

ested in the problem of the spirit and the letter and arrived at his position by reading St. Augustine's booklet on the subject. He was so impressed that he wrote a commentary on the treatise.[118] Since Carlstadt arrived at his position on this via Augustine it is not surprising that he would not influence Marpeck too greatly. The same is probably not the case in Carlstadt's treatment of the difference between the Old and New Testaments, for indirectly the radical distinction made between the two by Carlstadt influenced Marpeck as undoubtedly all of Anabaptism. It is possible that in Carlstadt the Anabaptists found the basic hermeneutical clue to which they clung tenaciously in the sixteenth century: the radical difference between the Old and New Testaments. Again it is clear, however, that Marpeck's debt to Carlstadt is minimal.

Positively, however, there is little doubt that Marpeck owes most to that noble group of martyrs and missionaries from Tyrol and South Germany, men like Hans Schlaffer, Leonhard Schiemer, Ambrosius Spittelmayer, and Hans Hut. The same love for the church and missionary drive characterize all of these men. Only Marpeck and Scharnschlager were called to consolidate the gains that had been made by these men in the brief months of their labors. Differences that emerge are the result not only of differences of temperament, but, most important, of tactics. The Anabaptist movement had changed from a first-generation pneumatic movement to a second-generation group, surging still with vibrant energy, but seasoned by years of costly and bitter experience. The Reformers, too, had learned that the Anabaptist movement could not be eradicated by the shedding of blood, for the more they killed the leaders, the faster the movement seemed to forge ahead.

It would be unfair to infer that Marpeck was indebted only negatively to non-Anabaptists and positively to Anabaptists. The man who made the most profound effect on Marpeck was Martin Luther; indeed, the indications that Marpeck is indebted to Luther are so extensive they cannot be pursued here.

Conclusion

It has not been the major purpose of this chapter to delineate the various strands that make up Marpeck's hermeneutic. This would be a task in itself. Rather the purpose

---

[118] Barge, *op. cit.*, I, 72; II, 533f.

was to indicate some possible positive sources and also to indicate why certain emphases gained the importance they did. It became apparent that Marpeck's strong antispiritualistic strain came about through his contacts with spiritualists: the radicals—Franck and Bünderlin, the moderates—Bucer and Schwenckfeld.[119] We noted that it is possible that both Hofmann and Carlstadt influenced Marpeck in so sharply differentiating between the Old and New Testaments but that he owed nothing to either of these men on the view he took on spirit and letter. The way in which he saw the letter enslaving his fellow Anabaptists did not force him to go either the way of the spiritualists or that of Luther, but compelled him to find his own way. That he did so stands as a tribute to this man who never had a formal theological education.

[119] Urner (*op. cit.*, col. 331) says that we will need to reckon Schwenckfeld as a spiritualist even though we remain aware of the differences between him and Franck.

V

RETROSPECT AND PROSPECT

Our study has revealed that Marpeck's hermeneutic was determined by two major problems. These two problems have plagued not only the Anabaptist-Mennonite church but have also been a thorn in the flesh of the ecumenical church throughout the centuries. No group has ever claimed to have fully solved the problem of the Old Testament or the tension between the spirit and the letter.

Marpeck resolved these problems by viewing the Old Testament as being secondary to the New and superseded by the full revelation of the Son of God. At no point could the Old Testament be brought in to attenuate the Christian ethic or to revert the Christian church from freedom to bondage. The provisional role of the Old Testament was fulfilled; and while it was important for the Christian to read the record of God's dealing with his people, the practices and standards of the Old Testament dare not become normative for the church. In doing so there are some indications that Marpeck borders on Marcionitism, particularly when he discusses the wrath of God (*KB*, fol. 12b) in the Old Testament or when he says that "the law of revenge was given through Moses, grace and truth came to us through Christ" (*KB*, fol. 171). It may be that Marpeck's style carried him away here. At any rate one looks in vain for any extended dualism between the God of the Old Testament and the New. His emphasis on history, on the centrality of the covenant, but especially on the promissory nature of the Old Testament makes the continued use and appreciation of the Old Testament inevitable. Only when parts of his position have been isolated from the whole does the Old Testament become as unimportant as it has been in many subsequent Anabaptist-Mennonite churches.

The same is true of Marpeck's position with respect to the letter and the spirit. During his time the one who insisted on the letter was venerated for "holding the line," and this has often been repeated. Those who have emphasized the Biblical concepts of freedom and responsibility, whether it be of the individual conscience or of the congregation, have been looked at with suspicion. Perhaps this was deserved insofar as this emphasis on liberty was reactionary; but where it is wedded to the Pauline emphasis, as was the case in Marpeck's thinking, one cannot escape the conviction that the better road, albeit the harder one, was chosen. He who is in Christ is free, but he who is not in Christ is the most enslaved of all, regardless of how free he may consider himself to be. Marpeck's position has exerted no influence at all in the group where he had such prominence in the early years, and it may well be that this accounts in some measure for the development of that group.

The point at which his hermeneutic speaks directly to the modern church situation is in its rejection of rampant individualism. The Bible cannot be studied alone; it must always be studied with the brother. The modern church, especially the ecumenical church, is acutely aware of this, but in the sixteenth century there is less evidence that this was of great importance. It should also be noted that Marpeck thinks of the church in its widest sense. He did not restrict his conversations to Anabaptists, but in Strasbourg conversed with Capito, Bucer, and Sturm, and in Augsburg with Wolfgang Musculus. On this point, too, Marpeck speaks to those who would claim him as a founder of what is known as the "free-church tradition." Discussion with the brother proceeds with the one closest, moving on into ever-widening spheres of conversation. Such discussion is Christologically based because the church is the body of Christ and cannot be rent by divisions. Marpeck's followers already in the sixteenth century actively pursued union discussions with the Moravian Brethren, thus giving us the only clear instance of Anabaptists exploring church union with Christians not of their group.[1] Surely here is clear evidence that all free-church people, by remaining aloof from

---

[1] See J. Th. Müller, "Die Berührungen der alten und neuen Brüderunität mit den Täufern," *Zeitschrift für Brüdergeschichte*, IV (1910), 180-208. Müller gives extracts of the record of these conversations in German. J. K. Zeman kindly informed me that these are substantially accurate but that he has published the complete Czech original in *Pravda*, XXXIX (1958, Chicago, Ill.), under the title: "Rozhovory ceskych bratri a novokrtenci na Morave."

ecumenical discussions, betray not only their Lord but also their own heritage!

This aloofness is the more lamentable since one of the hermeneutical issues in the current ecumenical conversations deals with the relation of the Old and New Testaments.[2] Whether Marpeck has anything to say to his own confession or to the ecumenical church would depend upon the degree to which his approach is that of the Scriptures themselves. He himself would insist that at each point the brotherhood subject his position to the penetrating ray of God's Word. Whether Kiwiet is right in asserting that Marpeck is closer to the Hebraic mentality than his contemporaries only a detailed exegesis of the Biblical material and comparison with Marpeck's position can decide.[3] Perhaps with the increasing interest in this unusual person this task will some day be undertaken. It could well be an important contribution to Anabaptist theology and might also help us to determine in how far the Anabaptists were Biblical Christians. It is apparent in any event that Marpeck deserves a wider hearing than he has received.

Excursus II: Marpeck and the descensus ad inferos

The sentence in the Apostles' Creed, "He descended into hell," has been a source of embarrassment to the church ever since the second century. Some have regarded it as a fossilized relic, which ought to be disposed of;[4] others have felt that it deserves a place in the Creed and has some Scriptural support.

During the Reformation this became a topic for extensive discussion.[5] This discussion was to some extent a break with the scholastic formulation of the problem where both the topography of "hell" and the chronology of the visit were of considerable interest. Jesus entered only that part of hell in which the patriarchs dwelt, but his influence extended to all

[2] *The Ecumenical Review*, XI:4 (July, 1959), 447.

[3] Kiwiet, *op. cit.*, p. 150.

[4] Adolf Harnack (*Marcion*, p. 169) says: "Was heute in den Kirchen eine vertrocknete Reliquie ist, war damals nicht nur *ein* sondern nahezu *das* Hauptstück der Verkündigung vom Erlöser."

[5] See Vogelsang, *op. cit.* Werner Bieder (*Die Vorstellung von der Höllenfahrt Jesu Christi* [Zürich, 1949]) deals with the Reformation only in passing.

parts. To the lowest hell where the damned dwelt he brought a glorious manifestation of his victory, which would frighten the demons and convict the damned of their unbelief and eternal lostness. To those in purgatory he brought comfort and hope. The most important aspect of his mission was to free the pre-Christian saints who were waiting in the vestibule of hell and take them to heaven in his glorious train of victory. Conspicuous by its absence is any reference to the implications of this view for the Christian in the present.

Under the influence of mysticism topography became less important and personal influence took on greater significance. Both Eckhardt and the *Theologia Deutsch* related Christ's *descensus* to the believer's *resignatio ad infernum* which puts an end to all self-love and self-will. This interpretation is directly correlated with Christ's descent.

Vogelsang notes in connection with Luther's view of the *descensus* that the element "*pro nobis*" comes strongly to the fore. The totality of demonic forces was routed by Christ's descent so that the Christian need no longer fear the devil. Any moralism connected with the descent was rejected and Luther had increasingly less interest in the location of "hell." His *descensus* doctrine is an integral part of his theology of the cross (cf. also *RGG*, III, cols. 408f.).

Zwingli, Bullinger, Oecolampadius, and Martin Bucer more or less viewed the *descensus* as merely a surrogate for the burial of Christ. To Calvin the *limbus* view is nothing but a fable (*Institutes*, II, XVI, 9) and the substitutionary value of Christ's suffering was prominent. The *descensus* was necessary for Christ and for him alone because by it he felt the severity of the divine vengeance, in order to appease the wrath of God and satisfy his justice (*Institutes*, II, XVI).

The Anabaptists apparently adopted the traditional view on the *descensus*, and it is discussed in three Anabaptist commentaries on the Apostles' Creed. For Schiemer, Hut, and Schlaffer, the *descensus* is a point at which the Christian identifies himself with his Lord; and unless he does so he will not be permitted to ascend with Christ (*vide supra*, p. 133). Schlaffer uses the term "*tiefe Christi*," and may be the source for Marpeck's use of this term.

Marpeck's view consists of the following points:

(1) The insistence that the *descensus* was the turning point in the status of the patriarchs of the Old Testament.

(2) The identification of the Christian in both the victorious and the humiliating aspects of the *descensus*.

(3) There is a fuzziness on the exact place to which Christ descended, partly because of the various Biblical terms, and partly because this is not the most significant aspect.

It would appear from this that Marpeck's interest in this part of the Apostles' Creed is stimulated by motifs from mysticism. These he blends with some strands of scholastic teaching, and perhaps also with Luther's. It is not impossible that his interest was fostered by reading the Gospel of Nicodemus, for many editions of this book were published in German in the sixteenth century. The fact that the strand of humiliation so prominent in Marpeck is almost totally absent from the Gospel of Nicodemus militates against this view.[6]

[6] *ME*, III, "Nicodemus, Gospel of," offers an inadequate survey of the influence of this book, even as far as Marpeck is concerned. It should also be noted that the Apostles' Creed did not have the *descensus* sentence until A.D. 370 (so Bo Reicke in *RGG, loc. cit.*).

BIBLIOGRAPHY

A. PRIMARY SOURCES PERTAINING TO PILGRAM MARPECK
(listed chronologically)

(Pilgram Marpeck) *Ain klarer vast nützlicher vnterricht / wider ettliche Trück / vnd schleichendt Geyster / so jetz in verborgener weiss aussgeen / . . .* , 1531 (photostatic copy of title page in MQR, XXXIII [1959], 20). Photostatic reproduction of British Museum copy, Associated Mennonite Biblical Seminaries (AMBS) Library.

(Pilgram Marpeck) *Clare verantwurtung ettlicher Artickel / so jetz durch jrrige geyster schrifftlich vnnd mündtlich ausschweben / von wegen der ceremonien dess Newen Testaments . . .* , 1531. Photostatic reproduction of Stuttgart Library copy, AMBS Library.

Krebs, Manfred, and Hans Georg Rott, *Quellen zur Geschichte der Taüfer*, VII. Band, Elsass, I Teil Stadt Strassburg, 1522-1532 (Mit Benutzung der von Joh. Adam hinterlassenen Material-sammlung), Gütersloh, 1959 (Marpeck's *Confession* of 1532).

Wenger, John C., ed., "Pilgram Marpeck's Confession of Faith, 1531 (!), A Hitherto Unpublished Document Transcribed and Edited from the Original," MQR, XII (1938), 167-202. This text of the *Confession* is here followed and checked with the photo-static copies of the original supplied by Wenger.

Das Kunstbuch, ed. Jörg Propst Rothenfelder, auch genant Maler, 1561 (Manuscript) containing sixteen letters by Marpeck. Samuel Geiser's transcription in typescript deposited in GCL. Sources were checked with the microfilm deposited at Bluffton College Library through the courtesy of Delbert Grätz, Li-brarian.

(Pilgram Marpeck) *Vermanung auch gantz klarer gründtlicher un(d) unwidersprechlicher bericht zu warer Christlicher ewigbestendiger pundtsvereynigung allen waren glaubigen frummen und gutt-hertzigen menschen zu hilff . . .* (1542?). Hege's edition in the *Gedenkschrift* was checked with a photostatic reproduction of the British Museum copy.

187

188 COVENANT AND COMMUNITY

(Pilgram Marpeck) *Verantwurtung über Casparn Schwenckfelds Judicium . . .*, Johann Loserth, ed., *Quellen und Forschungen zur Geschichte der oberdeutschen Taufgesinnten im 16. Jahrhundert. Pilgram Marbecks Antwort auf Kaspar Schwenckfelds Beurteilung des Buches der Bundesbezeugung von 1542*, Vienna and Leipzig, 1929.

Bergsten, Torsten, "Two Letters by Pilgram Marpeck," *MQR*, XXXII (1958), 192-210.

(Pilgram Marpeck) *Testamenterleütterung. Erleütterung durch ausszug auss Heiliger Biblischer schrifft / tail vnd gegentail / sampt ainstails angehangen beireden . . .* (no date, no place), microfilm in AMBS Library.

Röhrich, T. W., "Zur Geschichte der strassburgischen Wiedertäufer . . . ,"*Zeitschrift für die historische Theologie*, 1860, pp. 3-121.

Fast, Heinold, ed., *Der linke Flügel der Reformation*. Bremen: Carl Schünemann Verlag, 1962, pp. 105-137.

B. SECONDARY SOURCES PERTAINING TO PILGRAM MARPECK

Bender, H. S., "Pilgram Marpeck, Anabaptist Theologian and Civil Engineer," *MQR*, 38 (1964), 231-265.

Bergsten, Torsten, "Pilgram Marbeck und seine Auseinandersetzung mit Caspar Schwenckfeld," *Kyrkohistorisk Årsskrift*, 1957 and 1958, pp. 39-135 (offprint).

Fast, Heinold, "Pilgram Marbeck und das oberdeutsche Täufertum. Ein neuer Handschriftenfund," *ARG*, 47 (1956), 212-242.

Källstigen, Olof, *Der Mensch Christus als Eckstein*, Stockholm Diss., 1964.

Kiwiet, Jan J., *Pilgram Marbeck, ein Führer der Täuferbewegung der Reformationszeit*, Kassel, 1957.

Klassen, William, "Anabaptist Hermeneutics," *MQR*, 40 (1966), 83-111.

Loserth, Johann, "Zwei biographische Skizzen aus der Zeit der Wiedertäufer in Tirol," *Zeitschrift des Fernandeums für Tirol und Vorarlberg*, III, Folge, Heft 39, Innsbruck (1895), pp. 279-288.

Quiring, Horst, "Die Anthropologie Pilgram Marbecks," *Menn. Geschbl.*, 1937, pp. 10-17.

Wenger, John C., "The Life and Work of Pilgram Marpeck," *MQR*, XII (1938), 137-166.

————, "The Theology of Pilgram Marpeck," *MQR*, XII (1938), 205-256.

————, "Additional Note on the Life and Work of Pilgram Marpeck," *MQR*, XII (1938), 269-270.

Widmoser, Eduard, "Das Täufertum im Tiroler Unterland," Diss. Leopold Franzens Universität in Innsbruck, 1948.

————, "Das Tiroler Täufertum," *Tiroler Heimat*, XV (1951), 45-89; XVI (1952), 103-128.

Wiswedel, Wilhelm, "Die Testamentserläuterung. Ein Beitrag zur Täufergeschichte," *Blätter für württembergische Kirchengeschichte*, 41 (1937), 64-76.

––––––, *Bilder und Führergestalten aus dem Täufertum*, Kassel, Vol. I (1928), Vol. II (1930), Vol. III (1952).

Wray, Frank J., "The 'Vermanung' of 1542 and Rothmann's 'Bekentnisse,'" *ARG*, 47 (1956), 243-251.

C. PRIMARY SOURCES PERTAINING TO THE REFORMATION AND ANABAPTISM

Acta Des gesprächs zwüschen Predicantenn Vnnd Teuffbruderenn Ergannen, Inn der Statt Bernn von xj^a Mertzenns biss vf den xvij^a Desselben Monats Im MDXXXVIIIten Jar, GCL.

Althamer, Andreas, *Diallage, Hoc est, concilatio locorum scripturae, qui prima facie inter se pugnare uidentur*, Nürenberg, 1527.

Ambergius, Andreas, *Disputatio contra Anabaptistarum errores*, Wittenberg, 1598 (not accessible).

Andree, Jakob, *Drey / und / dreissig Predigen Von dem fürnembsten Spaltungen in der Christlichen Religion. . . .*, Tübingen, 1568.

Bergsten, Torsten, and Gunnar Westin, *Balthasar Hübmaier: Schriften*, Gütersloh, 1962.

(Bild, Veit) S. V. P., *Grund und schriftliche Anzeigungen aus heiliger Schrift des einen artickels halber unsers Glaubens, nämlich dass Christus zur Hoelle hinuntergestiegen und gefahren sei*, Philip Ulhart: Augsburg (?), 1525.

Bucer (Butzer), Martin, et al., *Bericht auss der heyligen geschrift von der recht gottseligen anstellung und haushaltung Christlicher gemeyn, Eynsatzung der diener des worts, Haltung vnd Brauch der heyligen Sacramenten*, Strasbourg, 1534.

––––––, et al., *Ein Summarischer vergriff der Christlichen lehre vnd Religion . . .*, Strasbourg, 1548. Reprint in *Revue d'histoire et de philosophie religieuses*, 31 (1951), 12-100.

––––––, *Grund und Ursach aus gotlicher schrift der neuerungen . . .*, Strassburg, 1524.

––––––, *Enarrationum in Evangelia Matthaei, Marci & Lucae*, Strasbourg, 1527 (especially the section "De discrimine veteris et novi testamenti . . .," pp. 148-159), Swift Library, University of Chicago.

––––––, *Enarratio in evangelion Johannis, praefatio, summum Disputationis & Reformationis . . .*, Strasbourg, 1528 (especially the section "Defensio paedobaptismi et verum populi veteris et novi discrimen" from fol. 39-54).

––––––, *Quid de baptismate infantium iuxta scripturas Dei sentiendum*, 1533 (letter to Rothmann).

––––––, *Wie leicht unnd füglich Christliche vergleichung der Religion, und des gantzen kirchendiensts Reformation . . .*, Strasbourg, 1545.

––––––, ed. Max Lenz, *Briefwechsel Landgraf Philipps des Grosmüthigen von Hessen mit Bucer*, 3 Teile, Leipzig, 1880, 1887, 1891.

————, ed. Henri Strohl, *Traite de l 'amour du proclaim*, Paris, 1949 (edition of Bucer's *Das ym selbs niemandt . . .* [Strasbourg, 1523], and French translation in *Cahiers de la Revue d'histoire et de philosophie religieuses*, No. 32, Paris, 1951).

Bullinger, Heinrich, *In omnes apostolicas epistolas . . . commentarii . . . de Testamento dei unico & aeterno*, Tiguri, 1549.

————, *Von dem einigen vnnd ewigen Testament oder Pundt Gottes*, Zürich, 1539 (?).

————, *De Testamento seu foedere Dei unico & aeterno . . .* , Tiguri, 1534.

————, *Den Widertoufferen ursprung, fürgang, Secten wäsen, furnemen und gemeine jrer leer, Artickel . . .* , Zürich, 1561.

————, Lütge, H. A. J., and G. Oorthuys, *Heinrich Bullingers Het Eenige en Eeuwige Testament of Verbond Gods*, Groningen, 1923.

————, Schiess, Traugott, *Bullinger's Korrespondenz mit den Graubündnern*, I-III (*Quellen zur Schweizerischen Geschichte*, 23), Basel, 1904ff.

Bünderlin, Johannes, *Eine gemeyne Einlaytung in den aygentlichen Verstand Mosi, und der Profeten, wie man sie lesen und in Allegorien mit dem neuen Testament vergleichen und auslegen soll. . .* , 1529 (but not the first edition).

————, *Aus was ursach sich Gott in die nyder gelassen und in Christo vermenschet ist, . . .* , Strassburg, 1529.

————, *Eine gemeyne Berechnung über der Heiligen Schrift Inhalt*, Strassburg, 1529.

————, *Erklärung durch Vergleichung der biblischen geschrifft, das der Wassertauff sampt anderen éusserlichen gebrauchen in der Apostolischen Kirchen geübet. On Gottes befelch und zeugniss der Geschrifft von etlichen dieser Zeit wider efert wird. . .* , (no place), 1530.

Concordantz und Zeiger der namhafftigsten Sprüch aller Biblischen Bücher alts und news Testaments, no place, no date.

Concordantz und zeyger der sprüch und historien, aller biblischen bücher alts news Testaments . . . , Lienhart Brunner, ed., Strassburg, 1530.

Denck, Hans, *Schriften 2. Teil, Religiöse Schriften*, Walter Fellmann, ed., Gütersloh, 1956.

Eder, George, *Evangelische Inquisition Wahrer und falscher Religion*, Ingolstadt, 1590 (Preface dated 1573).

Ein schoens Gesprech / zwischen aim Edelman / vnd seinem Knecht / vom Apostolischen Tauff / vnd die gehorsam der Oberkait belangend / Vnd wie der Knecht sich durch den Edelman vnnd sein Pfarherren / mit hailiger Schrifft weysen lasst, Augsburg, 1527 (?).

Eleutherobios, Stoffel (Christoph Freisleben), *Vom warhafftigen Tauff Joannis, Christi, und der Aposteln. Wann und wie die Kindertauff angefangen und eingerissen hat*, no place, 1528.

Erhard, Christoff, *Gruendtliche kurz verfasste Historia von Münsterischen Widertauffern . . .* , München, 1598.

Faber, Johannes, *Christliche vndterweisung an die Widertauffer von dem Tauff der Jungen Kindlein*, Ingolstadt, 1550.

———, *Von dem Ayd Schwoeren, Auch von der gemainschaft der Widertäuffer*, no place, 1550.

Franck, Sebastian, *Paradoxa ducenta octoginta das ist / CCLXXX Wunderred vnd gleichsam Räterschafft / aus der heiligen schrift*, no place, no date (1534?), Princeton Theological Seminary Library copy; Ziegler edition of Jena, 1909.

——— (?), *Unterschied des Alten und Neuen Testaments* (Title page missing, place and date missing), in Sammelband LXXIII, SL; contains other writings by Franck, Schwenckfeld, and Oecolampadius.

———, *Das verbütschiert mit siben Sigeln verschlossen Buch, das recht niemandt auffthun, verstehen, oder lesen kan, dann das Lamb, und die mit dem Thaw bezaichnet* . . . , 1539.

———, *Die guldin Arch darein der Kern unnd die besten hauptsprüch, der Heyligen Schrift, alten Leerer und Vater der Kirchen* . . . , 1557.

———, *Chronica, zeytbuch und geschychtbibel von anbegyn biss inn diss gegenwertig* . . . *jar*, Strassburg, 1531.

Gansforth, Wessel, *Life and Writings*, ed. Edward Waite Miller and Jared Waterburg Scudder, London, 1917.

Greyffenberger, Hanns, *Ein tröstliche ermanung den angefochtenen im gewissen / von wegen gethoner sund wye vnd wamit / Sye getröst werdenn / Den sathan / sich nit erschrecken lassen,* . . . , no place, 1524.

Hätzer, Ludwig, *Der Prophet Maleathi mit ausslegung Joann Ecolampadij, durch in im latein beschriben, mit fleyss verdeutscht,* 1526, SL.

———, *Eyn Urtayl Gottes unsers Eegemahels, wie man sich mit allen götzen und bildnussen halten soll, auss der heyligen geschrifft getzogen*, Breslau, 1524.

Hedio, Caspar, *Chronica der Altenn Christlichen kirchen aus Eusebio, Ruffino, Sozomeno, Theodoreto, Tertulliano, . . . und Plinio durch C. H. verteutcht*, Strassburg durch Georgium Ulricher von Andlo im Jenner 1530 gedruckt, SL.

Hofmann, Melchior, *Der Leuchter des alten Testaments ussgelegt*, Strassburg, 1529.

Hübmaier, Balthasar, W. O. Lewis, and G. D. Davidson, eds., "The Writings of Balthasar Hübmaier," an unpublished translation of Hübmaier's collected works in the Library of William Jewell College, Liberty, Missouri, dated 1939.

Jenny, Beatrice, *Das Schleitheimer Täuferbekenntnis, 1527*, Thayngen, 1951.

Kessler, Johannes, *Sabbata*, Emil Egli and Rudolf Schoch, eds., St. Gallen, 1902.

Krebs, Manfred, *Quellen zur Geschichte der Täufer*, Vol. IV, *Baden und Pfalz*, Gütersloh, 1951.

Menius, Justus, *Der Widdertäuffer lere und geheimnis*, Wittenberg, 1530.

Mosheim, Johann Lorenz, *Versuch einer unpartheiischen und gründlichen Ketzergeschichte*, Helmstaedt, 1746.

Müller, Lydia, "Unpublished Collection of High German Anabaptist Materials," planned as a second volume of her *Glaubenszeugnisse*, no place, no date, microfilm in GCL.

————, *Glaubenszeugnisse oberdeutscher Taufgesinnter*, Leipzig, 1938.

Müller, J. Th., "Die Berührungen der alten und neuen Brüderunität mit den Täufern," *Zeitschrift für Brüdergeschichte*, IV (1910), 180-234.

Musculus, Wolfgang, *Ain frydsams vnnd Christlichs Gesprech, ains Euangelischen, auff ainer, vnd ains Widerteüffers auff der anderen seyten, so sy des Aydschwurs halben mit ainander thund*, Augsburg, Preface dated July 28, 1533.

Oecolampadius, Jo., *Underrichtung von dem Widertauff, von der Oberkeit und von dem Eyd . . .* , Basel, 1527.

Ottio, Joh. Henrico, *Annales Anabaptistici, hoc est, Historia universalis de Anabaptistarum origine . . .* , Basel, 1672.

Protocoll. Das ist Alle Handlung des Gesprechs zu Franckenthal inn der Churfürstlichen Pfaltz, mit denen so man Widertäuffer nennet, Auff den 28, May angefangen, und den 19. Junii dises 1571 jars geendet, 1573.

Rhegius, Urbanus, *Wie man fürsichtiglich und ohne ärgerniss reden soll von den fürnemesten artikeln christlicher lehre 1536* (reprinted in *Quellenschriften zur Geschichte des Protestantismus*, Vol. 6).

————, *Zwen wunderseltzam sendbrieff / zweyer Widertauffer . . .* , Augsburg, 1528.

Rothmann, Bernhard, *Zwei Schriften des Münsterschen Wiedertäufers Bernhard Rothmann*, Heinrich Detmer and Robert Krumbholtz, eds., Dortmund, 1904.

Schwenckfeld, Caspar, *Corpus Schwenckfeldianorum*, C. D. Hartranft, E. E. S. Johnson and S. G. Schultz, eds., vols. I-XVIII, Leipzig, 1907-1961.

Spittelmayer, Hans, *Entschuldigung Johannes Spitelmayer, Prediger zu Nicolspurg . . .* , 1524.

Tauler, Johann, *Predigten*, Leopold Naumann, ed., Leipzig, 1923.

————, *Die Predigten Taulers, Deutsche Texte des Mittelalters XI*, Ferdinand Vetter, ed., Berlin, 1910.

Thormann, G., *Probier-Stein oder Schriftmässige und auss dem wahren innerlichen Christenthumb hergenommene Gewissenhafte Prueffung Dess Taufferthums In der Forcht dess Herrn . . .* , Bern, 1693.

Wenger, John C., "The Schleitheim Confession of Faith," *MQR*, 19 (1945), 243-253.

Williams, George Huntston, and Angel M. Mergal, *Spiritual and Anabaptist Writers*, Philadelphia, 1957.

Zieglschmid, A. J. F., *Die älteste Chronik der Hutterischen Brüder*, Ithaca, New York, 1943.

Zyegler, Clement, *Von der waren niessung beim leibs und bluts Christi . . . Und von dem tauf*, Strasbourg, 1524.

D. SECONDARY SOURCES PERTAINING TO THE REFORMATION
AND ANABAPTISM

Adams, J., *Evangelische Kirchengeschichte der Stadt Strassburg bis zur Französischen Revolution*, Strassburg, 1922.

Aland, Kurt, "Luther as Exegete," *ET*, LXIX (1957), pp. 45-48; 68-70.

Althaus, Paul, "Martin Luther über die Kindertaufe," *Theologische Literaturzeitung*, Vol. 73 (December 1948), cols. 705-714.

Anrich, Gustav, *Martin Bucer*, Strassburg, 1914.

Argyle, A. W., " 'Outward' and 'Inward' in Biblical Thought," *ET*, LXVIII (1957), 196-99.

Armour, Rollin, *Anabaptist Baptism*, Scottdale, Penna., 1966.

Augustine, *De spiritu ac litera*, The Nicene and Post-Nicene Fathers, First Series, V, 80-115 (written about 412).

Bainton, Roland, *Bibliography of the Continental Reformation, Materials Available in English*, Chicago, American Society of Church History, 1935.

————, "The Immoralities of the Patriarchs according to the Exegesis of the Late Middle Ages and of the Reformation," *HTR*, XXIII (1930), 39-49.

Baring, Georg, "Neues von der 'Theologia Deutsch' und ihre weltweiten Bedeutung, *ARG*, 48 (1957), 1-10.

Barth, Markus, *Die Taufe, Ein Sakrament?*, Zollikon-Zürich, 1951.

Baum, J. W., *Capito und Butzer, Strassburger Reformatoren*, in *Leben und Ausgewählte Schriften der Väter und Begründer der reformierten Kirche*, Teil III, Elberfeld, 1860.

Baumgärtel, F., *Verheissung: Zur Frage des evangelischen Verständnisses des AT*, 1952.

Bender, Harold S., *Conrad Grebel*, Goshen, Indiana, 1950.

————, "Recent Progress in Research in Anabaptist History," *MQR*, VIII (1934), 3-17.

————, "Bibliographical and Research Notes: I, General and Bibliographical," *MQR*, XXIV (1950), 88-91.

Bergfried, Ulrich, *Verantwortung als theologisches Problem im Täufertum des 16. Jahrhunderts*, Wuppertal-Elberfeld, 1938.

Bieder, Werner, *Die Vorstellung von der Höllenfahrt Jesus Christi*, Zürich, 1949.

Blanke, Fritz, "Beobachtungen zum ältesten Täuferbekentnisse," *ARG*, 37 (1940), 246-47.

————, "Täufertum und Reformation," *Reformatio*, VI (1957), 212-223.

————, *Brüder in Christo*, Zürich, 1955.

Bornkamm, Heinrich, "Studien zu Luthers Anschauung vom Alten Testament," *ARG*, 40 (1943), 30-61.

————, *Luther und das Alte Testament*, Tübingen, 1948.

————, *Martin Bucers Bedeutung für die europäische Reformationsgeschichte*, Gütersloh, 1952.

194 COVENANT AND COMMUNITY

Bossert, Gustav, "Aus den nebenkirchlichen religiösen Bewegungen der Reformationszeit in Württemberg," *Blätter für württembergische Kirchengeschichte,* 33 (1929), 1-41.

Brinkel, Karl, *Die Lehre Luthers von der fides infantium bei der Kindertaufe,* Berlin, 1958.

Burckhardt, Paul, *Die Basler Täufer, Ein Beitrag zur schweizerischen Reformationsgeschichte,* Basel, 1898.

Burrage, Champlin, *The Church Covenant Idea, Its Origin and Development,* Philadelphia, 1904.

Calvin, John, *Institutes of the Christian Religion,* John Allen, trans., 6th American edition, Philadelphia, no date.

Castrén, Olavi, *Die Bibeldeutung Calvins,* Helsinki, 1946.

Cohen, Boaz, "Note on Letter and Spirit in the New Testament," *HTR,* XLVII (1954), 197-203.

Coppens, J., *Vom christlichen Verständnis des Alten Testaments,* Louvain, 1952.

Cornelius, C. A., *Geschichte des Münsterischen Aufruhrs,* 2 vols., Leipzig, 1860.

Danièlou, Jean, *Holy Pagans of the Old Testament,* London, 1957.

Dedic, Paul, "Forschungen zur Geschichte des Oesterreichischen Protestantismus. Sammelbericht über die Epoch 1918-1939," *ARG,* XXXV (1938), 277-281.

Detmer, Heinrich, "Das Religionsgespräch zu Münster (Westfal.) am 7. und 8. August 1533. Ein Beitrag zur Geschichte Bernhard Rothmanns und des sogenannten Anabaptismus," *Monatshefte der Comenius-Gesellschaft,* IX (1900), 273-300.

————, *Bilder aus den religiösen und sozialen Unruhen in Münster während des 16. Jahrhunderts,* Münster, 1903-1904.

Diehl, W., *Zur Geschichte der Konfirmation,* Giessen, 1897.

Döllinger, J., *Die Reformation, ihre innere Entwicklung und ihre wirkungen im Umfange des Lutherischen Bekentnisses,* 3 vols., Regensburg, 1846, 1848.

ten Doornkaat Koolman, J., "Leupold Scharnschlager und die verborgene Täufergemeinde in Graubünden," *Zwingliana,* IV (1926).

von Dunin Borkowski, Stanislaus, "Untersuchungen zum Schrifttum der Unitarier vor Faustus Socini," *75 Jahre Stella Matutina, Festschrift,* II (1931), Feldkirch, Austria.

————, "Quellenstudien zur Vorgeschichte der Unitarier des 16. Jahrhunderts," *75 Jahre Stella Matutina, Festschrift,* I (1931), Feldkirch, Austria, pp. 91-138.

Ecke, Karl, *Schwenckfeld, Luther und der Gedanke einer apostolischen Reformation,* Berlin, 1911.

Eells, Hastings, "The Failure of Church Unification Efforts during the German Reformation," *ARG,* 42 (1951), 160-174.

————, *Martin Bucer,* New Haven, 1931.

Estep, W. R., *The Anabaptist Story,* Nashville, Tenn., 1964.

Fast, Heinold, *Heinrich Bullinger und die Täufer,* Heidelberg, 1961.

Feldner, August, *Die Ansichten Sebastian Franck's von Woerd nach ihrem Ursprunge und Zusammenhange dargestellt*, Berlin, 1872.

Ficker, J., and O. Winckelmann, *Handschriftenproben des 16. Jahrhunderts nach strassburger Originalen*, 2 vols., Strasbourg, 1902-1905 (inaccessible).

Friedmann, Robert, "Eine Dogmatische Hauptschrift der hutterischen Täufergemeinschaften in Mähren," *ARG* (1931), 80-111; 207-241.

————, "Die Briefe der oesterreichischen Täufer, IV: Bibliographie," *ARG*, XXVI (1929), 170-187.

————, "Conception of the Anabaptists," *ChHist*, IV (1940), 341-365.

————, *Mennonite Piety Through the Centuries*, Goshen, 1949.

Gerbert, Camill, *Geschichte der Strassburger Sectenbewegung zur Zeit der Reformation, 1524-1534*, Strasbourg, 1889.

Gerdes, Hayo, "Zu Luthers Lehre vom Wirken des Geistes," *Luther-Jahrbuch, Festgabe für Paul Althaus*, Franz Lau, ed., XXV (1958), Berlin, 1958, pp. 42-60. Extensive critique of Regin Prenter's *Spiritus Creator*.

————, *Luthers Streit mit den Schwärmern um das rechte Verständnis des Gesetzes Mose*, Göttingen, 1955.

Goeters, G. F. Gerhard, *Ludwig Hätzer*, Gütersloh, 1957.

Grant, R. M., *The Letter and the Spirit*, New York, 1957.

Gritsch, E. W., "The Authority of the 'Inner Word,' " Yale Diss., 1959.

Gschwind, Karl, *Die Niederfahrt Christi in die Unterwelt*, Münster, 1911.

Gussmann, Wilhelm, ed., *Quellen und Forschungen zur Geschichte des Augsburgischen Glaubensbekentnisses*, Leipzig and Berlin, 1911.

Harnack, Adolf, *Marcion: Das Evangelium vom Fremden Gott*, Leipzig, 1921.

————, *History of Dogma*, Boston, VII (1901).

Hase, Carl Alfred, *Sebastian Franck von Wörd, der Schwarmgeist*, Leipzig, 1869.

Hauth, L., *Les anabaptistes à Strasbourg au temps de la Reforme*, Strasbourg, 1860.

Heberle, Adolf, "Capito's Verhältnis zum Anabaptismus," *Zeitschrift für historische Theologie*, 1857, pp. 285-310.

Hege, Christian, "Pilgram Marbeck und die oberdeutschen Taufgesinnten," *ARG*, 37 (1940), 249-257.

Hein, Gerhard, "Leupold Scharnschlager. Ein Mitarbeiter Pilgram Marbecks," *Menn. Geschbl.*, 4 (1939), 6-12.

Heitz, Charles, *Das Zunftwesen in Strassburg*, 1856 (inaccessible).

Heitz, P., and K. A. Barack, *Elsässische Büchermarken*, Strasbourg, 1892.

Hendry, George S., *The Holy Spirit in Christian Theology*, Philadelphia, 1956.

————, "The Holy Spirit and the Renewal of the Church," *Moravian Theological Seminary Bulletin* (Fall, 1962), pp. 1-31.

Hershberger, Guy F., ed., *The Recovery of the Anabaptist Vision*, Scottdale, Penna., 1957.

Heyer, Fritz, *Der Kirchenbegriff der Schwärmer*, Leipzig, 1939.

Hillerbrand, Hans, "Die gegenwärtige Täuferforschung, Fortschritt oder Dilemma?" in *Lebendiger Geist, Festschrift für Schoeps, Beihefte der Zeitschrift für Religion und Geistesgeschichte*, Leiden-Köln, IV (1959), 48-65.

————, *Die politische Ethik des oberdeutschen Täufertums*, Leiden, 1960.

Hirsch, Emanuel, "Zum Verständnis Schwenckfelds," *Festgabe für Karl Müller*, Tübingen, 1922, pp. 145-170.

Holl, Karl, "Luther und die Schwärmer," *Gesammelte Aufsätze*, Tübingen, I (1923), 420-467.

Hollweg, Walter, "Bernhard Buwo, ein ostfriesischer Theologe aus dem Reformationsjahrhundert," *Jahrbuch der Gesellschaft für bildende Kunst und vaterländische Altertümer zu Emden*, 33 (1953), 71-90.

van 't Hooft, A. J., *De Theologie van Heinrich Bullinger in betrekking tot de Nederlandsche Reformatie*, Amsterdam, 1888.

Horsch, John, *The Principle of Nonresistance as held by the Mennonite Church*, Scottdale, Penna., 1939.

————, *Mennonites in Europe*, Scottdale, Penna., 1942.

Hulshof, Abraham, *Geschiedenis van de Doopsgezinden te Straatsburg van 1525 tot 1557*, Amsterdam, 1905.

Husner, F., "Zwei unbekannte Wiedertäuferdrucke?", *Stultifera Navis, Mitteilungsblatt der Schweizerischen Bibliophilen-Gesellschaft*, III (1946), 84-88.

Hutchinson, Harry, *Why Baptize Infants?*, New York, 1957.

Joest, Wilfried, *Gesetz und Freiheit*, Göttingen, 1956.

Jones, Rufus, *Spiritual Reformers in the 16th and 17th Centuries*, Boston, 1959[2].

von Karlstadt, Andreas Bodenstein, *Ein Sermon Vom Stand der Christglaubigen seelen von Abrahams schoss und fegfeuer, der abgeschydnen seelen*, no place, no date.

Kawerau, Peter, *Melchior Hoffman als religiöser Denker*, Haarlem, 1954.

Keller, Ludwig, "Zur Haltung Strassburgs in den Religionshändeln des 16. Jahrhunderts," *Monatshefte der Comenius-Gesellschaft*, V (1896), 310-13.

————, *Die Reformation und die älteren Reformpartien*, Leipzig, 1885.

Kiwiet, Jan J., "The Life of Hans Denck," *MQR*, XXXI (1957), 227-259.

Klassen, Herbert C., "The Life and Teachings of Hans Hut," *MQR*, XXXIII (1959), 171-205; 267-304.

Köhler, Walter, "Das Täufertum in der neueren kirchenhistorischen Forschung," *ARG*, XXXVII (1940), 93-107; XXXVIII (1941), 349-364; XL (1943), 246-270; XLI (1948), 164-186.

————, *Dogmengeschichte, als Geschichte des christlichen Selbstbewusstseins, Das Zeitalter der Reformation*, Zürich, 1951.

Kolde, Theodore, *Andreas Althamer der Humanist und Reformatur in Brandenburg-Ansbach*, Erlangen, 1895.

Kraeling, Emil, *The Old Testament Since the Reformation*, London, 1955.

Krahn, Cornelius, "The Historiography of the German Reformation During the Past Twenty Years, IV: Research in the History of the Anabaptists," *ChHist*, XIII (1944), 182-209.

————, *Menno Simons*, Karlsruhe, 1936.

Kraus, Hans Joachim, *Geschichte der historisch-kritischen Erforschung des Alten Testaments von der Reformation bis zur Gegenwart*, Neukirchen, Kreis Moers, 1956.

Kreck, Walter, "Wort und Geist bei Calvin," *Festschrift für Günther Dehn*, Neukirchen, Kreis Moers, 1957, pp. 167-181.

Kuczynski, Arnold, *Thesaurus Libellorum Historiam Reformationis Illustrantium; Verzeichniss einer Sammlung von nahezu 3000 Flugschriften Luthers und seiner Zeitgenossen*, Leipzig, 1870.

van der Laag, Albertina, *Index to the Mennonitica in the Amsterdam Mennonite Library*, 1919; Goshen, Indiana, 1950.

Lammert, F. R., "Martin Bucer's Activity for a United Protestantism," University of Chicago, M. A. Diss., 1941.

Lang, August, *Der Evangelienkommentar Martin Butzers und die Grundzüge seiner Theologie*, Halle, 1900.

Lawson, John, *The Biblical Theology of St. Irenaeus*, London, 1948.

Leendertz, W. I., *Melchior Hofmann*, Haarlem, 1883.

von Liliencron, R., "Zur Liederdichtung der Wiedertäufer," *Mitteilungen aus dem Gebiet der öffentlichen Meinung in Deutschland während der zweiten Hälfte des 16. Jahrhunderts*, 1875.

Littell, Franklin H., *The Anabaptist View of the Church*, American Society of Church History, 1952.

Loserth, Johann, "Der Anabaptismus in Tirol," *Archiv für österreichische Geschichte*, 78 (1892), 429-604; 129-276.

————, "Zur Geschichte der Wiedertäufer in Mähren," *Zeitschrift für Allgemeine Geschichte . . .*, VI (1884), 438-457.

————, "Anfängen der Reformation in Steiermark, Die Visitation und Inquisition von 1528 und ihre Ergebnisse," *Jahrbuch der Gesellschaft für die Geschichte der Reformation . . . Oesterreich*, 54 (1933), 86ff.

————, "Ueber die Beziehungen der mährischen Wiedertäufer zu ihren Glaubensgenossen in Augsburg und Graubünden," *Zeitschrift des Deutschen Vereins für Geschichte von Mähren und Schlesien*, 27 (1925), 48-50.

Lüdemann, H., *Reformation und Täufertum in ihrem Verhältnis zum christlichen Prinzip*, Bern, 1896.

Maurer, Wilhelm, "Luther und die Schwärmer," *Schriften des Theologischen Konvents Augsburgischen Bekentnisses*, Heft 6 (1952), Berlin, pp. 7-37.

McClelland, Joseph C., "Covenant Theology: a Re-evaluation," *Canadian Journal of Theology*, III (1957), 182-87.

————, *The Visible Words of God*, Grand Rapids, 1957.

McNeill, John T., "The Significance of the Word of God for Calvin," *ChHist*, XXVIII (1959).

Meyer, Christian, "Die Anfänge des Wiedertäufertums in Augsburg," *Zeitschrift des historischen Vereins für Schwaben und Neuburg*, I, 2 (1874), 207-253, continued by F. Roth in 27 (1900), 1-45.

Müller, Lydia, *Der Kommunismus der mährischen Wiedertäufer*, Leipzig, 1927.

von Muralt, Leonhard, *Glaube und Lehre der Schweizerischen Wiedertäufer in der Reformationszeit*, Zürich, 1938.

Nicoladoni, Alexander, *Johannes Bünderlin von Linz*, Berlin, 1893.

Niesert, Joseph, *Münsterische Urkundensammlung*, Coesfeld, 1826.

Oyer, John, *Luther and the Anabaptists*, Nijhof, 1964.

Pauck, William, "The Historiography of the German Reformation During the Past Twenty Years, IV: Research in the History of the Anabaptists," *ChHist*, IX (1940), 335-364.

Peschke, Erhard, *Die Theologie der Böhmischen Brüder*, Stuttgart, 1940.

Pestalozzi, Carl, *Heinrich Bullinger*, Vol. V of *Leben und Ausgewählte Schriften der Väter und Begründer der reformierten Kirche*, Elberfeld, 1856.

Peter, Rodolphe, "Le maraîcher Clément Ziegler, l'homme et son oeuvre," *Revue d'histoire et de philosophie religieuses*, 1954, pp. 225-282.

Peuckert, Will-Erich, *Sebastian Franck, Ein Deutscher Sucher*, München, 1943.

Prenter, Regin, *Spiritus Creator*, Philadelphia, 1953.

Putnam, G. H., *Censorship of the Church of Rome and its Influence upon . . . Literature*, 2 vols., New York, 1906, 1907.

Räber, Kuno, *Studien zur Geschichtsbibel Sebastian Francks*, Basel, 1952.

Rathgeber, Julius, *Strassburg im sechszehnten Jahrhundert, 1500-1598*, Stuttgart, 1871.

Reid, J. K. S., *The Authority of Scripture. A Study of the Reformation and Post-Reformation Understanding of the Bible*, London, 1957.

Reicke, Bo, *The Disobedient Spirits and Christian Baptism*, Kobenhavn, 1946.

Reimann, Arnold, *Sebastian Franck als Geschichtsphilosoph*, Berlin, 1921.

Ritter, F., "La police de l'imprimerie et de la librairie a Strasbourg . . . ," *Revue des Bibliotheques*, 32 (1922), 161-200.

————, *Histoire de l'imprimerie alsacienne aux XVe et XVIe siecles*, Strasbourg, 1955.

Rödel, Friedrich, *Die anarchischen Tendenzen bei den Wiedertäufern des Reformationszeitalters*, Erlangen Diss., 1950.

Röhrich, T. W., "Martin Butzers Testamente, nach dem Original herausgegeben und mit erläuternden Anmerkungen begleitet," *Beiträge zu den theologischen Wissenschaften von der theologischen Gesellschaft zu Strassburg*, 2 (1851), 193-230.

————, *Geschichte der Reformation im Elsass*, I (1830); II (1832); Strasbourg.

Roth, F. W. E., "Die Schriften des Otto Brunfels 1519-1536," *Jahrbuch für Geschichte, Sprache und Literatur Lothringens*, 16 (1900), 256-288.

Roth, Friedrich, *Augsburg Reformationsgeschichte*, I-IV (1901-1911), München.

Rudolphi, E., *Die Buchdrucker-familie Froschauer in Zürich, 1521-1595*, Zürich, 1869.

Rupp, Gordon, "Word and Spirit in the First Years of the Reformation," *ARG*, 49 (1958), 13-25.

Sachse, Fdr., *Die Anfänge der Büchercensur in Deutschland*, Leipzig, 1870 (or 1871).

Saint Bernard on the Love of God, De diligendo Deo, London, 1950.

Saint Bernard on the Song of Songs: Sermones in Cantica Canticorum, London, 1952.

Salig, Christian August, *Vollständige Historie der Augsburgischen Confession und derselben zugethanen Kirchen*, Halle, 1735.

Schäufele, Wolfgang, *Das missionarische Bewusstsein und Wirken der Täufer*, Neukirchen-Vluyn, 1966.

Schiess, Traugott, "Aus dem Leben eines Ilanzer Schulmeisters," *Bündnerisches Monatsblatt*, 1916, pp. 73-89.

Schoeps, Hans Joachim, *Vom Himmlischen Fleisch Christi*, Tübingen, 1951.

Schottenloher, Karl, "Beschlagnahmte Druckschriften aus der Frühzeit der Reformation," *Zeitschrift für Bücherfreunde*, N. F. 8 (1916/17), pp. 305-321.

————, *Philipp Ulhart, Ein Augsburg Winkeldrucker und Helfershelfer der "Schwärmer" und "Wiedertäufer"* (1523-1529), München and Freising, 1921.

————, "Buchdrucker und Buchführer im Kampf der Schwärmer und Wiedertäufer, 1524-1568," *Buch und Papier, Buchkündliche und papiergeschichtliche Arbeiten Hans Bockwitz zum 65. Geburtstag dargebracht*, 1949, 69-78.

Schrenk, Gottlob, *Gottesreich und Bund im älteren Protestantismus vornehmlich bei Johannes Coccejus*, Gütersloh, 1925.

Schultz, Selina Gerhard, *Caspar Schwenckfeld von Ossig* (1498-1561), Norristown, Penna., 1946.

Schumann, F. K., "Schwärmerei als Gegenwärtige Versuchung der Kirche," *Schriften des theologischen Konvents Augsburgischen Bekentnisses*, Berlin, 1952.

Seeberg, Reinhold, *Textbook on the History of Doctrines*, Charles E. Hay, trans., Grand Rapids, 1952.

Selwyn, Edward Gordon, *The First Epistle of St. Peter*, London, 1952.

COVENANT AND COMMUNITY

Sick, Hansjörg, *Melanchthon als Ausleger des Alten Testaments,* Tübingen, 1959.

Simpson, William John Sparrow, *St. Augustine on the Spirit and the Letter,* London, 1925.

Sippell, Theodor, "Eine unbekannte Schrift, Sebastian Francks Zweintzig Glauben oder Secten, allein des einigen Christenglauben," *Theologische Studien und Kritiken,* 95 (1923/24), 147-150.

Smith, Preserved, "The Methods of Reformation Interpreters of the Bible," *The Biblical World,* 38 (1911), new series, pp. 235-245.

Steck, Karl Gerhard, *Luther und die Schwärmer,* Zollikon-Zürich, 1955.

von Stetten, Paul, *Lebensbeschreibungen zur Erweckung und Unterhaltung bürgerlicher Tugend,* Augsburg, 1782.

————, *Geschichte des Heiligen Römischen Reichs Freyen Stadt Augsburg . . . ,* Franckfurt und Leipzig, 1743.

Strauss, Gerhard, *Schriftgebrauch, Schriftauslegung und Schriftbeweis bei Augustin,* Tübingen, 1959.

Stupperich, Robert, "Melanchthon und die Täufer," *Kerygma und Dogma,* III (1957), 150-170.

————, *Bibliographia Bucerana: Schriften des Vereins für Reformationsgeschichte,* No. 169, Vol. 58, Heft 2, pp. 27-96.

————, "Buceriana," *ARG,* 43 (1952), 106.

————, "Stand und Aufgabe der Butzerforschung," *ARG,* 42 (1951), 244-259.

————, *Das Münsterische Täufertum,* Münster, 1958.

Sullivan, Frances A., *The Christology of Theodore of Mopsuestia,* Rome, 1956.

Terry, Milton S., *Biblical Hermeneutics,* New York, 1890.

Teufel, Eberhard, "Täufertum und Quäkertum im Lichte der neueren Forschung," *Theologische Rundschau,* XIII (1941), 24-57, 103-127, 183-197; XIV (1942), 27-32, 124-154; XV (1943), 246-270; XVI (1948), 164-186.

————, "Religiöse Nebenströmungen der Reformation. Wiedertäufer und Schwenckfelder . . . ," 1946, typescript in GCL.

————, "Luther und Lutherthum im Urteil Sebastian Francks," *Festgabe für Karl Müller,* Tübingen, 1922, pp. 132-144.

Thompson, Bard, "Bucer Study Since 1918," *ChHist,* XXV (1956), 63-82.

Thudicum, F., "Die 'deutsche Theologie,'" *Monatshefte der Comenius-Gesellschaft,* V (1896), 44-62.

Torm, Frederik, *Hermeneutik des Neuen Testaments,* Göttingen, 1930.

Tresmontant, Claude, *Saint Paul and the Mystery of Christ,* Donald Attwater, trans., New York, 1957.

Trinterud, L. J., "The Origins of Puritanism," *ChHist,* XX (1950), 37-57.

Uhlhorn, G., *Urbanus Rhegius in Leben und ausgewählten Schriften,* 1861.

Urner, Hans, "Die Taufe bei Caspar Schwenckfeld," *Theologische Literaturzeitung,* 73 (1948), cols. 329-342.

Usteri, Johannes Martin, "Die Stellung der Strassburger Reformatoren Bucer und Capito zur Tauffrage," *Studien und Kritiken*, 1884, pp. 456-525.

Verduin, Leonard, *The Reformers and Their Stepchildren*, Grand Rapids, 1965.

Vogelsang, Erich, "Weltbild und Kreuzestheologie in den Höllenfahrtsstreitigkeiten der Reformationszeit," *ARG*, 1941, 90-132.

Wach, Joachim, "Caspar Schwenckfeld: A Pupil and a Teacher in the School of Christ," *Journal of Religion*, XXVI (1946), 1-29 (also in *Types of Religious Experience*, London, 1951, pp. 135-170).

Wendel, Fr., and P. Scherding, "Un Traité d'exégèse pratique de Bucer," *Revue d'histoire et de philosophie religieuses*, 26 (1946), 32-75.

Will, G. A., "Althamers Unterricht," *Beiträge zur Geschichte des Anabaptismus in Franckenland*, Nürnberg, 1773, p. 115.

Wiswedel, Wilhelm, "Oswald Glait von Jamnitz," *Zeitschrift für Kirchengeschichte*, 56 (1937), 550-564.

————, "Zum Problem, 'Inneres und äusseres Wort' bei den Täufern des 16. Jahrhunderts," *ARG*, 46 (1955), 1-19.

Wittmer, Charles, and J. C. Meyer, *Le livre de bourgeoisie de la ville de Strasbourg 1440-1530*, Texte II, Strasbourg, 1954.

Wolf, Hans Henrich, *Die Einheit des Bundes. Das Verhältnis von Altem und Neuem Testament bei Calvin*, Neukirchen, Kreis Moers, 1958.

Wolkan, Rudolf, *Die Lieder der Wiedertäufer*, Berlin, 1903.

————, *Geschicht-buch der Hutterischen Brüder*, Macleod, Alberta and Vienna, 1923.

Wood, James D., *The Interpretation of the Bible*, London, 1958.

Wray, Frank J., *History in the Eyes of the Sixteenth Century Anabaptists*, Yale Diss., 1953.

Yoder, John Howard, *Die Gespräche zwischen Täufern und Reformatoren in der Schweiz, 1523-1538*, Basel Diss., 1957.

Zuck, Lowell H., *Anabaptist Revolution through the Covenant in Sixteenth Century Continental Protestantism*, Yale Diss., 1954.

————, "Anabaptism: Abortive Counter-Revolt within the Reformation," *ChHist*, XXVI (1957), 211-226.

E. GENERAL REFERENCE WORKS

Bender, Harold S., ed., *The Mennonite Encyclopedia*, 4 vols., Scottdale, Penna., 1955-59.

The Catholic Encyclopedia, New York, 1913.

Galling, Kurt, ed., *Die Religion in Geschichte und Gegenwart*, 6 vols., 1957-62, Tübingen. All references are to the third edition unless otherwise noted.

Grotefend, H., *Taschenbuch der Zeitrechnung des Deutschen Mittelalters und der Neuzeit*[4], Hannover and Leipzig, 1915.

Hege, Christian, and Christian Neff, eds., *Mennonitisches Lexikon*, Frankfurt am Main and Weierhof (Selbstverlag), 1913f.

Kittel, Gerhard, ed., *Theologisches Wörterbuch zum Neuen Testament*, Stuttgart, 1933, Vols. I-VII complete. English trans. by G. Bromiley, Grand Rapids, 1964, Vols. I-IV complete.

Koehler, Ludwig, and Walter Baumgartner, *Lexicon in veteris testamenti libros*, Grand Rapids and Leiden, 1958.

Schmeller, J. Andreas, *Bayerisches Wörterbuch*, 2 vols., Leipzig, 1939.

Schottenloher, Karl, *Bibliographie zur Deutschen Geschichte im Zeitalter der Glaubensspaltung, 1517-1585*, Leipzig, 1933-1940, 6 vols.

INDEX OF SUBJECTS

203

INDEX OF PERSONS AND PLACES

207